Toward World Prosperity

*Reshaping the Global
Money System*

by

IRVING S. FRIEDMAN

Lexington Books

D.C. Heath and Company • Lexington, Massachusetts • Toronto

Library of Congress Cataloging-in-Publication Data

Friedman, Irving Sigmund, 1915–
The international financial system.

Includes index.
1. International finance. I. Title.
HG3881.F74   1987   332′.042   86-20959
ISBN 0-669-11564-9 (alk. paper)

Published simultaneously in Canada
Printed in the United States of America
International Standard Book Number: 0-669-11564-9
Library of Congress Catalog Card Number: 86-20959

The paper used in this publication meets the minimum requirements of American National Standard for Information Sciences—Permanence of Paper for Printed Library Materials, ANSI Z39.48-1984. ∞™

86 87 88 89 90 8 7 6 5 4 3 2 1

Dedicated to
ANDREW N. OVERBY
whose steadfast devotion to
the International Monetary Fund
kept it alive during its
troubled fledgling years
and to
GEORGE D. WOODS
whose creative initiatives as
President of the World Bank
have flourished to the benefit
of all mankind

Contents

PART III
The International Debt Problem

PART IV
Ending the Crisis

PART V
Proposals for Strengthening
the International Financial System

Prologue

I T is June 1986 as the manuscript for this book is being completed. Many still consider the international financial crisis to be alarming; others, expert and inexpert, are more optimistic. Falling oil prices and interest rates are easing the balance of payments of many borrowing countries that are having external debt servicing difficulties. Debt restructuring is also easing the immediate problems of servicing these difficulties. Optimism may be becoming fashionable again, but such fads and fashions, however illfitting, have repeatedly led analysts, commentators, financial institutions, and governments astray. The history of the past 30 years in international finance could be aptly entitled "Errors in Persuasion."

This book sets forth my own views; it does not summarize or popularize the views of others. It is addressed to experts and general readers alike, and it aims at readability, but not simplicity. My views have often differed from those others. For example, I have strongly advocated the use of commercial sources of external finance for developing countries. I have refused to accept the view that the debt crises would lead to collapses of major banks and banking systems. For years, I have insisted that despite the difficulties in servicing external debt, the developing countries would continue to borrow and their external debt would increase substantially. I have refused to accept the argument that the cause of the debt crises is excessive borrowing or that the existing large debts make it virtually impossible to restore creditworthiness. I have advocated expanded multilateral lending, but I have refused to advise countries to cut back growth to the levels made possible by such lending. For decades, I have been convinced that official sources would be inadequate to meet the growth needs of developing countries and that private sources of external finance would be essential for satisfactory growth. Developing countries would need to change existing national policies substantially to attract such capital. I have refused to regard reductions in imports, resulting in reduced balance-of-payments deficits, as evidence of improved economic conditions or performance for developing countries. I have insisted on the need for developmental as well as monetary criteria in judging the economic management of developing countries—a conviction resulting from more than 25 years of senior responsibilities in the International Monetary Fund and the World Bank. Moreover, I have emphasized for decades that inflation is the corrosive enemy of economic growth and equitable income distribution as well as of external financial strength.

As an executive in the world's largest international banks, I became aware of how banks can accept and manage international risks on the basis of professional investigation, thoughtful risk/reward analyses, and portfolio management. I have emphasized that commercial banks are borrowers before they are lenders—that they, too, have debt problems like those of the entities that borrow from them. There is no shortage of the world savings needed for development; they can be tapped if the conditions for creditworthiness are established. Borrowing developing countries must compete, however, with huge domestic demands for consumer credit, extended by lenders at attractive rates, as well as business credit. Moreover, borrowing countries may need to attract back into international lending the banks which have virtually withdrawn, such as the smaller and middle-sized banks in the United States.

I do not consider debt restructuring a way to restore creditworthiness. Indeed, I maintain that debt restructuring has often diverted attention away from the need to create viable economies that are able to borrow extensively on a voluntary basis. For years, I have believed that the International Monetary Fund and the World Bank should collaborate much more closely and should maintain continuous dialogue with member countries on economic policies and practices. I have refused to accept prevalent views that such collaboration is not desirable or practical, and I welcome the very recent steps in this direction as well as other innovations in development finance.

I remain an optimist, in that I believe that the international financial system can be reformed to provide the foundation and framework for a prosperous world economy. I consider the international financial system to be 50 years behind national financial systems. This gap must be closed, and it can be closed. National banking systems have long recognized the risks and vulnerabilities inherent in banking, and effective defenses have been created to deal with these vulnerabilities. Similar defenses have not been erected for international banking, and they cannot be a simple duplication of national defenses. A basic problem is the reconciliation of global business and a world political system based on nation-states.

The international financial system *can* be modernized to meet modern conditions. This book gives suggestions and presents a program of action to achieve this end. Hundreds of millions, if not billions, of people in developed and developing countries are now being victimized by the inadequacies of the international financial system, but these conditions can be remedied. The remedies do not involve fundamental changes in economic and social systems; rather, they require changes in the economic and financial management of countries and the roles of the private and public international financial institutions.

I realize that the thesis of this book can easily be misinterpreted. It envisages large increases in the external debts of developing countries to private lenders, but it does not present this increase in debt as a "solution" to the debt problem. Rather, the solution is found in the reestablishment of creditworthiness with private lenders and their consequent willingness to increase their loan exposures substantially in now-troubled countries. More fundamentally, the solution is found in establishing the domestic and international conditions necessary for reestablishing creditworthiness.

The book does not advocate more borrowing to solve the existing debt problems. It does, however, advocate development goals and policies that will require much larger inflows of capital than are now available. It is assumed that such inflows can be met only partially by official bilateral or multilateral sources and that equity and private direct investment will also provide only a small fraction of the required external capital. The conclusion drawn is that large inflows must come from private lenders. The primary subject matter of the book is how this can be accomplished.

Because of the depth of the international financial crisis, and because it is so widespread, many have reacted from perspectives much wider than the economic, financial, and narrowly political. Many ethical questions have arisen because of the poverty and other adverse social conditions in most of the troubled borrowing nations, and a "just" solution to the external debt problem has been sought.

It is hoped that those concerned with ethical questions will be helped by the analyses given in this book. The starting point, however, is an examination of the social and economic development of the less industrialized countries of the world and a determination of how international financial assistance can, in practice, perform efficiently in this process.

Many have advocated massive increases in official assistance to the poorer countries. However, donor governments have not been willing to provide these massive increases. Foreign assistance for social and economic development has a high priority, but only for relatively small amounts. For large amounts, it meets strong resistance from other national needs. Fortunately, other sources have been able to offset the reluctance of governments to provide official support. At present, to build hopes of progress in development on expectations of huge increases in budgetary expenditures is to build on quicksand. The alternative is to take advantage of world finance—to seek funds originating from private sources and intermediated through private institutions, often with the active assistance of official institutions. The role of official institutions is crucial. Without a much larger and more diversified role for the official institutions, private sources of savings will still not be available in adequate amounts and maturities for many developing countries. Through the combined actions of the borrowing countries and the private and official institutions, the needed international flows of capital can be generated with little need to call on national budgetary funds.

I consider implementation of the suggestions made herein to be feasible in the foreseeable future. They are not offered as "optimal" solutions, nor are goals of huge increases in official aid advocated in the hope of influencing public opinion and governmental actions. Such advocacy is left to others. My lifework has been problem solving in the real world of official and private economies and finance. This book is rooted in that experience.

Many will doubt the feasibility of the suggestions made herein because they differ sharply from common, widespread views on the international financial system and the external debt crises. I believe, however, that these views are not grounded in realities. They assume an unchanging reluctance of private lenders to lend to countries that are now in difficulty. I suggest that the skeptical consider the following: Would the international financial system still be in crisis if Argentina, Brazil, and Mexico were restored to creditworthiness and if Korea maintained its creditworthiness? Are not these restorations and maintenance feasible? I believe they are feasible and, if they are achieved, that the world will be well on its way to ending the international financial crisis. The problem will still remain of preventing recurrences, perhaps in even more virulent forms. Thus, this book addresses not only the present external debt crises but also necessary alterations to the international financial system to prevent such crises in the future.

Introduction
and Statement of the
Problem

1

Introduction

THE international financial system is failing to meet the needs of a large majority of the world's population. The most dramatic manifestation of this failure is the great external debt crisis of the 1980s. The countries most involved in this crisis are in Latin America and Africa. Countries in Asia have also been seriously affected, however, and the future of all developing countries has been made more difficult and more uncertain. For the United States and other developed countries, the failure of the system has meant the loss of markets for their exports, reduced opportunities for profitable investments, and new strains in political relations with friendly nations. For the global economy as a whole, the crisis has demonstrated the deep conflicts and tensions between the conditions of international business, which is now conducted as an unbroken process involving many countries simultaneously, and the political organization of the world into nation-states. It is not surprising that multilateral financial institutions have grown in importance because they consist of nations but deal with the world of global business, economics, and finance.

The international financial system must be strengthened. The great external debt crisis must be brought to an end and become part of past history, like World War I debts and reparations. This Sword of Damocles must not be allowed to paralyze private and official actions; it must be cut down and thrown away. This book is meant to contribute to the understanding of the international financial system and the external debt problem. It suggests changes and reforms designed to strengthen the system, end the debt crises, and prevent their recurrence. The thoughts contained herein are based on 40 years of experience of the author. The published literature in these areas is extensive and covers many aspects of this book. Particular attention is drawn to the publications of the International Monetary Fund; the World Bank; the African, Asian, and Inter-American Development Banks; the Organization of European Cooperation and Development (OECD); and the Bank for International Settlements (BIS). The commercial banks are also excellent sources of information and analyses, and doctoral theses and other academic studies are further sources of knowledge and insights.

This book is not a substitute for more extensive reading in these fields; rather, the book is intended to help the reader think about these matters of major importance and absorb future studies and experiences more effectively. The issues involved are those of public policy and private concern and action. No one can be indifferent to the workings of the international financial system; each reader is an active participant whose future will be shaped significantly by the international financial system.

This book about the international financial system originated as a book on international lending and the external debt crises of many developing countries. I had intended to entitle the book "The Return to Creditworthiness." My first desire was to focus on how the developing countries, whose ability to obtain international credits and loans from commercial banks and other private lenders had been severely damaged, could restore their creditworthiness. Many developing countries, especially in the 1970s, had been able to achieve and sustain high growth rates and rising living standards with funds obtained from foreign private sources. In the 1980s, this process was disrupted. Growth rates had to decline and become negative, and living standards fell. The loss of access to private sources of finance contributed in a major way to these adversities. The revival of these economies requires the reestablishment of the creditworthiness of these countries—that is, their ability to obtain foreign loans on a market basis, meeting the lending criteria of commercial banks.

In writing this book, my perception changed. My preoccupation with the restoration of creditworthiness remained, but it became a part of a broader preoccupation with how to improve the international financial system as a whole. In addition to international banking, the international financial system also includes the international monetary system and the International Monetary Fund; official sources of development finance, especially the World Bank and the regional multilateral development banks; and the private international capital market, as distinct from credit markets. Each of these institutions has a different financial role in the international economy. They interrelate and function simultaneously, together forming the international financial system. The system thus combines different private and public, national and international institutions; the behavior of financial markets, especially international financial markets; and the codes of international behavior agreed upon by countries in these areas. No one aspect can be understood apart from the others. Prior to the great external debt crisis, it was the entire system that enabled countries to borrow to assist their efforts to grow, become more efficient, and provide better living conditions for their people. The return to creditworthiness with commercial banks and its maintenance in the future requires an orderly and efficient functioning of the entire international financial system. Private sources of finance are critically important, and international banking is the most important mechanism for access to private finance. Measures to restore international lending by commercial banks can be successful, but that success will be only temporary unless the entire international financial system functions satisfactorily.

It was the failure of the total international financial system that led, in the early 1980s, to the withdrawal of commercial banks from much lending to developing countries in Latin America, Africa, and elsewhere. Unless the weaknesses of the system are remedied, such crises can occur again and can be duplicated in other countries. Fortunately, mechanisms already exist and function well that, if better interrelated and managed differently, can provide an efficient international financial system. The world is already overburdened with difficulties and complexities. Achieving a world economy capable of meeting the needs and aspirations of a rapidly expanding and mobile population is, at best, a most difficult task, and it need not be greatly handicapped, as it is at present, by a poorly functioning international financial system. The necessary changes or improvements are feasible. They do not raise critical issues of ideology or principle, and they are compatible with the existence of the nation-state and with existing socioeconomic systems.

With this perception, I refocused this book on the entire international financial system, considering the restoration of creditworthiness with commercial banks as a major aspect and benefit to be derived from the suggested improvements in the system.

The book is intended to provide a way out of the painful dilemmas now troubling the developing countries and poisoning their relations with industrial countries. It calls for major changes. Nothing remains the same, but nothing would remain the same whether or not the changes suggested herein were accepted. The world cannot eliminate uncertainty and risk, failures as well as successes, retrogression as well as progress. It can, however, make progress more achievable and the process of change less unstable, less disruptive, and less painful.

2

Breakdown of the System:
Unresolved Issues

I s the international financial system suited to the world economy?
How can the external debt crisis be solved? Can the developing
countries cope with existing conditions? Will national banking systems in the United States and elsewhere be undermined by these
conditions? These questions are being raised and discussed throughout the world but are still unanswered. Solutions are still being
sought, because those applied thus far have been inadequate.

The functioning of the international financial system in recent
years has come under closest scrutiny and criticism worldwide.
Scholars, practitioners in international finance and banking, multinational institutions, governments, administrators, politicians,
statesmen, and journalists have written about it at great length with
sobriety and sophistication. Once the international financial crisis of
the early 1980s became a reality, joking and cynicism went out of
style. To talk of the crash of 1979 in the mid 1970s was fun; to talk
of the crash of 1989 in the early 1980s was gruesome.

In the 1970s, when the system worked well, pessimism was fashionable—disaster was thought to be around the corner. Paradoxically, as the situation became more serious in the 1980s, optimism
became more fashionable. The existing crises could be overcome by
domestic management—feasible austerity measures taken by the
troubled debtor countries. Creditor banks could accept multiyear
debt rescheduling so long as countries followed adjustment programs
endorsed by the International Monetary Fund (IMF). The IMF
could extend extensive financial help on medium-term maturities
without seriously jeopardizing its own liquidity and viability; the

World Bank could play a large, more immediately helpful role by moving massively from project financing to quicker disbursing financing, called structural adjustment loans. The world economy needed to grow "only" at about 3 percent or 4 percent per annum in real terms for world trade to provide the borrowing countries with the growth in export earnings needed to reduce the relevant ratios of debt servicing or interest servicing obligations to other national aggregates, such as gross national product, national income, export earnings, and the like. Continuing world inflation would erode the real magnitudes of debt and debt servicing.

The year 1984 became the year of relative relief from the intensive worry that was prevalent in 1982–83. Crisis management had worked. "Only if" the U.S. economy would maintain its recovery, and the rest of the industrial world would accelerate and maintain its recoveries, acute concerns could be laid to rest. However, the fundamentals had not changed. Many people noted that the austerity programs in the borrowing countries were creating social and political instability, or worse. Capital flight from the developing countries was still strong, despite "rational" arguments pointing to the conclusion that flight capital should return, as holding assets in the borrowing countries became more attractive to savers and investors than holding assets abroad. Countries like Brazil could take advantage of the overvalued U.S. dollar to sell manufactures to the United States, but how long could they do so before protectionist measures would be taken to protect troubled U.S. industries? How would the IMF be repaid ("repurchased" in IMF terminology) by its borrowing countries? Would the creditor nations of the IMF be willing to employ its ability to create "paper gold"—that is, special drawing rights (SDRs), approximately equivalent to one U.S. dollar—in large magnitudes, thus increasing international liquidity without a corresponding increase in debt? Some sober voices even hinted at the need for large-scale debt forgiveness.

Yet all these questions and concerns did not undermine the prevailing complacency. Just as the voices that argued in 1982–83 that the crisis was manageable were politely ignored by scholars and practitioners alike, so worried but muted voices in 1984 were listened to, duly noted, and then ignored. In 1985, the budding complacency gave way to deeper concerns.

A new understanding was beginning to prevail about the nature of the debt crises. The simplistic approaches of 1982–83 to resolving the problems were not working. The focal point of concern had been the international banking system collectively and its separate institutional parts, and the harm that could come to them from wholesale defaults on external debts by borrowing countries in severe balance-of-payments difficulties. Whatever the reasons or origins, by 1980, international lending to developing countries by commercial banks had reached magnitudes that could cause severe damage to the financial viability of the commercial banks if wholesale defaults were experienced. It took only the most simplistic analysis to demonstrate that the debt servicing obligations to the commercial banks were high proportions of their total earnings and capital. It was not hard to accept the argument that developing countries with balance-of-payments difficulties would find it most difficult to service their debts, and would eventually be unable to avoid repudiation or defaults as a way out of their difficulties.

This quality of reasoning dominated thinking and action in 1982 and 1983. Articles in learned journals and headlines in newspapers echoed the same themes. Warning signals were given that no one could fail to see or hear. The risks of international lending now clearly outweighed the benefits; "collapse" was imminent. Latin America was the most obvious region for alarm, because countries in this region had come to rely most heavily on commercial banking as the source of external finance. Many had been "graduating" from reliance on official sources of external finance. They had come to rely on their creditworthiness with market sources of finances and had done quite well in so doing in the 1970s. Brazil, Chile, Ecuador, Mexico, and Venezuela exemplified this evolution. The countries deemed most creditworthy in the 1970s were deemed to be the most suspect and vulnerable in 1982–83. This phenomenon repeated the experience in domestic banking—that is, the strongest and biggest borrowers during favorable times frequently become the biggest headaches during adverse times.

In the United States and other developed countries, "collapse" referred to the foreseen harm to their national banking systems from financial panics, bank failures, disrupted financial markets, and the like. Experts in Latin America, as in industrial countries, warned of the impending collapse of banks and banking systems. Use of words like *collapse* became commonplace. To an expert in Latin America, "collapse" referred to the breakdown of the international financial system that had been financing the balance-of-payments deficits of

Latin American countries that accompanied the satisfactory growth rates and export diversification achieved in the 1970s. Export earnings of these countries had improved greatly during this period in magnitude, commodity diversification, and marketing. Sources of borrowing had increased visibly. Balance-of-payments deficits had also grown, as increased exports do not diminish the need for imports. Without a large inflow of funds, Latin America could not grow at a satisfactory rate, and living conditions would deteriorate seriously. Thus, the experts in Latin America were not wrong in seeing the adverse implications of a collapse of international lending. What was wrong was their emphasis on past lending as being wrong, reinforcing the new cautious views of many lenders and thus reinforcing their refusal to lend to Latin America.

Brazil was the bellwether example; it dramatically illustrated the issues and choices confronting developing countries. In the 1970s, Brazil could not have grown at the high rates achieved with its improved export composition and its rising living standards if it had not found the means to finance large external deficits. High oil prices, higher interest rates, and higher costs of capital goods required more foreign exchange to meet the needs of a very large industrializing and urbanizing economy. Huge shifts from domestic consumption into investments, resulting in increased export earnings, could eventually provide the needed additional foreign exchange, but not without major social disturbances nor within a time period related to practical needs. What was at issue was the governing of a country, not the performance of an individual firm or entity.

Brazil was fortunate enough, in the 1970s, to understand the potentials of the international banking system. It induced the financial flows of the world economy into financing Brazilian growth. It created a large external debt, but with great expansion in domestic growth and in export capacity. Its creditors shared the risks in Brazilian growth in exchange for revenues and profits. Brazil entered the troubled 1980s with a much stronger economy than it otherwise would have had. Between 1950 and 1960, Brazilian exports in U.S. dollars virtually stagnated at about $1.4 billion. From 1960 to 1970, Brazil's exports about doubled, reaching $2.7 billion in 1970. In 1973, when the oil crisis began, exports had already risen to $6.2 billion, and imports had reached about the same levels. In 1974, Brazil's import bill more than doubled as the high oil prices became effective. In one year, 1974, imports amounted to over $12.6 billion.

The strategic choice was clear: Brazil could drastically slow down modernization and thus cut down domestic demand to bring oil and other import demand close to export earnings, or it could choose to accelerate export-led growth. Brazil chose the latter. In 1979, exports reached over $15 billion, about seven times their level in 1969. Imports again exceeded exports in 1979 because of the second oil price increases, but the economy had $15 billion of export earnings. By 1982, exports exceeded $23 billion, nearly ten times those of 1970 and four times those of 1973–74, when the strategic decision to restrain or grow had to be made.

Living standards improved despite the huge population expansion, the dependency on oil imports, and the oil price blows. In this process, Brazil ceased to be dependent on three main primary products for export earnings: coffee, soybeans, and sugar. In 1983, these commodities accounted for less than 25 percent of Brazil's export earnings, compared with 50 percent in 1970. The Brazilian growth strategy did not start in 1973–74, but it was the deliberate decision in that period to keep on this strategic path that enabled Brazil to make the huge progress it did between 1973 and 1980. This was the basis for Brazil's ability to borrow extensively from private sources of finance during these years. Brazil's strategy also had its Achilles heel—it required continuous new net borrowing from abroad, mostly from private banks. These credits were needed to make the engine run; without them, even a strong economy would be in deep trouble.

Private creditors of Brazil were becoming concerned with its economic management in the late 1970s and early 1980s as domestic inflation accelerated, reminding the world of Brazil's horrendous history of rapid inflation in earlier decades, which had resulted in the end of civilian government. Ironically, inflation was again accelerating in the early 1980s, when Brazil was moving back from military to civilian government. Despite these warning signals, enough private lenders were impressed with Brazil's economic growth and export strength to be willing to lend to Brazil on acceptable market terms.

In 1982, Brazil lost its creditworthiness through the folly of its government management, caused by complacency and fed by self-deception and by political exigencies. However, the fact that Brazil was a major external debt problem during the recessions of the early 1980s need not have disturbed lenders to Latin America as much as it did if they had kept their eyes on their compasses. The Brazilian economy of the 1980s was in trouble—deep trouble—but its chances for finding responses mutually satisfactory to its creditors and itself were good, because it was a strong, viable economy, with a vigorous private sector and essentially good economic management, even though it was going through a troublesome period of political change. The Brazilian economy entered a painful period of adjusting to its loss of creditworthiness, jeopardizing decades of gains. In 1985, Brazil elected its first civilian government in 21 years. In February 1986, the government of President José Sarney announced a new stabilization program, and in March 1986, Brazil reached a new commercial bank rescheduling agreement. It remains to be seen whether the new economic program will work. Most critical is the effort to halt virulent inflation by price freezing, a technique that has repeatedly failed in the past.

Intense negotiations are taking place among the many borrowing countries, lending banks, and other interested parties regarding how to handle the outstanding debt. Many suggestions have been made by governments, bankers, and others, including myself. They include limiting debt service to a certain percentage of foreign exchange earnings; postponing servicing by extending amortizations and converting interest due into principal; relating, and presumably reducing, interest rates to rates of world inflation; converting medium-term and longer-term debt into much longer-term debt with generous grace periods; marking down debt to reflect market values; selling unwanted debt to world investors; and converting debt into equity. These suggestions are not mutually exclusive; they can be combined in seeking compromises and agreement. Hard bargaining is inevitable and desirable; it will help gain acceptance for whatever may be agree upon. In retrospect, the terms of agreement will not be as important as resolving the issue of what to do. The test of success should be that the restoration of creditworthiness and the resumption of incremental, voluntary lending by banks and other private sources of finance are no longer inhibited by the overhang of the past debt.

The issues raised by the Brazilian experience remain unresolved. The international financial scene continues to be dominated by two different, though interrelated, concerns: the viability of banking systems in the United States and other industrial countries and the harmful effects, in borrowing countries, from loss of access to commercial banks and other private sources of finance. Instead of *growth*, *austerity* became the fashionable word, until events made clear that austerity, which does not lead to restoration of creditworthiness and resumption of growth, cannot endure in developing countries. New approaches emphasize growth but with little focus on how growth is to be accomplished.

Before delving further into the international financial situation and the debt crisis, it may be useful to look briefly at the world economy and the role of the international financial system. It is the nature of the world economy that determines the structure and functioning of the international financial system.

3

The World Economy and the Mixed International Financial System

T HE primary role of money and credit is to facilitate the efficient functioning of national economies. The secondary role, which is often dominant, is to help national economies achieve social and political objectives. These generalizations also apply to the international financial system. The international financial system consists of many institutions, policies, and practices. From the viewpoint of the developing countries and the current international financial crisis, the principal institutions are the private banks, the International Monetary Fund, the global and regional development banks (the World Bank and the African, Asian, and Inter-American Development Banks), and the official bilateral aid institutions.

Private and public institutions, policies, and practices function simultaneously. Each can be examined and analyzed separately but cannot be understood well unless examined in the context of the other elements in the system. The closest analogy is the financial system of a country. The financial system in the United States, for example, is very complex and encompasses myriad public and private institutions. Fully describing the system is nearly impossible, because it includes a wide variety of official institutions and practices—the public finance of the federal government, with its revenues, expenditures, and financing of deficits (or disposal of surpluses when, or if, they occur); the Federal Reserve System; the fiscal institutions and practices of the state and local governments; governmental specialized lending institutions in housing, agriculture, energy, and the like; such policies as state-supported industrial bonds and subsidies; bond issues of local school boards; and so forth. In addition, there are hosts of private financial institutions, which can be categorized as being in the credit or money markets or in the capital markets. Whereas banks function in the credit or money markets, insurance companies and trusts provide funds through instruments issued and traded in capital markets. Capital market instruments are usually of much longer duration or maturity than credits or loans made by banks. In practice, however, the dividing lines are obscure and are often ignored. For example, floating rate notes, issued in markets by banks to investors, have the characteristics of capital issues but are also similar to bank deposits; and certificates of deposits range over a wide spectrum of maturities.

In addition to lending by commercial banks, investment banks, insurance companies, venture capital firms, and others, also provide funds on varying terms. Moreover, private financial institutions are strictly regulated and supervised by officials at all levels of government. Regulations on certain interest rates, on lending, and on deposit taking are enforced at various levels of government by bank supervisors and regulatory authorities that operate simultaneously.

In addition to these lending institutions and practices, there are mechanisms for raising and marketing of equity—that is, shares in ownership•and earnings. The stock markets are the principal and most visible mechanisms, but many others exist, such as the private placement markets. Many governmental regulations control these institutions. In the United States, the Securities and Exchange Commission is the most important and most visible regulator, but again, many other regulations issued by federal, state, and local authorities also affect the functions of these markets.

A true picture of finance in the United States would fill an encyclopedia devoted only to this subject. Its many parts work simultaneously, efficiently, and with relatively little friction, and it provides the financial services that are necessary for the economy. However, much controversy arises regarding the policies that should guide these financial institutions—for example, "public" finance, the budget, and the Federal Reserve System. Such controversy concerning the management of the money supply never ends and is rarely resolved to everyone's satisfaction. Deficits in the budget also cause much controversy—even regarding whether they are desirable or undesirable.

The financial system meshes these great varieties of institutions and practices and allows policy objectives to be pursued with the confidence that these institutions will work reasonably well. Indeed, policy approaches assume that changes in policies will result in changes in the behavior of all institutions, because they are assumed to be interlinked efficiently by markets and institutional practices, which are assisted, in turn, by modern technology. The fact that they involve public and private institutions complicates matters, but not to the extent that the system is unable to function reasonably well. The different institutions reflect society's desired division of labor among them, and public policies, markets, and managements integrate these institutions into an efficient system.

The international financial system has not reached this stage of sophistication and efficiency. Just as financial panics in the nineteenth century and the first half of the twentieth century plagued the U.S. economy because of the immaturity of its domestic financial system, so do international debt crises in the second half of the twentieth century reflect the immaturity of the international financial system.

The environment in which the international financial system operates is essentially made by the conditions and policies of national economies. Within national economies, however, economic decisions are affected by conditions in all other national economies. Global markets create the demands for final products, and the output and sale of any one product involves elements and activities in many countries. As thousands—even millions—of transactions go on simultaneously, the global character of economic behavior creates interconnecting webs of many layers. The organizing mechanism that creates order out of this incredible complexity is the existence of markets, which are the coordinating poles in the system of webs. When markets are disrupted, the global economic system ceases to be a system within countries as well as among countries. The global economic system is composed, however, of national economies governed as nation-states.

The world lives with the tensions created by the simultaneous existence of different nation-states. National policies aim to achieve national objectives—output, employment, growth, investments, savings, living standards, and so on. The instruments used to achieve these objectives are national instruments, especially fiscal policies and practices and monetary measures, such as credit creation and interest rates, exchange rates, foreign trade, and investment laws. Although the objectives and mechanisms are national, they function in a global economy. Thus, the achievement of such national objectives as growth, employment, profitability, investments, and living standards depends on the national policies of other countries. Even the largest economies—such as the United States, Japan, and the USSR—cannot achieve their national objectives through their own endeavors. They need imports from other countries to meet production requirements or consumption needs and demands. They also need exports to create large enough markets to make domestic output profitable and to earn the foreign exchange needed to pay for imports. More complicated is the functioning of national interest rates, which are intended to affect domestic levels of demand and prices but cannot achieve their goals if other countries or their nationals act counter to their aims. For example, high interest rates may be designed to reduce domestic demand for credit and dampen economic activity. However, if nationals of other countries decide to bring their money into a country because the interest rates are relatively attractive, the effect is expansionary rather than the desired contractionary situation. The impact of the United States on Canada and Mexico is obvious; less obvious, however, is the impact of the world on the United States. It has been repeatedly demonstrated, in great detail, that employment and income in the United States are significantly affected by U.S. exports. Capital inflows into the United States during the last few years have made possible its huge external deficit in goods and services, which has reduced inflationary pressures. These inflows have helped finance the U.S. budgetary deficit while facilitating the decline in interest rates. However, they have escalated the global adjustment problem by helping to keep the U.S. dollar overvalued.

Thus, the world economy is an integrated global economy. It could be otherwise, but only with great costs in lower output, consumption, and technological progress.

Furthermore, it is not merely a question of foreign countries reacting as governments to the policies of some other government. Again, such reactions are easy to comprehend. An import quota to keep out foreign goods that are being dumped in a country is obvious retaliation to prevent the gains of dumping from being realized. More subtly, however, the conditions created in other countries by national policies can frustrate those policies without government actions. Thus, the devaluation of the dollar may well increase U.S.

exports, but if it discourages U.S. imports at the same time, it may make it less possible for countries to earn the foreign exchange they need to buy more exports from the United States and thus may cause them to take measures to restrict their purchases from the United States.

These dilemmas let loose powerful forces. They cannot be wished out of existence or left out of our thinking merely because they are difficult to perceive and even more difficult to resolve in ways that are acceptable to the countries involved. It may be well argued that many of these dilemmas would resolve themselves if markets were allowed to operate without being affected significantly by government policies. Evidence of the validity of this view is found in the nearly miraculous way in which the intricacies of the world economy are coordinated continuously by markets, even during conditions that are considered very adverse. Nevertheless, it is necessary to recognize the profound role of national governments in modern societies and their economies. At one extreme is the way markets are highly regulated under wartime conditions. National aims of self-preservation and military victory result in policies that determine economic behavior. Consumption and investment levels, production and distribution, labor force structure, wages, profits, availability of raw materials, transportation, credit, international trade, and so forth, are made part of the national effort to win the war. Governments provide the leadership, and economic incentives and disincentives are employed to military ends. Markets become the mechanisms for achieving governmental objectives, and the economic behavior of individuals and firms becomes explainable only in terms of governmental policies.

What is less obvious is the economic impact of the cold war. Unlike "hot" wars in the past, which ended and were followed by peacetime behavior based on economic market-driven conditions, the cold war is continuous. Its justification, ultimately, is to preserve societies and economies and to maintain their freedom from outside interference or even abolition. Weight is added by the fact that it is the two superpowers—the United States and the USSR—that are ideologically in conflict, and their ideological conflict is about the entire system of organized societies. Their coexistence is not an issue; they do coexist. The tensions arise because of the fear that each system is threatened by the existence of the other and that the other has the military means to impose drastic change.

In the United States, the cold war means the central preoccupation of government with political-military considerations. Although the size of the defense budget is usually the most publicized aspect of this preoccupation, a closer examination reveals that political-military influence is much more pervasive. For example, the United States cannot be indifferent to its sources of oil, to the vulnerability of its international communications system, to the export of technology applicable to war efforts, or to the economic and social conditions in countries deemed of strategic importance in the cold war. The list of such factors could go on indefinitely. These are matters that cannot be left to markets and to market incentives and disincentives. Often, market considerations go contrary to national interests of defense, as has happened repeatedly in various embargoes by U.S. presidents, which have been regarded as necessary for the national interest but have been hurtful to the industries involved. The U.S. government maintains considerable regulation over private business, although efforts have been made to deregulate in recent years. The government can deregulate some activities, and has done so, but the fundamentals of a cold war economy remain.

Other countries outside NATO and the Soviet bloc do not consider themselves participants in the cold war, but they are involved in the proverbial competition for the hearts and minds of their own people. Each country is eager to have a socioeconomic system that commands the loyalty of its people, and governments follow policies intended to give them this loyalty. Occasionally, governments that ignore this condition fall, and their place is taken by those who promise to be concerned and to make successful efforts to meet the aspirations of their people. Again, although markets are global and integrated, national policies are dominated by such domestic, social, and political conditions.

A common response to the aspirations of modern societies is the welfare state, which had its roots in the conditions and thoughts of the nineteenth and early twentieth centuries. The Great Depression and World War II gave a sense of urgency to problems of unemployment, living standards (housing, food), illness, education, old age, and the like. Solving these problems was not to be left to the play of market conditions, especially because of the repeated recurrence of severe economic or business cycles. Governments had to act to prevent widespread social distress and social discontent. They did so and achieved the desired social and political order. The government plays a determining role in the welfare state. In the post–World War

II period, the governments in industrial countries disagreed on the details of the welfare state, but they did not disagree fundamentally. Even governments that are ideologically committed to market-oriented free-enterprise systems do not dismantle the welfare state. They stop well short, thus perpetuating the strong role of dominating government, irrespective of political party. Yet these governments cannot determine national conditions by their own actions; they are limited by conditions in other countries and by the policies of other governments.

At the same time, the market-oriented free-enterprise system has adapted to these conditions. It has done so by making itself compatible with, or even the instrument of, the welfare state. The system conflicts with government policies that interfere with the operations of the market, but the worldwide network of markets, which guides global production and distribution, operates within governmental parameters. Reflecting this mixture of private and governmental factors, the international financial system involves the operations of private and official institutions—national, regional, and global—and government policies greatly influence all of them.

Given these conditions, the international financial system does not serve the interests of the private sectors or the goals of governments alone. It endeavors to serve both simultaneously, but these interests often conflict. Thus, repeated disruptions are experienced in the financial system. For example, in the 1970s, the private banking world was able to develop an efficient international banking system to meet the external credit needs of many developing countries. This was most acceptable to the governments of lenders and creditors alike. The borrowing entities and the borrowing countries, whether private or governmental, had to meet the lending criteria of the banks. The banks acted on the basis of the credit standing of the borrowing entity, the risks that arose from being in a particular country, considerations of portfolio management, and profitability. Strong country risks made many borrowers ineligible for credits from private sources, even though they were prepared to pay otherwise attractive interest rates and had the goodwill of the governments in the creditor countries. Official institutions performed the external financing role for such countries.

A mixed mechanism of public and private financial institutions worked well and led, in the 1960s, to an expansion of branch banking throughout the developing countries. In the 1970s, the expansion resulted in the well-known large increases in commercial bank lending to many developing countries. At the same time, the World Bank and the regional multilateral development banks greatly increased their project financing, as other poorer developing countries increased their absorptive capacities and creditor/donor countries supported the expanded lending programs of these official banks. The principal preoccupation was the felt need to provide more official funds on a grantlike basis to the poorer countries. The multilateral development banks increased their "soft loan" lending; the International Development Association of the World Bank was by far the most important of these banks; but it was not the only one. During this period, the International Monetary Fund had to be only a minor or occasional provider of international finance.

When the world recession occurred in the 1980s, the weaknesses in the international financial system became evident. The mechanisms of the international financial system were there to deal with external financial needs, but the elements were too small, too slow to respond, or unwilling to act. The cautiousness of the commercial bank lenders (always more risk-averting than official lenders) resulted in a sharp reduction in net lending to developing countries, especially, as noted earlier, to their formerly largest borrowers in Latin America.

In a rational, efficient system, the international governmental institutions would have stepped into the breach and would have provided the needed external financing to avoid more damaging consequences of the world recession than was inherent in the changed global conditions. This did happen to a considerable extent. Most important was the expansion of the financial role of the International Monetary Fund, whose net lending to developing countries rose from nearly zero in 1979 to about $11 billion in 1983. These amounts were large, however, only in the context of the IMF; they were small in terms of the need. The member countries could have productively used much more from the IMF. In addition, the other official entities—such as the World Bank and the Inter-American Development Bank—expanded their activities and modified their practices to be of quicker assistance. Much was done, but not nearly enough to avoid the need for drastic reductions in imports by the developing countries in Latin America and Africa, thus adding to the depressed conditions in the exporting nations of North America and Europe. The international political will to act collaboratively to limit the damage to the world economy was too weak to do more. It was, however, much ahead of the world's responses to the world depression of the 1930s. Protectionism and "beggar-thy-neighbor" policies did not flourish in the 1980s as they had in the 1930s, although they increased as protectionist pressures grew. The international machinery put in place after World War II proved helpful and durable, though inadequate and often too slow.

In the 1980s (and in the future) the world needed official international institutions—comparable to the Federal Reserve System in the United States or central banks in other countries—that were able to provide international financing quickly, orderly, and adequately. That financing need not have been automatic and indiscriminate. It could have had conditions similar to those that were used. The effect would have been very different, however, if the funds had been adequate in magnitudes and available when needed, avoiding the time-consuming need for mobilization and packaging while countries were hemorrhaging. Progress in raising living standards and growth rates in countries like Brazil and Mexico and the positive impact this would have had on the entire world economy could not be sustained during the world depression of the 1980s, but the setbacks need not have been as damaging and enduring if the international official agencies had been able to act more quickly and effectively. They had the mechanisms, but they were not in a state of readiness because the available resources were much too small.

Although it cannot be proved, it is arguable that if the international official system had been adequate, the private system would not have retreated so much from its role. A major element in that retreat was the obvious absence of adequate support from other external sources. With an adequate international financial system, the events of 1980–82 need not have resulted in the major setbacks that it may well take the world over a decade, if not more, to recover from—with all this means in human, social, and political terms.

The past cannot be undone, but the lesson for the future can be drawn and acted on in time to avoid compounding the harmful effects of past inadequacies. The alternative is not to turn to governmental or private institutions; this is not a true alternative in the world of "mixed" economies and competing political systems. Rather, the need is to understand that private institutions cannot perform like official institutions, and vice versa, even when they seem to be nearly alike. Their responses to conditions are different, and they become inefficient and even counterproductive when they are made to act contrary to their fundamental characteristics. A private bank operates for profit, and its shareholders, managers, and employees are the beneficiaries of its actions. It is not in the "foreign aid" business—its managers are not "statesmen," and they do not run governments or take responsibility for government. They cannot undertake to follow the lead of governmental institutions without jeopardizing their efficiency and viability. The reverse is also true. Governmental institutions are not run for profit, even though some make profit incidental to pursuing their political purposes. Their justification is the validity of these political purposes. If the purposes are not valid, the institutions cannot gain legitimacy by showing profits. Although helping private entities, including private institutions, might be part of their political purpose, their real purpose is the public interest. Where that public interest is not served, governmental institutions cannot be reliable supports or aids to private commercial banks.

The efficient meshing of the private and official financial institutions requires recognition of their separate and different characteristics. It is necessary for official international financial institutions to step in when private financial institutions falter—not to rescue the private institution but to protect the world economy and its constituent elements, the national economies.

To understand the working of the international financial system, it may be useful to expand further on the role of government in modern societies and economies. As noted earlier, the political systems of countries reflect the deep involvement of government in economic matters. The great domestic political issues in most developed countries—such as the franchise, representation, the judicial system, separation of powers, or freedom of speech, assembly, press, and so on—are not usually political. More often, the principal issues are economic and closely related social issues, such as employment, interest rates, education, health care, the environment, and the family. The issues are about what governments should *do*, rather than what they should *not* do. Political parties are organized to represent economic interests and groups; they are pro-labor, pro-business, pro-Medicare, or pro-deregulation. Those concerned with economic issues form special-interest groups to further their economic interests through the political process. Thus, all economic issues become political issues. Instead of the invisible hand of the market governing and coordinating economic behavior of individuals and firms, it is the highly visible public clash of special-interest groups, and their political instruments, that determines most economic behavior and conditions. The belief in giving to government as little as possible and taking from government as much as possible is not generally considered socially or politically immoral. Governments are to be used to further special interests.

In international economic relations, governments are pressured quite openly by special interests to serve their special needs. Other special interests are expected to oppose these pressures if it serves their interest to do so. Monetary and financial actions of governments in such areas as exchange rates and foreign aid are political acts, and what governments will do cannot be deduced from economic analysis alone. This is of critical importance in judging the role of the international financial organizations. To the degree that they are dominated by national politics, they are less able to act as economic institutions. Governments have to make the political decision to allow these institutions, which they govern, to act on technical grounds. Otherwise, these institutions are severely constrained in their ability to make their needed contributions to the world economy.

Another fundamental characteristic of the world economy that enhances the role of government is the phenomenon of accelerated development of the developing countries that constitute a large majority of the world's populations. Leaving aside, at least for the moment, the question of whether governments could do relatively more or less and the private sector could do more or less, the basic fact is that the modernization of the developing countries is not left to the workings of competitive markets that are relatively free of governmental influences. Governments provide vigorous leadership and often direct control and command. The head of state is often designated the country's chief economic planner. As in the industrial countries, private enterprises and markets are usually the mechanisms for implementing government purposes and policies, but the economic life in the country is decisively determined by government. Government intervention in economic matters is taken for granted.

The aim of government is to accelerate changes in economic and social conditions. These changes may be regarded as undesirable by some, but the demand is then for different governmental policies, not for the withdrawal of government as the primary influence in economic affairs. The issues in a developing country include government subsidization of consumption versus government encouragement of domestic investment; investment in social capital, such as schools and hospitals, versus investment in power generators or manufacturing plants; more food production for domestic consumption versus more primary product production for export; cheap interest rates for entrepreneurs versus higher interest rates to induce more savings; and indexation of wages with inflationary rises in living costs versus flexible wage policies to raise profitability, increase output, and reduce inflationary pressures. Although this litany could go on and on, what is important for understanding the world economy as it is and the international financial system as it is, is that these issues are issues of government and that the critically important decisions in these areas are those of government. The international financial system provides the credit (and some equity) for this world. The behavior of the systems, however, is determined by these actions of governments, even though the working out in individual consumption and investment decisions is done largely through private enterprises operating in markets. Thus, the lender is dealing with borrowing entities, but judgments on the creditworthiness of the lender and its future as a business organization are also judgments on the governing of the country and about the borrowing entity.

Again, as in the industrial, highly capitalized, modernized countries, nationalism reinforces a strong role for government. In developing countries, there are often disturbing and, at times, violent ethnic problems and international threats of invasion and war. Governments are expected to solve social and economic problems in ways that serve immediate national interests. If depressed conditions hit the country, the government must expel the previously welcomed foreign workers and prohibit immigration. If foreign-owned enterprises seem more profitable than competing domestically owned enterprises, the government must limit the foreign firm's ability to obtain credit or must give domestic firms credit on cheaper terms. Domestic import substitution (that is, keeping out foreign goods) is extolled as economically virtuous, even by those who ought to know better. Agreeing to an international code of behavior, as in the IMF, is a major step for a developing country. It involves trying to reconcile the pursuit of nationalistically defined goals with an internationally agreed-upon code of financial behavior. Conflicts are frequent, and the nationalistic values usually prevail.

Thus, for a developing country to agree to follow domestic policies that are acceptable to (or even drafted by) an international organization can create nearly violent internal tensions. This is a major issue in the current international financial crises, since countries are being required to follow IMF programs. Where nationalism prevails—and it prevails nearly everywhere—national pride and even suspicion of foreigners is taken for granted. In international financial relations, this aspect is not so troublesome when borrowers know that international agreement on national policies will result in substantial external assistance. It becomes very troublesome, however, when borrowers are told that the policies of their countries disqualify them for foreign loans or that available funds are inadequate to meet politically defined needs. Salt is added to the wounds when the lender insists that foreigners judge whether policy changes that are regarded as necessary are adequate and are being implemented. The national pride of the developing country is often outraged, and the deeply rooted resentments of earlier colonial periods are rekindled. In an international financial system made up of private lenders to private borrowers, such attitudes might be less important, so long as the private lenders are regarded as profit seekers, not meddlers in domestic politics. In an international system made up of private and governmental lenders to private and governmental borrowers, these nationalistic attitudes are often of prime importance.

Other aspects of the international financial system closely related to the role of government are technology and management. Modern technology is complex and expensive, yet it is applicable in all countries, irrespective of their economic systems. In developing countries, governments are frequently the instruments for the introduction of technology, even when the users are in the private sector. The government is expected to obtain the needed financing, technical assistance, and managers. It looks, in turn, to governmental institutions, such as foreign aid programs or the World Bank, and to private sources to provide the needed financing and experts. The international financial system again comes into play in a mixed way. Besides equity, the private commercial banks are involved in financing technology transfer and application, whether the borrower is a private firm or a government agency. However, financial requirements often exceed the creditworthiness of the borrower. Official funds may then be required, and the financing can be a combination of private banks, official lenders, and private equity raised in capital markets in various forms, such as limited partnerships or equity pools. These combinations of financing are particularly suited to projects that result in profit-making enterprises, such as tourist recreation centers, industrial parks, or airports and harbors. In these activities, private merchant and investment banks play an important mobilization and coordinating role—or these functions may be performed by smaller entities, called "boutiques" because they are relatively small and specialized. These are traditional activities in international finance, and they are performed in a manner much like banking in earlier centuries, when bankers were merchants, or close associates of merchants, whose own equity was at stake in their financial operations. In these combined merchant banking activities, the banker must know all the sources of international finance and must combine them in new mixtures suited to the particular activity that requires financing.

In modern banking, the commercial bank proudly insists that it performs financial services and earns interest, commissions and fees. It is usually not an investor, in that it does not seek equity or profits from the enterprises it helps finance. Whether a merchant or commercial banker, the banker must be fully aware of the nature of the economy and government in which the new or expanding activity is located. The banker takes this mixed world as it is. Some of the funds sought are available from private financial markets on market-determined financial terms. Others are obtained from official sources. The merchant banker is thus a negotiator seeking the best combination of financial terms for the client. This, in turn, depends on the best (I hesitate to use the word *optimal*) combination of sources of finance, which are by no means uniform nor determined by formula. The banker acting as a negotiator and coordinator is performing a very different financial function from that of the banker whose institution accepts deposits, or otherwise borrows from financial markets, and then lends these funds at a margin above costs to earn its profits. A commercial bank creates or destroys money and thus adds to or subtracts from the world money supply. A merchant or investment banker taps the available sources of money for a particular use. Thus, money supply watchers correctly pay much more attention to the activities of commercial banks than to those of investment or merchant banks.

In examining the fundamental aspects of the world economy that significantly affect the international financial system, it is also necessary to add the phenomenon of persistent inflation, which was briefly mentioned earlier and will be mentioned again because of its pervasive importance. Throughout the past 40 years, inflation has been important in all economies, though at differing rates. Even during the recent global recession of the early 1980s, inflation continued in the developed countries. In many of the developing countries, inflation rates are as high as or higher than ever. This persistent global inflation has destabilized the international monetary system and has kept it unstable for decades.

Exchange rates have become chronically volatile and uncertain. Speculative international movements of funds or capital are induced by the uncertainty of exchange rates and differing domestic interest rates as national governments deal differently with their domestic inflationary pressures. Exchange rates govern all international movements of funds, whatever their causes. With the uncertainties and disturbances created by persistent global inflation, it becomes most difficult to judge the likely course of exchange rates. In the more distant past, before World War II, relative changes in national price levels tended to be closely reflected in exchange rate movements (commonly called *purchasing-power parity*). Other determinants of exchange rate behavior were relative national changes in gold supplies, productivity, balance of payments, international trade, and central bank or monetary policies. Exchange rates have obeyed no predictable rule of behavior. The undervaluation of the U.S. dollar in the late 1970s and its overvaluation in the 1980s—both unexpected—greatly influenced domestic and international conditions throughout the world. With the overvalued U.S. dollar, U.S. industry experienced unfair competition from foreign suppliers and unnecessary burdens in competing in foreign markets. The U.S. automobile industry was depressed while non-U.S. automobile manufacturers expanded their sales in the United States, taking advantage of the overvalued dollar.

The world system of exchange rates works in the sense that markets exist in which currencies are bought and sold. These markets are technically very efficient; they are tied by electronic devices and they operate around the globe on a continuing 24-hour basis. All transactions, even huge ones, are consummated virtually instantaneously; and risks of most sorts can be hedged immediately, even though they involve buyers and sellers of currencies thousands of miles apart. This efficiency, however, is not to be mistaken for efficiency of the international monetary system. The international monetary system, of which the International Monetary Fund is the central manager, is designed to promote world prosperity by encouraging growth, productivity, and international trade. It aims to achieve a system of exchange rates that promotes these goals. A world of volatile, unrealistic exchange rates, combined with high levels of unemployment and low levels of growth in most countries, is not fulfilling the objectives of the international monetary system, however efficiently the exchange markets operate.

A reasonable degree of exchange rate predictability is needed for a healthy world economy. This predictability is not being provided by the international monetary system as it exists, but it would be facilitated by the creation of noninflationary conditions in most developed countries. However, the international financial system cannot, by itself, end inflation or create exchange rate stability. Until these conditions of stability are established, the international financial system will be buffeted by waves of international speculation and currency instability. Nevertheless, the system has to operate. The real world goes on, though much less efficiently and with otherwise avoidable distress to millions of people. In these disturbed conditions, the simultaneous existence of private and governmental institutions makes it more possible to reduce the adverse effects of an inherently disturbed system.

The international financial system cannot create stability, but it can be prepared for instability. The key is anticipation—recognizing the inevitability of disturbances. Financial institutions can have policies and practices that allow them to be ready for such disturbances or that help prevent them. Crisis management can be orderly, efficient, and flexible, but not if crisis means surprise and lack of preparation, as in 1982. With the mixture of private and public institutions, it is possible to shift gears from one set of institutions to another set quickly, without unnecessary friction, delay, and disturbances.

Sources of
International Finance

4

International Banking:
Conceptions and
Misconceptions

T HE most important single source of international finance, especially for developing countries, is the commercial banking
system; therefore, banking is given more detailed attention than
other sources. In discussions of international banking, confusion and
misunderstanding are constantly created because people are unfa-
miliar with some elementary facts and concepts. Even very careful
commentators make critical errors—critical in the sense that they
result in profound misunderstandings, and attitudes on policy issues
become thoroughly distorted. The intent here is to clarify some of
the basic concepts that are most relevant to the subject of this book,
especially the external debt crisis and the functioning of the international financial system.

An International Loan: What It Is

An international loan is one in which the lender and the borrower
are residents of different countries. Whereas the loan originates from
the country of the lender, the obligation is regarded as domiciled in
the country in which the borrower resides. Moreover, the lending
institution may be owned by shareholders outside the country in
which the lender legally resides. Thus, a branch of an American
bank in the Bahamas or Britain is lending from these countries even
if the bank's owners are in New York, Chicago, or San Francisco.
The loan is described as "booked" in the Bahamas or Britain, because

that is where the lending institution resides and where it is chartered by the local banking authorities to be in the banking business. Central banks are usually responsible for issuing such charters. In the United States, banks can be chartered on the federal or state levels, and there are many different layers of federal and state bank regulators, reflecting the federal character of the U.S. political system.

Moreover, a loan can be made by private entities or by official entities, but this does not affect its geographic designation. When a loan is made by multilateral institutions, such as the World Bank, it is categorized as multinational, not according to the country in which the multilateral lender is located. Thus, World Bank loans are not regarded as loans from the United States.

What Constitutes International Debt

An international debt is the obligation resulting from an international loan; it is categorized according to the location or residence of the borrower. Thus, when a German-owned subsidiary of Mercedes-Benz that is located in Sao Paolo, Brazil, borrows from an American bank in Dallas, Texas, it results in "Brazilian" debt. If the loan is guaranteed by some entity in the credit-extending country, such as the Export-Import Bank of the United States, it is still categorized by some as "Brazilian" debt, even though the lender has recourse to a non-Brazilian guarantor if the debt is not repaid. The same situation holds if collateral held outside the borrowing country is given for a loan. The dominant principle is that the country in which the borrower is an entity is the country "at risk." Again, as in the case of loans, debts incurred by a multilateral institution are not attributed to the countries in which the institution resides. For example, the borrowings of the African Development Bank, which is headquartered in the Ivory Coast, are not regarded as debts of the Ivory Coast. The borrower can be any entity—a government or state-owned enterprise, a private business firm, a nonprofit institution, or an individual—and the maturities of the loan can vary from hours to years. Thus, statistics on "Brazilian" debt sum all kinds of loans, with greatly differing borrowers, degrees of risk, and financial terms. Aggregate national statistics on lending and debt cover an incredible mixture of borrowers and lenders. Thus, generalizations about lending and debt, which ignore these differences and complexities, are frequently wrong and misleading.

Risks in Lending

Whatever kind of lending a bank does—domestical or international—banking is a risk acceptance business. In this respect, an international loan or debt is fundamentally the same as a national or domestic loan or debt.

To the lending bank, a loan is an income-earning asset—a risk asset, to be precise. When a loan is made, the borrower's account is credited with the loan proceeds. Deposits are also created by monies deposited in the bank by others. Reserve requirements—say 20 percent—act as a brake on total deposit creation, but a bank has built-in multipliers that make it possible to run profitably on the basis of a low return per loan.

The bank's total risk assets constitute its portfolio of loans, which is usually the main source of bank income. Risk assets are acquired because they are deemed profitable after consideration of the risks involved. The principal risk is that the borrower will not honor its obligation to repay or service the loan and interest thereon fully and promptly. All loans are risky. Interest earned on the loan must compensate the lending bank for risk. Thus, there is a risk/reward equation, or ratio, to guide lending decisions. The banks rely on established credit analyses to judge risk and to decide whether the risk/reward ratio is acceptable to the bank. In addition, knowing that any judgment may prove wrong in practice, the bank diversifies its risks to avoid holding too many eggs in any one basket—that is, its portfolio. However, diversification does not guarantee future avoidance of bunched loan servicing difficulties. Banks may have made many loans to different borrowers in a particular industry, such as the oil industry, or in a particular foreign country when such loans were acceptable risks. Then, adverse conditions—especially downturns in business cycles, prolonged inflation, slow growth of an economy, or collapse in a commodity price—can affect many firms in the industry, or even in a combination of industries. Thus, many loans originally judged credit-acceptable and spread over a large number of borrowers can become doubtful more or less simultaneously, resulting in unwanted concentration. Similarly, loans in one country can become doubtful simultaneously, even though they were originally regarded as diversified and sound. These are the hazards of the banking business.

Banks have capital and reserves to meet adversities. Their reserves are invested in such holdings as U.S. Treasury securities or

otherwise readily marketable securities. Banks can also borrow from
central monetary authorities, such as the Federal Reserve in the
United States. Banks are also borrowers from others—ordinary depositors, holders of their certificates of deposits and commercial
notes issued, or other banks. Thus, banks need to defend their own
creditworthiness as borrowers. If they are seen to be in danger of
becoming unable to meet their obligations, even temporarily—that
is, becoming illiquid—their creditors, especially other banks, will
withdraw their deposits or loans, and others will refuse to substitute
for these withdrawals. A bank might become unable to meet its obligations and might even have to close its doors. This condition occurs from time to time. When it is widespread, there is a financial
crisis or what used to be called a financial panic.

In modern banking, capital and reserves are only a small fraction
of total risk assets—about 6 percent. Serious problems of simultaneous default on many loans, whether the problems arise in the domestic economy or abroad, can add up to more than the total capital
and reserves. When this happens, banks are threatened with insolvency. However, more urgent and truer to actual conditions is the
threat of illiquidity—that is, when the income from loan assets of
the banks are not currently adequate to meet the banks' own obligations and when they do not have sufficient cash assets to make up
the difference. Their creditors are not willing to continue to lend to
the banks that are having difficulties, and their borrowers cannot
accelerate their payments to the banks. Their loan assets may well
be mostly sound in the longer run, but they are not readily marketable, except at great losses. Such banks are not really insolvent, but
they are short of cash to meet the demands of their obligors. It is on
such occasions that central monetary authorities, acting as "lenders
of last resort," come to help. In many circumstances, individual depositors are protected by governmental insurance up to designated
limits.

These factors are shared by all risk assets, domestic or international. An international loan is not fundamentally different from a
domestic loan. For these reasons, loan portfolios usually combine
domestic and international loans. In the Eurocurrency markets—that
is, financial markets in which foreign currency loans are booked outside the country in which the used currency is issued—there are no
reserve requirements. The magnitudes of these loans are not constrained; they can rise, and have risen, explosively. When interna-

tional loans are spread among a number of countries, when they are not in difficulty in several foreign countries simultaneously, or when they constitute a small portion of the total portfolio, concern with international lending is not great. It is when the domestic portfolios are in trouble, when loans to troubled countries aggregate large numbers, or when there is a combination of both conditions that concern becomes keen and widespread. Then total loans in a troubled country are compared with a bank's capital and reserves and found to be relatively large. The same is done in domestic sectors, such as real estate, farming and oil. Such ratios of loan assets to capital and reserves often focus attention on capital accumulation as the primary way to deal with uncertainty and risk in banking.

The very existence of high ratios between loan risk assets and capital, and the fact that bank lending requires that banks be able to borrow and that bank deposits created by loans can be withdrawn by borrowers, means that the banks are always vulnerable to illiquidity and even to insolvency. Banks must have access to extraordinary sources of funds, such as a lender of last resort. This function may not be automatic, and it cannot be taken for granted by the lending bank, but it must be a viable alternative if required. Since the bank is being monitored by the central bank or monetary agency that will be the lender of last resort, the lender of last resort can help avoid difficulties by the way it exercises its regulatory authority or cooperates with other banking supervisory authorities.

Banking is also made more vulnerable by the network of banking that characterizes national banking systems and that is transformed into a global network by international lending and borrowing. Banks lend largely to each other. Smaller banks tend to hold their surplus funds on deposit with larger banks. Banks also hold balances in other countries; for example, Japanese banks hold balances in the United States, and vice versa. In the United States, funds of so-called regional banks and foreign banks are usually held in the major money center banks in New York, Chicago, Boston, and so on. Money center banks are always faced with the potential withdrawal of such deposits. The depositing banks are very cautious and sensitive to risks, since their own solvency and liquidity depend on the security of their deposits with the major banks. This is particularly true of the smaller banks. In the case of Continental Illinois, for example, rumors of difficulties with a portion of the bank's portfolio led to large withdrawals by foreign and domestic banks. A financial diffi-

culty was thus transformed into a financial crisis for Continental Illinois. Such situations have happened before, and they are likely to
happen again.

Regarding international lending, the smaller banks are affected
by adversities of their own borrowing clients, but they are also mindful of potential adversities for the major banks in which they have
deposits. They often believe that the larger banks will be rescued by
the monetary authorities if necessary because of their importance to
other banks and to the business community in general. They cannot
be certain of this, however, and must assume, at least, that delays
will be experienced. Thus, banking by small and large banks is a
high-risk, sensitive business, whether lending is done domestically
or internationally.

Special Risks in International Lending and Offsets

Special risks arise in international lending because the borrower resides in a country different from the country of the lender. In addition, governments or "sovereigns" are often the borrowers. Sovereigns are subject to contractual obligations, but they can act to
protect a general or national interest in a way that makes the fulfillment of an individual loan contract impossible or changes its profitability for the lender. The most general risk in international lending
is that the private or official borrower will not be allowed to purchase
the foreign exchange needed to service its foreign debt. This *transfer
risk* is common to all recent cases of external debts.

Restructuring of debt is a time-honored way of dealing with a
loan when a debtor has trouble meeting the servicing obligations. It
is widely used in domestic and international lending. It takes on
heightened importance and is transformed when the restructuring
covers a large number of borrowers simultaneously and a large number of creditor banks.

Restructuring of external debt is designed to reduce the amount
of foreign exchange needed during an agreed period for the servicing
of past debt. The restructuring nearly always involves extending the
maturity; in theory, it can also apply to interest payments. In practice, banks are much more reluctant to restructure interest payments,
as these are critical for the earnings of the bank. A bank's profitability
usually depends mostly on income from risk assets, and the bank's
financial statements reflect actual and anticipated earnings based on

existing loan contracts. Failure to receive such interest payments means less attractive income statements, because the unrealized revenue is subtracted from current income statements. Such a "nonperforming" loan means less income than was expected and publicly forecast. Lenders to banks, especially institutional lenders and other banks, carefully scrutinize these financial statements. Regulatory authorities are responsible for ensuring that these financial statements are realistic and that they can be used to judge a bank's financial condition. Thus, banks give great weight to validating their income statements. If loans are declared to be substandard in performance, this results in charges against income to set up special reserves. However this is done, it means less income, lower profitability, and reduced confidence in the lending institution. Thus, international lending is more risky than domestic lending mostly because of the transfer risk, which does not exist within a country for a domestic loan.

On the other hand, there are aspects that diminish risk in international lending compared with domestic lending. First, the choice of borrowers can be very selective. This is especially true of borrowers in developing countries. The bank is in a strongly favorable position, even when the borrowers have strong credit standings—as the Brazilian and Mexican governments had in the 1970s and Korea and Singapore have in the 1980s. No bank wants unlimited assets in any of these countries, even those that meet the credit-extending criteria of the bank. Lending competitors are there, and they are usually constrained by similar lending limits. A forgone loan can be replaced with another one. Thus, there is no excuse for knowingly accepting a poor credit risk in international lending to a developing country. Of course, there is also no way to ensure that a carefully assessed credit will not turn sour at some time during the maturity of the loan.

It is not because of accident or carelessness that the biggest loan problems arise in cases that originally met strict credit assessment criteria, including professional projections of future cash flows. The fact that some projections prove to be wrong in time does not indicate that the techniques of projection making were poor or were applied poorly. In our highly complex world economy, projections of monetary phenomena that reflect the interaction of many dynamic factors always have a significant probability of proving to be wrong. This is not an argument against using projections; rather, it is an argument against portfolio management based on the assumption that projections will prove to be accurate. Projections are helpful in making analysis more thoughtful, but in banking, where the ability and willingness to service loans depend on numerous interacting factors, judgment is all-important—not only in choosing the assumptions for the projections but also in determining the best combination of risk assets to hold at any time. Portfolio management is neither an art nor a science; it is a profession. Defining lending standards and abiding by them to the best of one's ability are the best available defenses against risk and uncertainty.

Closely related to the point that lenders can be choosy is the point that they are less likely to be called on to finance activities of long-established customers that have special claims on the lending bank's loyalty. The borrower–lender relationship in international lending is more impersonal, thus creating a more favorable environment for objective decision making.

In addition, international loans are often made to governments and their various agencies—and countries do not go bankrupt and cease to exist. Their need to defend their creditworthiness endures beyond current difficulties, and their obligations are inherited by successor governments. They may repudiate their debts, but the immediate penalties for doing so are great: seizure of assets held abroad, loss of creditworthiness, and even virtual stoppage of international trade, combined with the likelihood that these critical adversities will be perpetuated. Unless adequate alternative sources of foreign exchange are available despite the repudiation, very few countries can tolerate these consequences. There is much talk of possible repudiation of external debt, but it is mostly nonsense. Perhaps the best argument is that if a country is finding, at a particular time, that its servicing costs in foreign exchange exceed inflows of funds from such sources, it cannot simply stop paying. A country does not—cannot—choose to disappear. The government must look to the future. It cannot simply let the future take care of itself, no matter what its political leaders say for contemporary domestic or international consumption. Private borrowers can threaten to disappear, and they often choose to do so. Governments of countries also can and do disappear, whether or not they choose to do so. Their countries, however, cannot and do not choose to disappear. Thus, even the poorest countries in the most adverse circumstances strive to maintain their external creditworthiness. They are happy to renegotiate their debt, and they are often in arrears in servicing, but these are not preludes to repudiation. The fact that the very different significances of arrears, defaults, restructuring, and repudiations in international lending compared with domestic banking are often treated as the same has resulted in major misconceptions about international lending and international debt and about what needs to be done and what can be done about debt problems.

It is, perhaps, desirable to note at this point that governments have access to external credits that are not available to private borrowers. Bilateral aid programs, the International Monetary Fund, the Bank for International Settlements, the World Bank, and the various regional development banks are all examples of sources of assistance that are not available to domestic borrowers. These institutions strengthen the ability of borrowing governments to deal with external payments difficulties. Moreover, such sources are not available to make possible defaults by borrowing countries; rather, they are available, in effect, to help prevent such defaults. Only the possible existence of alternative sources of external finance that are indifferent to how a country handles its existing debt can be regarded as helping to create conditions more favorable to default on debts to other lenders. From time to time, the cold war has created something close to such conditions—as when Egypt, under Nasser, turned to the Soviets for finance. This happens only rarely, however, as the major antagonists in the cold war share a common need to have a functioning international financial system, whatever the mix of lending institutions might be at any time. The behavior of Poland, the USSR, and other Soviet bloc countries attests to this.

Repayment of Loans and Reduction of Debt

Another popular misconception arises from the misunderstanding of individual debt repayment compared with the total external debt of a country. The question frequently asked is how the country can repay its debts. This question seems particularly pertinent when the debt is very large by any criteria—as the Brazilian and Mexican external debts are. It is also a question that arises frequently about a country's domestic debt. For example, can the United States repay its astronomically high internal debt?

International loans are made on the assumption of full and prompt servicing of the contractual terms of the debt. Loans are to be repaid, and servicing includes amortization of principal as well as payment of interest. The interest may be fixed or variable—that is, subject to change according to an agreed formula that is usually related to changes in interest rates in money and credit markets.

In domestic and international banking, individual loans are sometimes not serviced fully and promptly. At times, private loans are defaulted or renegotiated; that is, new terms are agreed upon between lender and borrower. However, very few loans are not ultimately repaid. Even when collateral is provided, repayment is preferred and is the usual course of action. Lending institutions do not usually want to be in the business of acquiring, managing, or disposing of real property or other assets offered as collateral. Lenders and borrowers more often renegotiate the original terms and, in effect, replace the original loan with a new loan. Where necessary, this process can be repeated again and again. If the borrower can maintain interest payments, the lender is likely to be well disposed to renegotiate the maturity of the principal. This happens on a grand scale in the restructuring of debt of countries, whereby many, if not all, of the individual loans or debts are pooled together and new terms are negotiated for the entire pool.

There is no question of forgiveness of debts by private lenders. They have no authority to forgive debts voluntarily, since the debts are the assets of the institutions. Shareholders do not give bank managers the power to forgive debt, but bank managers *can* use their authority to renegotiate terms. They can also declare a loan in default and seize collateral, if available. Thus, they can accept losses, but not voluntarily, for such losses jeopardize the liquidity, solvency, and therefore the very viability of the financial institutions.

Therefore, returning to the question of whether a country can repay its debts to a lender, if the question is whether a particular loan will be repaid or serviced, the answer must be yes in the majority of cases. Given the capital/assets ratios referred to earlier, banks can afford only a very small percentage of loan losses. If there are payments difficulties, loan contracts will be renegotiated or "rolled over"—that is, renewed at the end of the agreed maturity period. These renegotiations result in new loans, not loan losses. The total outstanding loans of a bank are expected to increase over time; this is a sign of a prosperous and well-managed bank. Individual loans are repaid, but total loans increase as the bank expands the total volume of its business. Often, total loans to an individual borrower also increase, but individual loans of that borrower must be repaid or new terms must be negotiated. Again, the fact that total loans to a borrower are increasing is not a sign that the borrower cannot repay or is not repaying its debt; rather, it is a sign of a need for credit and of the borrower's creditworthiness to obtain additional debt.

The external debt of a country will consist of thousands or hundreds of thousands of individual loans, or their equivalent. These individual loans must be repaid. Thus, the total debt of a country consists of myriad loans that are being serviced separately. If individual loans are not serviced, the borrower ceases to be creditworthy. Regarding the question of whether a country can repay its debts, countries, as such, do not repay debts—borrowers within the country, be they private or official, do the repaying. The question, rather, is whether the external financial position of a country will enable individual borrowers to meet their obligations or whether governments will intervene to prevent such payments. The answer is not found in the size of the debt or in trends of borrowing. Individual loans will be repaid, but finding the needed foreign exchange involves all aspects of economic behavior. If the question is whether the total debt of all borrowers is likely to rise or fall, the total debt of most countries tends to rise over time. If nothing else is operative, inflation means that increases in money magnitudes are necessary merely to keep up with inflation. In addition, real expansion in national economies and in international trade increases the need for international flows of funds or savings. International savings flows more often take the form of loans or credits rather than equity, especially flows to developing countries. An expanding total external debt, like an expanding domestic debt, is by itself not a sign of adverse or poor economic or financial conditions. It does not lead to a loss of creditworthiness. It is often a sign of a healthy economy that is strengthening a country's creditworthiness and benefiting from this strengthening.

The question of whether a country can repay its debt becomes more understandable if what is meant is whether a country could reduce its total volume of external debt outstanding if it wanted or needed to do so. It would normally have no reason to want to do so, because individual borrowers, including official or governmental borrowers, would normally be servicing their debts. So long as credits were available on acceptable terms, borrowers would be repaying old debts and contracting new ones. Declines in total debt take place when the demand for new loans declines or the availability of new credits declines while old ones are being repaid. This happens quite frequently in the case of an individual borrower. For a country, with its external debt as an aggregated total, this decline in loan demand is likely to take place only when domestic conditions are depressed or when the government sharply reduces its demand for external funds—for example, when it decides to cut its public investment program drastically. By reducing its new external borrowings and continuing to service its past borrowings, total debt can decline. This also happens occasionally when the borrowing entities are in an industrial country that is normally a capital exporter rather than a capital importer. For example, Japan borrowed heavily in response to the oil price increases in the early 1970s; the oil had to be purchased and paid for. Because of the fundamental strength of the Japanese economy, however, Japan soon adjusted to the larger import bill for oil so that its total debt could decline. As another example, Spain could use the benefits of the recent decline in oil prices to reduce its external debt and increase its holdings of international reserves. Even a developing country Brazil could do likewise, but only for a relatively short period of time.

For developing countries, total declines in debt may be signs of strain and adversity. The degree of strain depends on the importance of the net inflow of resources from abroad and the availability of substitute nondebt sources of external finance, such as direct equity investment or grants. As a generalization, a developing country can bring down its total debt only by severe reductions in domestic consumption and investment. This is done mostly by constraining private and public investment, which are needed to maintain or increase output, improve productivity, and provide employment. Except for extraordinary windfalls—such as Nigeria and Venezuela benefiting from the large OPEC price increases—or for short periods of time, the total debt of a developing country will tend to rise. Good economic management will affect the use of the net inflow of resources, may change the terms and conditions on which the funds are borrowed, and may, to some extent, reduce the rate of increase in external debt, but the total debt to all lenders will rise. The new loans are of crucial help in servicing the old debt, because new loans provide additional foreign exchange to meet any and all international payments, including servicing of past debts.

The fundamental diversity of the external debt of a country is obscured by the fact that during periods of foreign exchange shortage, all servicing of debt is centralized through the central bank of the borrowing country. The separate loans do not lose their individual identities, but the availability of foreign exchange to service all loans in foreign currencies is subject to an official authority. This does not mean that all debts are necessarily treated uniformly by the central authority; distinctions are made. For example, the central bank may give a high priority to servicing debts incurred in importing such necessities as pharmaceuticals; to servicing debts incurred for fuel imports; to making payments to a multilateral agency, such as the World Bank or the Inter-American Development Bank; or to meeting its obligations to the International Monetary Fund. However, loans that are bunched together for restructuring purposes are likely to be treated uniformly. Thus, when foreign exchange shortages cause the monetary authorities to establish rules for servicing of certain categories of debt, the separate character of each loan becomes much less important. In effect, the credit analysis on which the original loan was made is superseded by the regulations on international payments. It is common to refer to the bunch of loans being restructured as if they were one loan. Indeed, following this concept, analysts and commentators often treat all of the external debt of a country or all of the debt in the category of loans being restructured as the equivalent of one loan, even though only loan payments falling due in a given period in the future—say, 6 months or 1 or 2 years—are actually restructured, leaving untouched payments falling due in other categories or in later periods. Headlines greatly magnify the amounts being restructured and overstate the implications of what is being done. Much of the economy of a country, including its international trade, continues to function during periods of massive debt restructuring.

The environment that created a foreign exchange shortage—such as a world recession—may also cause certain debtors to be unable to service their debt in the ordinary sense. Private borrowers are often unable to service domestic and international debt in adverse economic periods. They cannot find the local or national currency needed to buy the foreign exchange to service their foreign debt. In such cases, some borrowers will simply default, unless they are rescued by their governmental authorities or have other extraordinary sources of foreign exchange. In most cases, defaults do not happen.

A firm usually can provide local funds to the central monetary authorities to purchase the needed foreign exchange. The central authority may even regard the private lender as servicing its debts and may take on the responsibility of providing the foreign exchange to the foreign lender. Nevertheless, whereas private lenders may be short of needed domestic funds, governments are an entirely different matter. Governments can almost always provide the needed national currency to service debt, including external debts. They obtain such funds from taxation or by borrowing from the banking system. Governments can find it difficult, however, to gain access to needed foreign exchange when international conditions are adverse. Theoretically, a government can buy its foreign exchange, but a government is often very reluctant to sell its national currencies at exchange rates or prices that are attractive to potential foreign buyers of the currency. In practice, there may be no feasible price at which it can induce foreigners to purchase its currencies for the foreign exchange needed by the government. This is often true even when a country's own citizens, residing in their own country, are holding amounts of foreign exchange outside the country. These citizens usually avoid selling their foreign exchange holdings to their own central bank for national currencies.

Centralization of debt servicing helps expedite the process of restructuring external debt. It does not, however, eliminate the diversity of debt or the significance of this diversity. When new voluntary lending is considered, the borrowers are again individual. Credit assessments are again the first line of defense for a bank. This continues to be true in lending to countries that do not require debt restructuring. At some point, when debt restructuring is no longer necessary, the diversity of lenders and borrowers will again appear at the normal level of importance. In the meantime, however, the fact that debt servicing and other regulations on external payments are the responsibility of the governmental monetary authorities gives a bias in favor of new lending to governmental borrowers rather than to private firms.

The "What If" Syndrome

The centralization of responsibility for debt servicing in the monetary authorities gives more credibility to the "what if" and "dominoes" syndromes frequently cited by commentators, writers, and experts in international lending and debt. The "what if" syndrome is a worst-case approach. It usually poses the question of "what if" a country were to default on its entire external debt or on all debt owed to commercial banks, or it assumes this contingency in analyses. The usual context is an examination of the likely effects on lending banks or on the banking system. It is a worst-case approach because it focuses not on individual loans owed to individual banks but on all debts or all debts in a very broad category, such as debts to all private banks considered together. What if all these debts were defaulted simultaneously?

It is impossible to argue logically that this cannot happen. It is also impossible to argue that for banks that have substantial portfolios in external risks assets, a default or repudiation of debt by a major borrowing country, or a group of such countries, would not have very serious consequences for the bank's income, creditworthiness, and financial viability. Much would depend on how important the default or repudiation was in relation to the bank's income and capital and on what importance or significance was given to this adversity by the banking authorities. In terms of capital, if all international loans to one developing country or group of countries in difficulties account for, say, 5 percent of a total portfolio, a 5 percent loss will be equal to the entire capital of the bank. Since, in case of repudiation, the bank might well have to charge these losses to capital, it could be wiped out. Even much smaller losses could affect a bank's financial standing.

Modern commercial banks, as we have seen, are highly vulnerable in terms of asset/capital ratios. Similar scenarios could be envisaged if there were widespread bankruptcies in major sectors of developed countries or if a major bank reached a state of illiquidity and could not meet its obligations. There is no eliminating this vulnerability. At present (1985–86), U.S. banks are being requested to increase their capital (9 percent has been suggested), but even so, the capital/asset leveraging will be high, and banks will continue to be vulnerable in this respect. From the viewpoint of earnings, the situation can be quite different. Declines in income are not welcome, of course, but banks can absorb substantial declines in income without becoming unprofitable over an accounting period of, say, a year. In addition, experience has repeatedly shown that banks can weather losses without losing their own creditworthiness if the losses are regarded as being due to general market conditions, not to individual

bank mismanagement. Not even the largest developing country borrowers, such as Brazil or Mexico, account for more than a small fraction of a lending bank's earnings. On the other hand, even a relatively small decline in earnings can be serious for a bank's standing
and creditworthiness if the loss is interpreted in financial markets as
being due to poor management.

It has been argued that the monetary authorities would come to
the rescue of banks in serious trouble. The general public interest is
usually seen as being served by avoidance of serious banking difficulties. Extraordinary rescue measures are accepted by the public,
as demonstrated in recent cases of difficulties in savings and loan
institutions in the United States, and efforts are made to protect depositors and other creditors. Such assistance does take place, but it
is not always a certainty. In assessing their risks in international lending, banks cannot operate on the principle that, if necessary, they
will be rescued by their governments. Lending criteria must assume
no rescues. A bank that needs to be rescued is in deep trouble. The
ripple effect on the entire system may be reduced by a rescue operation but the effects will still be there.

Thus, it is easy to spell out a frightening scenario for lending
banks, individually or as a group, based on the "what if" scenario. It
is a highly tempting scenario to financial writers and debt experts,
because it dramatizes the international debt problem and because the
conditions of banks are of wide general interest and concern. In the
United States, tens of millions of people hold their savings in banks.
For commentators, publicists, and writers interested in public attention, dramatizing conditions in banks has proved to be a bonanza.
Again, it is to be stressed that the "what if" scenario is not illogical
or impossible. In the 1930s, it was the Kredit-Anstalt in Austria that
led the way into an era of long delays in debt servicing and widespread defaults. These defaults resulted in a global financial crisis
that deepened the existing recession and made the decade of the
1930s the decade of the Great Depression.

The difficulty with the "what if" scenario is that it is unbalanced
and simplistic. It approaches international lending to the developing
countries from the viewpoint of concern with the lending institutions, especially the commercial banks. The "what if" hypothesis assumes a condition in which borrowing countries decide that they
cannot, or will not, service their debt for some period, and this goes
beyond the existence of any willingness for or likelihood of success-

ful renegotiation and restructuring. The borrowing nation is assumed to have calculated that the relief obtained from renegotiation of debt servicing would be less than the costs of default or repudiation. This is a most unbalanced and unrealistic approach. No one knows the future. A defaulting country must assume that it will lose its creditworthiness with all private external lenders. It must assume that official lenders are likely to become more cautious in assessing the credit acceptability of the country according to their own particular lending criteria. (This is different from threats or hints at repudiation in what is perceived as international financial and political diplomacy.) If the reasons for the inability to service debt are self-evident—for example, a major earthquake—it is likely that all lenders, private and official, will have made clear their willingness to postpone debt servicing. This is, in effect, restructuring the debt, and the borrowing country will not have to repudiate or default. Repudiation would destroy the ability of a country to finance a net inflow of resources from abroad by private financing. If another source of financing is available that does not care, or even applauds the default, the borrowing country may be more prone to run the risks of the adverse effects of repudiation or default. From time to time, countries have shifted from a pro-Western to a pro-Soviet stance, and vice versa, but these are exceptional cases and have only rarely been occasions for repudiations of debts owed to private banks.

Thus, in practice, even the countries in deepest external payments difficulties have not defaulted or repudiated their external debts. Some debtors, such as those in the Sudan, have delayed so long in meeting their servicing obligations that the banks have to treat their loans as nonperforming loans, with resulting losses in income and the need to charge reserves. These conditions are not welcome to the banks, but they are far from repudiations. They are within the category of loans in difficulties for which borrowers and creditors are working out a new schedule of servicing. This is possible because the borrowers have not repudiated their debts.

During the recent turbulent years, I have been unwilling to speak or write in terms of the "what if" scenario. To do so would distract attention from the fundamental problem—namely, that the international debt crisis of the 1980s is a crisis in development, with grave dangers for the developing countries and serious but not catastrophic difficulties for the lending banks. I could not accept as useful a line of analysis based on most unlikely assumptions that were harmful to borrowers and lenders. The main issue, in my opinion, has not been how to prevent an international banking crisis, but, rather, how to prevent a world economic and political crisis because of the inability of major developing countries to manage their countries without the benefit of borrowing from external sources. I have been convinced that readily assuming that banks face dangers in foreign lending would lead to an overcautious reaction by the banks. This overreaction would make the adjustment process in the developing countries much more difficult and would exacerbate the problems of the banks. Many people have considered such views optimistic or unrealistic, because I would not accept the prevailing view of the pessimistic "what if" assumptions. At best, those assumptions were based not on current facts or analysis, but on logic and on the historical experience of the 1930s—half a century ago—and the elegant simplicity of recurring historical cycles.

It is perhaps worth noting that even a declaration by the president of Peru to the effect that only a certain proportion of the country's foreign exchange earnings (mostly from exports) would be devoted to servicing outstanding debts is not a threat of repudiation or default. It is a bargaining position in negotiations for debt restructuring. The amount that a borrowing country can spare to service past debt is nearly always an issue in renegotiating debt. Whether it is a good negotiating tactic to announce publicly, in advance, what the borrower or lender is prepared to do, is a matter of judgment. Lenders have done similar things—for example, announcing, in advance, that their willingness to restructure debt requires a prior agreement between the borrowing country and the IMF on an adjustment program. Negotiations to restructure can become acrimonious and even hostile. Veiled and unveiled threats are heard, but the foundation on which the process is based is that the outcome will not be repudiation or default. It was largely because of this conviction that I regarded the withdrawal of banks from lending to many countries in difficulties in the early and mid-1980s as overreaction. The starting point in analyzing country risk to a commercial bank is determining whether it is likely to be faced with repudiation or default. If it is, the highest degree of caution is needed. If it is not, the next question is the degree of likelihood of a need for debt restructuring and the forms it can take—how much, how long, its impact on earnings, capital, and reserves, and so on. Such considerations are part of a cautious lending posture, but the risk/reward ratio can be sensibly analyzed, without a prior presumption that no practical risk/reward ratio can offset a possible repudiation. Here, *possible* must be defined in terms of facts and conditions rather than in terms of unsophisticated intuition (often practiced by very sophisticated people).

Domino and Imitation Effects: A Lender's Perspective

Closely related to the "what if" assumption is the "domino" effect—the adverse chainlike impact that default or repudiation by a lender or borrower has on other lenders or borrowers. The "domino" effect also involves the notion of inevitability of the direction of the impact—as a series of standing dominoes are made to topple one after another by the initial fall of a single domino. The danger of the "domino" effect is usually argued by those whose concerns focus on the lending banks rather than on the borrowing countries. It is also often linked with the "what if" scenario, and the outcome of such a linkage is awesome and terrifying. The "domino" effect argument, like other bleak outlooks, is logical. It can be set forth in different ways, but the mechanisms and results are essentially the same. One of the mechanisms is imitation; the other is financial links. It assumes that if a bank declares a default of a borrower, other banks are more likely to do so. Banks may believe that failure to declare default deprives them of the opportunity to seize assets, if any, of the borrower. Therefore, if they do not also declare a default when other banks do so, the other banks may have the benefit of the seized assets, and the refraining bank would be left without this possible compensatory benefit.

This factor came up sharply in the mid-1970s, when Zaire was sufficiently behind in servicing arrears to enable banks to exercise default clauses in their contracts with their borrowers in Zaire. The banks did not wish to declare defaults, but they also did not wish to be delinquent in their efforts to protect their shareholders. They could not be sure that other banks would not declare a default or that they would announce their intentions enough in advance to enable others to take timely protective measures. For a time in 1975, it was touch and go, but default was avoided. Zaire was the first major experience in recent decades with the problems involved in declaring and implementing defaults in the case of countries. It became clear that default provisions in contracts were not a strong defense for the lending bank if the borrower was a foreign government. Country risk analysis and management, as it evolved during 1975–85, does not assume that default provisions protect the lending bank adequately. If defaults were nevertheless to happen, they would probably have a "domino" effect.

Another kind of imitation effect arising from the behavior of lenders is their willingness to lend to the same countries, or the same borrowers, for similar purposes on similar financial terms as other banks. The market sets the framework for any loan negotiation, and the terms are known to both lender and borrower. This similarity of marketing behavior and financial terms is usually not included in the concept of the "domino" effect, but it reinforces the likelihood of "domino" effects if they were to occur.

A further comment may be useful on the willingness of lenders to lend to certain countries because other lenders are doing so. This imitation effect is not the same as coming to the same conclusion about the creditworthiness of a country as a borrower. The importance of this distinction has become vividly apparent in recent years, especially in debt restructuring cases. Many banks had lent to Brazil and Mexico, for example, because they had separately come to the conclusion that these countries were creditworthy by their own criteria, even though these criteria were often not the same as those of other lenders. When payments difficulties arose in these countries, these banks quickly recognized the need to restructure and, incidentally, to examine their country risk evaluation and management systems. They did not blame others. Often, however, other banks— usually the smaller regional banks—had not done their own homework in evaluating risk. They had joined syndicates led by major banks, believing that imitation of such major banks provided adequate safeguards. When it did not, the regional banks reacted very strongly. They were usually the first to withdraw from new foreign lending; they were hardest to reconcile to major debt restructuring; and they resented finding themselves with problems because of judgments made by others, even though they had made the lending decisions for their own institutions to follow the lead of others. These institutions are likely to be the most reluctant to move back into lending to developing countries and the most vocal in expressing fears of serious, unavoidable risks in international lending. Some of these banks may appreciate that the fault was in their failure to have their own country assessment and risk management systems, but given the unfavorable experiences of the major banks, they do not see such systems as providing adequate protection. They do not believe that country risk and management systems avoid debt servicing difficulties and the need to restructure.

Another imitation effect has been the acceptance of certain borrowers and purposes, as distinct from countries. Before the 1970s, commercial banking concentrated on lending to banks, private individuals, or nonbanking firms. In addition, international lending was largely related to financing international trade. In the 1970s, governments became the major borrowers in developing countries, and often the purposes were to help finance long-term investment for economic and social development. Loan maturities were still relatively short—say, 2 years or less—but they increasingly became longer-term—that is, 5 to 10 years or even longer. Commercial bank lending became an important instrument of development and development finance, though usually on a floating rate basis. This shift to longer-term lending to governments often was not the result of careful, thoughtful analyses but, rather, was in imitation of a few major lending banks.

From the viewpoint of the dangers to banks from international lending to developing countries, the potential "domino" effect from financial linkages is dramatic and urgent. The most important linkage is the widespread use of interbank deposits, referred to earlier. Deposits received by some banks from other banks are major sources of funds for lending. The depositing bank distinguishes among banks by its assessment of their relative financial strength. In turn, the depositing bank may be a bank of deposit for other banks. The reputation of the bank affects the kinds of other banks it attracts as depositors, the magnitudes of deposits, and the financial costs of such deposits.

The most highly reputed banks do best in all of these categories, yet their own creditworthiness remains vulnerable. An important vulnerability comes from the composition of their risk assets. If a substantial portion of a bank's portfolio is in difficulty, this will become known, at least in the financial community and to the banking regulators and supervisors. As indicated elsewhere, if adversities occur among external borrowers, there can be instantaneous responses in the form of deposit withdrawals from the lending bank. The bank may find it difficult to replace these deposits, and it may have to liquidate some of its assets. Illiquidity threatens and, with electronic banking, the threat is transmitted instantaneously through the national banking system and through the international banking system. A similar situation can materialize if the regulatory authorities seem to be worried about a particular bank. When the Brazilian and Mexican external payments difficulties were experienced in 1982, there was widespread speculation about which banks could be adversely affected in significant magnitudes. Similarly, when oil prices fell, some banks were seen as having too many loan assets in the oil-related industries. The problem is multiplied when major banks lose confidence in each other. They are large lenders and large borrowers, and smaller banks rely on them for funds, if needed. If the large banks cannot provide such funds because they themselves are unable to raise funds, many smaller banks are in danger of immediate liquidity difficulties.

The "what if" scenario readily combines with the "domino" and imitation effects. They lead to frequent conjectures that the major lending banks will suffer serious losses and will be threatened by illiquidity. If the national banking system is said to be threatened, very quickly the entire international banking system is said to be threatened. A Brazilian or Mexican default is the first "domino," leading to worldwide financial collapse! Thus, the "domino" approach is simply a graphic way of dramatizing the national and worldwide interlinking of the banking system and the consequent transmission of the adversities of any one bank to others. Used with caution, the "domino" approach is a useful way to understand the possible implications—in fact as well as in logic—of adverse developments in a lending bank's external assets. It is also useful in making it clear that banks are dependent on their own ability to borrow and that their borrowings are largely from other banks. Incidentally, it also clarifies international debt statistics. When the statistics aggregate only loans of 1 year or more, most interbank depositors will not be included, because they are usually shorter-term. When estimates are made of credits or loans less than 1 year, interbank credits should be included. These interbank credits are not likely to be included in any debt restructuring. The lending bank needs these credits for its own liquidity. The depositing bank is concerned with the risk of making such credits or deposits in foreign countries if such deposits can be caught up in debt restructuring exercises along with external debt. The banks of deposit and the central bank authorities have strong reasons to treat these debts differently from others, and they usually do so in practice. That practice illustrates, again, the need for caution in interpreting total debt statistics of a borrowing country.

The "domino" and imitation effects underline the importance of the prevailing assumptions about the likelihood of default or repudiation. Repudiation by a major borrowing country—such as Brazil, Mexico, Venezuela, Korea, Argentina, or even Peru and Chile—could start the "dominoes" falling. Widespread balance-of-payments difficulties, by themselves, are not likely to do so, however, especially if the borrowing country is taking steps to avoid default, including renegotiation of its external debts with commercial banks.

Over the Barrel: Debtor versus Lender

It has long been a widely held view that in the world of huge debt creation, debtors have creditors "over the barrel." This homespun attitude is often applied to international lending and debt. In a recent television interview with the Mexican foreign minister, the interviewers claimed that Mexico had its creditors "over the barrel" because the creditors could not afford to have Mexico default or repudiate its very large external debt. The Mexican minister of foreign affairs gave a very diplomatic reply, evading a clear acceptance or rejection of this view. He was indeed correct to be evasive.

Again, it can be argued logically and persuasively that for a number of banks, a repudiation by Mexico would start the "dominoes" falling. No bank wants to start this slide into disaster for itself and other banks. A borrowing country of any significant size—such as Chile, Peru, Mexico, or even Thailand—could be the origin of a financial crisis and, therefore, is in a strong bargaining position once it is assumed that it has default as an acceptable option. However, as in the "what if" case, the flip side of this view is what happens to the debtor if it repudiates its debt and the banks are forced to declare defaults. Mexico, for example, is an open economy integrated into the world economy—especially the United States, Canada, Western Europe, and Japan. Not only could default cause Mexico's foreign trade to come to a standstill, but the capital flight from Mexico would be devastating.

In the past, Mexico has experienced a so-called dollarization of its economy because Mexican businessmen preferred to do business in U.S. dollars rather than pesos. With repudiation of external debt and resulting loss of access to external credit, Mexico's business community, its state-owned enterprises, (for example, its oil company), and its various state and federal governments would be in most serious financial straits. Perhaps most important is that the federal government of Mexico would run the serious risk of losing its internal creditworthiness. It would be unable to borrow from its own citizens in its national currency. With a loss of internal creditworthiness, people are unwilling to hold financial assets denominated in local assets. The public debt is brought into disrepute as holders unload these financial investments for whatever they can get. Money holdings are in jeopardy of huge discounting, setting the stage for hyperinflation of a disastrous character.

Repudiation of debt by a debtor country is not an alternative in the real world. Even a serious threat of repudiation and default can have incredible adverse effects. Loose and erroneous use of language by officials and commentators—for example, using the word *default* to describe a temporary delay—has had very costly adverse effects.

There are some advantages, however, in being a large debtor in the negotiating process of restructuring and in obtaining external assistance from noncommercial bank sources, such as the IMF, the World Bank, and the Inter-American Development Bank. Banks are likely to be eager to return to more normal banking relations with a major and formerly highly profitable country. Monetary authorities are more sensitive to the possibilities of starting a "domino" effect, and assistance may be more urgently and effectively mobilized, as it was by the U.S. authorities in the case of Mexico in 1982. However, the level of concern is much below that generated by fears of default and repudiation. Banks are able to insist on their terms and conditions for debt restructuring and new monies, as seen repeatedly in the cases of Brazil and Mexico. They can tolerate further delays in debt servicing, if needed, to get acceptable terms and conditions. The debtor country is in a good bargaining position, but so is the lender, particularly if, as happens in practice, it combines with other lenders in a collective relationship with the borrowing country. In considering the implications and risks in lending to Mexico or another borrowing country, the lending bank must consider the need to restructure as a real possibility. As a working assumption for portfolio management, it must attach some weight to the possibility of repudiation and default, enough to avoid the obvious trap of overexposure—that is, a high proportion of total assets of the bank—in any one country. At present, overexposure in a developing country would be about 3 percent to 4 percent or more of a total portfolio—the equivalent of half of the bank's capital.

Domino and Imitation Effects: A Borrower's Perspective

The foregoing analyses of the "what if," "domino," and "over the barrel" approaches focused primarily on concerns of lenders. The "domino" or imitation effect can also be viewed from the perspective of borrowers. One example is the popularity of debt restructuring with the private banks on a countrywide basis. Until the 1980s, such debt restructuring with private banks was extraordinary. The individual cases that did happen—such as Zaire, Peru, Jamaica, and Turkey—were regarded, at the time, as exceptional by borrowers and lenders, although world conditions had already become difficult. Oil prices were high after 1973–74, while other commodity prices were low; economic growth in the industrial world was hampered by concerns about accelerating inflation; interest rates were climbing to historically high levels; the U.S. dollar was undervalued, and speculative international capital movements were disturbing foreign exchange markets; private direct investments in developing countries remained small; and the international financial agencies, though expanded, continued to be inadequate to fulfill their agreed purposes. The developing countries were able to access the commercial banks, but there were increasing concerns within these banks about the ability of the principal borrowing countries to cope with chronically unfavorable world conditions. Some developing countries, such as Brazil, did encounter payments difficulties. Nevertheless, debt restructuring was a last-resort measure. New borrowings were too important and might be jeopardized by such highly publicized events as debt restructuring, which proclaimed that the country was in external payments difficulties. When debt restructuring did happen—as in Zaire, Peru, Turkey, and Jamaica in the 1970s—it was regarded as exceptional because it constrained new lending. As late as the restructuring of Poland's debt around 1980, such restructuring was not taken by others as a sign of easy acceptance of debt restructuring as a way of dealing with balance-of-payments difficulties.

With the actions of Mexico and Brazil in 1982, however, debt restructuring became the fashion, particularly in Latin America and Africa. Lenders, borrowers, such related institutions as the International Monetary Fund, and governments in creditor countries welcomed or at least accepted this mode of tackling balance-of-payments problems. Some appreciated that it meant severe constraints on new, incremental lending to these countries, but the authorities therein found the easy path of restructuring too attractive to resist. For the lenders, already poised to restrain new lending, it was an acceptable alternative to repudiation, default, or very prolonged arrears in debt servicing. For regulators of banks, it was an orderly way to deal with difficulties, compatible with long-established practices in domestic banking. For related institutions, especially the IMF, it gave them a role of great influence, extending much further than ever before, since the IMF could control private bank activities as well as its own financing. For creditor governments, restructuring meant a way to avoid potentially serious domestic banking troubles and a way to help borrowing countries that did not involve new budgetary expenditures on their part, at least in the short run. The whole approach was rationalized by assuming that the difficulties were essentially temporary and that the borrowing countries could reduce their external payments deficits—and even create external surpluses—by changing their domestic policies and practices. In the meantime, the world economic situation would become more favorable, facilitating the return to more "normal" conditions. The need to cope with structural changes in the world economy and in the economies of the borrowing countries could be held off until the current difficulties were resolved.

Much of this proved to be wishful thinking. However, it took a few years for enough individuals and institutions to gain sufficient insight even to begin to alter their conventional, fashionable attitudes and practices. Meanwhile, debt restructuring flourished, and more than thirty borrowing countries—mostly in Latin America and Africa—became involved. Discovering that the process did not restore creditworthiness, that it often had to be repeated within the same country, that the procedures were costly in personnel time and effort, and that the lender banks were losing their flexibility to act individually was not enough to dampen the acceptability of, even the enthusiasm for, the restructuring process.

Fortunately for the international financial system, nearly all countries in Asia, except the Philippines, either had no need for debt restructuring with private lenders or chose to avoid it. A number of such countries, including India and Pakistan, had extensive experience with restructuring of debt to governmental lenders. In some cases, such debts had even been forgiven. Unlike the Latin American countries, a number of Asian countries still relied mostly on concessional sources of financing—such as the International Development Association, the World Bank, and the Asian Development Bank—for development finance, combined with use of the IMF resources for short- or medium-term balance-of-payments financing. A few could begin to borrow from the private capital markets. Borrowing from commercial banks was relatively less important than it was in Latin America.

Commercial bank financing was important in these countries, but mostly in self-liquidating international trade financing. Thus, these countries did not have extensive external debts to the private banks and, equally important, never lost their creditworthiness during the 1980s—although they, too, experienced constraints and obstacles because of the poor performance of the world economy. The countries in Southeast Asia and the Far East that made more important use of commercial banks—such as Korea, Taiwan, Hong Kong, Singapore, Malaysia, Thailand, and the Philippines—mostly managed their economies well enough to avoid unmanageable balance-of-payments difficulties. If anything, their external creditworthiness was strengthened during this period, with the exception of the Philippines. The Philippine situation steadily deteriorated during this period and, by 1985, the Philippines was on the verge of losing its creditworthiness with private lenders. The Far East and Southeast Asian countries, by their avoidance of debt restructuring, demonstrated that large external debts could be managed without the need for restructuring, even during unfavorable periods in the world economy. Some foundation stones were thus left for rebuilding the role of commercial banks in financing the external deficits of developing countries. The falling "dominoes" of easy acceptance of restructuring stopped. Instead, these Asian countries took domestic measures in time to adjust their economies to adverse world conditions; thus, the adjustments were easier because these countries continued to have access to commercial sources of external finance.

Another imitation effect was the widening acceptance of the IMF as an intermediary between developing countries and commercial sources of finance. IMF programs with countries were not new; they had been going on for 30 years before 1980. A number of practices, however, were new. It was new to publicize that country changes in policies were taken at the insistence of the IMF. It was new to refer to country programs as IMF programs rather than as the programs of the countries themselves. It was new for commercial banks to state loudly and unequivocally that debt restructuring and new money depended on a country's having a program endorsed by the IMF and that their loans had to be accompanied by parallel use of IMF resources.

In the 1950s and 1960s, the IMF's jurisdiction over exchange restrictions and over exchange rate changes had been exercised with considered discretion, in the mode of central banks. The IMF now became the spotlighted actor on the world stage, playing the role of dictator. The IMF became front-page news, especially when heads of state of member countries publicly attacked the IMF for its policies. The IMF was coming perilously close to being the whipping boy of international finance, as it controlled the spigot through which flowed a large portion of external finance for developing countries in difficulties. In the 1940s and 1950s, I had witnessed the resistance to IMF "interference" in the affairs of member countries, even in areas in which countries had delegated sovereign powers to the IMF—namely, exchange rates and exchange restrictions. The spectacle of the IMF becoming deeply involved in domestic political processes and of such involvement becoming accepted by the bulk of countries has been astonishing indeed. In this evolution, the fact that such countries as Argentina, Brazil, Mexico, and Nigeria had accepted this role of the IMF, however reluctantly, made it much easier for the smaller nations in Latin American and Africa to accept it. It was an imitation or "domino" effect—the "domino" being resistance to the supranational role of the IMF in major fields of domestic policies in countries wherein it was necessary to restructure debt and/or obtain new incremental funds from commercial banks. It is notable that stronger developing countries—such as Brazil, Mexico, and Venezuela—have moved away from reliance on IMF assistance and IMF approval of their programs.

Closely related was the "domino" or imitation effect on the adjustment policies of the borrowing countries. Developing countries had debated for decades whether their economies should be centrally managed—with a high degree of government ownership and regu-

lation of public utilities and productive facilities and protectionism—
or should be more market-oriented, with mostly private ownership.
Another facet of this debate was whether the country should emphasize export diversification or expansion of import substitution—
that is, domestic manufacture of goods previously imported from
abroad or their substitutes. These differences were reflected in official attitudes on exchange rates. Market-minded, private enterprise–
minded, export-minded officials, businesspeople, and financial experts favored so-called realistic exchange rates—that is, exchange
rates that made a country's exports competitive in world markets.
Instead of governmental administrative restrictions on imports, they
believed that the exchange rate should bring the price of exports into
line competitively with world prices while allowing imports that
were competitive in domestic price terms. Those who favored the
government ownership, centralized approach did not give a high
priority to competitive exchange rates. They relied on administrative
controls to keep out imports, to protect home industries, to encourage new industries, and to manage their external financial accounts.
They agreed that devaluations of their currencies in terms of other
currencies accelerated inflation and disturbed the centralized planning objectives and policies of the country.

The 1980s saw a massive swing to export orientation and a gradual acceptance of currency devaluations. Some countries, such as
Nigeria, strongly resisted this trend and vigorously opposed pressures to adopt realistic exchange rates. Such pressures were de-
nounced as foreign interference. Indeed, few policy measures are
more powerful or pervasive in their effects than changes in exchange
rates. Employment, profitability, composition of production, level
of prices, budgetary receipts, deficits or surpluses, distribution of
income and wealth, levels and composition of consumption, and investment are all greatly affected by changes in exchange rates. It is
no wonder that the question of exchange rate determination always
has been central in economic theory and practice and never has been
universally agreed upon. The swing in the 1980s to acceptance of
market-oriented, private enterprise, realistic exchange rates was
partly the result of the inadequacies of other policies. It also was
partly the result of the fact that this orientation reflects IMF views
of desirable economic management and that these views had the support of the international banking community. In any case, the fact

that these changes in policies became increasingly accepted greatly facilitated their adoption by others.

Another example of the imitation or "domino" effect from the viewpoint of borrowers might also be useful. Borrowing countries had always regarded their loan obligations to the multilateral financial institutions—such as IMF, the World Bank, and the regional development banks—as being in a very different category from other debts. As noted elsewhere, these institutions have enjoyed a "preferred creditor" status, recognized by other lending institutions as well as by borrowers. During the period of widespread debt restructuring, lenders other than these institutions were asked to subordinate their individual interests in accepting rescheduling, and they did. The multilateral lending institutions were neither asked or expected to do so—quite the contrary. The multilateral financial institutions were seen as playing a major role in defending the international financial system, and they had to protect their own credit standings in the private capital markets—their principal source of funds for their lending operations. Everyone benefited from this activity. Therefore, even other lenders benefited from this preferred creditor position, even though payments to these institutions reduced the amount of foreign exchange available for the less preferred creditors. The trade-off was clearly deemed worthwhile and acceptable to lenders and was observed by borrowers, facilitated by the fact that debt servicing to the multilateral institutions was still relatively small. Lenders that were dubious of this approach were confronted by the widespread acceptance of this practice.

During 1984 and 1985, the preferred creditor position began to be undermined. Countries began to be in arrears to the multilateral financial institutions, as they were to commercial bank lenders. The IMF, the World Bank, and the regional development banks were confronted by a growing, though still small, group of countries that were not meeting their obligations to these multilateral lenders. The creditworthiness of these multilateral institutions could be hurt. The lenders to the multilateral development banks were private investors making investment decisions according to the criteria that guide private investors in capital markets. Would other lenders accept the preferred creditor position of these multilateral institutions if their own borrowing members did not respect it? Are we seeing another "domino" effect? Such questions are still unanswered.

The Umbrella Concept

The concept of the "umbrella" has come to play an important part in international finance. Like other concepts, it can have many different meanings and it is used to convey different meanings. Essentially, it has to do with the impact on a lender of the presence of other lenders, which can provide money or guarantees.

For the lender, a useful starting point is the *comfort level* in making a lending decision. Comfort for the decision maker is achieved by a combination of objective and subjective factors. It does not come from any set of numbers by themselves, though numbers may well play a major role in the decision-making process. In a decision to lend to a developing country, the decision maker has to decide whether or not to make a loan. In making that decision, the manager will be concerned with the views of his superiors, the board of directors, the shareholders, the public, other lenders, the requesting borrower, other borrowers, regulatory authorities, the internal comptrollers, the officers in the credit and country risk management, various government agencies, the alternative lending opportunities, and so forth. Saying no is not easy, but neither is saying yes. If the answer is no, the process ends unless a superior disagrees and the factors are reconsidered. If the answer is yes, questions arise about how much to lend, financial terms, security or collateral, guarantees or guarantors, the presence of other lenders, relations with other lenders, the impact on the portfolio, the precedent for other loans, the impact on the bank's financial reputation, the reaction of the bank's creditors and depositors, stock market reactions, implications for the earnings and the careers of loan officers, interpersonal relations with other officers and managers, and so forth.

These factors are not always carefully considered, nor do they always have the same weights. Often, factors arise that are unique to the particular loan. In public institutions, such as the multilateral institutions, relatively few lending decisions are made, so each decision can receive exhaustive attention. In a commercial bank, many more loan decisions must be made. Some processes can be made more or less uniform—for example, the credit assessment mechanisms or the management technique for deciding the distribution of risk assets by country—but individual lending decisions often have specific factors that require judgment by the decision makers. Thus, the concept of comfort encompasses a great diversity of factors—some peculiar to the particular loan and some common to many other loans. Discomfort and anxiety often accompany the decision-making process.

In this panorama of factors, the presence of other lenders or other parties can play an important part in creating the level of comfort necessary to say yes to a loan proposal. This is especially so if other lenders are perceived as providing a protective shield—that is, an "umbrella"—that would otherwise not be there. For example, if an export credit agency is willing to ensure 80 percent of the risk, or if insurance is obtained against certain political risks, or if a financially strong institution in the creditor country offers to guarantee servicing of the loan if the foreign borrower fails to perform, these kinds of actions can make the difference between a loan being approved or disapproved. Another example would be a situation in which a lender with special status, such as the World Bank, is a partner in the operation or is involved simultaneously, though separately, in the same project. The presence of the special creditor may be seen as reducing the risk of difficulties for the more ordinary bank lender. If a special institution, such as the Inter-American Development Bank, is amenable to linking its willingness to lend and disburse previously committed loan funds to the performance of the borrower vis-à-vis other private lenders to a project, the added comfort given to the private lender well may be of decisive importance. Another type of cooperative action is when banks lend together as syndicates or clubs, acting together and tied to each other by cross-default clauses. This may also give added comfort to the individual lender in making a positive decision to lend.

Besides being given by the presence of other lenders, comfort can also be given by the presence of collateral. Marketable collateral available to the lender is a great source of ease, depending, of course, on the nature and location of the collateral. Asset-based financing is often attractive, even during disturbed periods. Achieving a generally acceptable level of comfort for most lenders is a precondition for the maintenance and restoration of an efficient international banking system. For many borrowing countries, the comfort level needed cannot be reached without extraordinary measures, often involving the presence of others. The ways of creating more comfort are many, and new ways can be invented if necessary. Advance agreement on arbitration of disputes and the use of judicial systems regarded as acceptable to all parties are examples of the broad range of possible actions.

More and more, these concepts of comfort have a common aspect: the lender does not depend on default and seizure of the borrower's assets as a strong defense, if needed. In the world of private lending to private borrowers within the same country, provisions for declarations of default and seizure of assets can be powerful defenses for the lender. As noted earlier, this does not usually apply in international lending. Assets may be small or it may not be feasible to seize them; legal disputes may raise questions of which jurisdictions will handle the disputes; the issue of sovereign immunity may be raised if the foreign borrower is a government; and so forth. Thus, comfort has to be achieved in other ways.

In view of the events of the 1980s, however, the presence of other lenders will not readily achieve the needed level of ease—nor will vague and unenforceable guarantees, the presence of lesser lenders, collateral that is hard to obtain, and the like. To provide effective defenses, guarantees must be given by agencies that are able to perform the guarantees, if required. These agencies can be official within a developed country—for example, an export credit agency—or they can be multilateral—for example, the World Bank or a regional development bank. They must have adequate available financial resources if and when needed. If they do, some country risk to the lender still exists. It is at least a nuisance to have to look to guarantors, but this nuisance is much more tolerable than the nuisance of debt restructuring, not to mention repudiation and default.

As stated earlier, "umbrellas" based on declarations of default are usually less effective. However, if one of the lenders has a preferred creditor position, then such links to it as cross-default provisions become much more significant. Essentially, the protection lies in the preferred creditor position and in the judgment that the country servicing debt to the preferred creditor would also pay the other partners in the lending project. This gives added importance to whether the practice of honoring the preferred creditor position of the multilateral development bank will continue. If it does, the combination of guarantees of adequate financial resources to meet guarantor obligations, cross-default provisions, and preferred creditor position can transform the international lending scene. Without such ingredients or their equivalents, the "umbrella" may be seen as too "leaky" to be much use, except where countries are already close to reestablishing their creditworthiness as country risks.

Concluding Remarks

Because of the foregoing conceptions and misconceptions, naive notions of bank behavior have become prevalent, even among serious observers and analysts. Banks have been seen as "pushing," "hawking," or "selling" loans without concerns about risk. In the early 1970s, for example, there were many stories about how bankers had aggressively made loans to Pertamina, the national oil company of Indonesia, which, at the time, had recently become an important oil exporter.

Much of what was said reflected the "follow the leader" syndrome of many banks. Bankers seemed to be unconcerned about risk because they took for granted that if the major banks—Bank of America, Citibank, and Chase Manhattan—were lending, these banks had done the necessary risk analyses. The banks, having decided that a borrower—public or private—was creditworthy and that the country risk was acceptable, regarded such borrowers as the market for bank loans. There was competition in such markets, coming from other lenders in many different countries. At times, competition drove down profits to levels that a lending bank found unacceptable. As in all markets, some suppliers decided to compete at a loss, at least in the short-run, to protect their market positions or to improve them. As a consequence, borrowers were able to shop for the best available terms. Borrowers that were considered strong in creditworthiness usually took advantage of competitive positions to obtain the "finest" (least costly) financial terms. Other borrowers, perceived as creditworthy but not so strongly, had to pay somewhat higher rates.

Banks vary greatly in their willingness to lend at market-determined interest rates. Portfolio considerations are of major importance. Banks generally pursue a policy of diversifying their risk assets and avoiding concentration. Within these broad principles, bank managers have very different judgments and practices. Risk evaluations have much to do with the terms deemed reasonable. These considerations in bank lending are many and interacting, and they are even more complicated in international lending.

Explanations of lending and external debt that seem simple should be regarded as suspect. Some simplistic explanations, such as the irresponsibility of borrowing governments or the stupidity and ignorance of lenders, are easy to spot as simplistic. More difficult are explanations based on more rigorous scientific forms, using quantitative models and statistical ratios such as debt servicing or interest payments in relation to foreign exchange earnings, gross national product or income, or international reserves. All of these quantitative measurements are useful for some purposes—they are all tools of balance-of-payments analysis—but by themselves they are not indicators or measures of creditworthiness or country risk. Analysts of country risk are chronically in troubled waters, necessitating the use of personal judgment on many unpredictable matters.

Qualitative facts and relationships, as well as quantitative facts and relationships, are viewed differently by different lenders. Thoughtful lenders do not simply go through a checklist of facts and factors, although a comprehensive approach to country risk has sometimes been interpreted this way by analysts who ought to know better. Thoughtful lenders study all available facts and analyses and synthesize them into a judgment that, in the final analysis, is experienced intuition. Into this process the lender brings facts and factors other than those contained in the material that has been perused. Among such facts are the reactions of stockholders, the public, the board of directors, or the manager's superiors in the bank; the actions of others; and the long-run strategic aims of the bank in international lending. Does the bank wish to conduct its affairs on a current and relatively short-run defensive outlook, or does it give weight to longer-run market-share considerations—a view largely influenced by attitudes of regulators and by attitudes of boards of directors and the influences that determine their behavior?

In the 1980s, China offers an excellent example of the complexities in judging country risk. Responsible bankers in various countries have had to decide their China lending strategy. All start with a knowledge of China's size, location, resources, institutional structures, governmental policies and practices, past history and international relations, size of external debt, balance-of-payments position, and growth conditions and prospects. China can be described and analyzed professionally, recognizing the many lacunae in facts and the traps in international comparisons. However, the banker still does not have a firm basis for judgment of creditworthiness because he is judging the future when loans will have to be serviced. Among the many uncertainties is China's future creditworthiness for international borrowing. The banker can be reasonably sure that China will experience repeated foreign exchange shortages in the years ahead; he dare not assume otherwise. He can also be reasonably sure that other adversities will be encountered by the Chinese authorities and people. What does the banker deduce from these uncertainties? The banker knows that many bankers in different countries, knowing what his bank knows and facing the same uncertainties it faces, are deciding to expand their financial relations with China, including the whole range of financial services, and establishing branches or affiliates in China, if permitted. These lenders presumably expect China to cope satisfactorily enough with adversities. As lenders, they expect repeated periods of concern and even difficulties requiring special actions, such as debt restructuring. They probably do not expect extensive defaults, but they cannot be ruled out as impossible. No strong creditor institution outside China is guaranteeing China's obligations. What influence should such general views have on the individual bank?

The decision to lend, in its various forms, is greatly influenced by the willingness of the lender to accept the uncertainties and the possibility of repeated difficulties, because it calculates the benefits and profits on a long-term basis, not only on a current or short-term basis. The bank may or may not have a true choice between short-term and long-term approaches. It must look to its own sources of funding. If it is a government-owned commercial bank or is strongly supported by a government, it may feel at ease in assuming greater risks of future adversity than if it is privately owned and dependent on private sources of funds. Again, the decision is never simple. Governments can change their policies and practices; so can private sources of funds. In neither case are future attitudes and actions known or predictable. Studies and analyses can indicate the ranges of effects of different policies and possible events thereafter; much remains, however, that is uncertain and risk-laden. One line of response is to try to match the bank's lending with its own borrowing needs and requirements. Again, this is easy to enunciate as a generality but very difficult to do in practice.

Given these conditions, how should bankers react to China—a country that is seemingly adopting a high growth rate policy based on large external borrowings from private banks and other commercial sources. In the mid 1980s, the banking response is yes for China, at the very time when caution is still the guideline for Brazil and Mexico. A similar acceptance of uncertainty and risk for Brazil and Mexico would make them—again—strong, creditworthy borrowers. Brazil, for example, has continued to pay interest on its debts ($10.5 billion in 1985), but principal payments are under a moratorium. With such reestablished creditworthiness, Brazil and Mexico could easily manage, again, to service their very high levels of external debt. Without this creditworthiness, they have difficulties in domestic economic and social management as well as in servicing their past debt obligations. Part of the difference, of course, is that Brazil and Mexico have already been large borrowers and have fallen into arrears in debt servicing, whereas China has been a small borrower with a good servicing record. Again, simplicity is alluring and misleading. Many banks around the world that have relatively small exposures in Brazil and Mexico are among the most vigorous in trying to reduce their relatively small exposures. Banks with already large exposures are often more open to increasing them. When confronted by this fact, the logic then switches and again is applied simplistically. "Of course" banks with large exposures have no choice except to stay in order to protect their large exposures. Thus, large exposures become arguments both for decreasing and for increasing exposures—a realistic condition because, in fact, the size of exposure is only one factor in a great range of factors determining lending decisions.

China will again bring into focus the question of loan syndications. Banks do not join together to make loans because misery loves company, though this adage may seem to be guiding the debt restructuring exercises. Loan syndications became prevalent in the 1970s, when governments became the borrowers. Governments and their entities borrow in relatively large quantities. Governments of small countries borrow less when compared internationally, but they are still relatively large compared with private firms borrowing in their countries. A government loan will run up against the principle of portfolio diversification by lending institutions and avoidance of concentration. It is not difficult for a lending bank that has standing in financial markets to attract other partners in putting together a government loan. The lead bank will earn additional fees for its efforts, which adds zest to its actions. Its success, however, depends on its willingness to participate in the risk and its reputation for good loan decision making, including country risk assessment and management. Borrowing by China is likely to involve huge amounts for any one bank, either because many Chinese borrowers will be borrowing or because the government will choose to borrow large amounts, which, in turn, it will disburse among its various components. Borrowing countries have done it both ways—often in combination. The results are large total borrowings involving a wide variety of lenders, often in some form of combination, whether it is called a syndication, a club, cofinancing, or some other term.

These complexities of international lending give strong inducements for analysts and bankers to seek the critical factors that determine events. The understandable fear of being lost in a morass of facts and probabilities leads analysts to seek simplification, precision, and predictability. These endeavors are characteristic of economic analysis in all its aspects. International lending is not more complicated to understand than domestic finance, or inflation or income distribution. In all cases, however, there is a huge leap necessary from careful, thoughtful, logical analysis and reasoning to decisions requiring judgments about the future; what is certain is uncertainty about the future. Big, broad ranges of likely events become more predictable. Inflation is likely to lead to social discontent and anti-inflationary policies. Exchange rate rigidity will likely discourage international trade. Banks will seek to maximize profits and avoid losses. These broad probabilities—and they are still only probabilities—do not determine country risk assessments and lending decisions. Yet it is these decisions that determine the course of international lending, the ability of borrowers to service debt, and the ability and willingness of borrowing countries to provide the foreign exchange needed to service debt. As in many other endeavors, the observers and commentators will have their views on events and actions, but they are not authoritative and they can be very wrong. The public will constantly be confronted by varying and conflicting thoughts and analyses in finance. Fortunately, concepts and practices can be rather generally understood. If confidence is lost in their ability to judge, experts in international lending will no longer be able to function as experts. When both bankers and experts lose their self-confidence, the mechanism of international lending slows down, and many costs are incurred by lenders and borrowers. This is the prevailing stage in the 1980s. It is hoped that the foregoing discussions of the concepts of international bank lending will make readers more able to judge and understand what they hear or read about international finance and the world economy.

5

Other Sources
of International Finance

I N addition to the commercial banks, other major sources of international finance are the International Monetary Fund (IMF), capital markets for debt and equity, and official development assistance, bilateral and multilateral. The export credit agencies are also worthy of separate mention.

The International Monetary Fund

The IMF, also known as the Fund, plays a key role in providing international financial resources to help countries finance their balance-of-payments deficits. Its credit operations are not linked to individual projects or specific usage; rather, it deals with national economies and their total external financial needs. This section summarizes the Fund's policies and practices regarding the use of its resources; other aspects of the Fund's role in the international financial system are discussed elsewhere in the book.

Resources of the IMF

The resources that the IMF uses for extending balance-of-payments assistance to member countries include ordinary and borrowed resources. Ordinary resources consist of the currencies of members paid to the Fund as quota subscriptions and special drawing rights (SDRs), which are created by the Fund itself. SDRs combine a number of currencies (at present, five—the U.S. dollar, the Japanese yen, the German deutsche mark, the British pound sterling, and the French franc) into a single unit used for designated purposes in international finance. The SDR unit has usually been equal to slightly more than the U.S. dollar. The SDR combination has been changed from time to time; the weight of the various currencies in the combination reflect their relative economic strength.

Each member of the Fund has a quota, expressed in SDRs, that is equal to its subscription to the Fund. All members have to subscribe. The United States has the largest quota—nearly 25 percent of the total. Quotas determine voting rights. Twenty-five percent of the quota has to be paid in reserve assets specified by the Fund, rather than in national currencies. This requirement is to enable the Fund to obtain currencies of general use by members of SDRs, which are also of general use in international payments. A member is not eligible to use the Fund's financial facilities until it has paid its quota subscription in full. Various economic factors are used in determining the size of quotas, but, roughly speaking, the relative economic sizes of countries and balance-of-payments conditions are the criteria. The Fund's quotas have totaled about SDR 90 billion since the latter part of 1983. Mechanisms exist, and have been repeatedly used, to increase quotas to reflect the changing relative economic size of members and their special circumstances; to keep Fund quotas in line with the increases in world trade, imports, and payments; and to maintain an adequate financial base for the Fund. Quotas are the major part of the Fund's financial base, but it also includes borrowed resources.

Borrowing has provided an important temporary supplement to usable quota resources from time to time. The need for borrowed resources originates in the Fund's financial policies, which have enlarged its members' access to its financial resources much beyond the point at which the access could be financed from quota resources alone. In this calculus, a major factor is that many of the quotas are paid in national currencies, which are not generally usable in international payments and settlements. Members "borrow" from the Fund by purchasing, with their own national currencies, the currencies they need to make international payments and settlements. Only a few national currencies have this general use. Members "repay" the Fund by buying back their currencies with generally usable currencies. Therefore, at any time, the liquidity of the Fund that the Fund can use to help members is only a fraction of its total holdings of currencies of all members. The Fund has wide authority to borrow from any source, so long as the issuers of the borrowed currency (for example, the United States, Germany, Japan) consent. In fact, the Fund's borrowing has been wholly from official sources, rather than from nonofficial private sources.

The Fund's borrowings, like its other operations, are denominated in SDRs. Their maturities have been, for the most part, 4 to 7 years, so as to match the maturities of Fund credit to member countries. The Fund pays its creditors a market-related rate of interest. Most important is that almost all lenders to the Fund are entitled to early repayment of their loans if they have balance-of-payments problems. Therefore, loans to the Fund are highly liquid and can be treated as part of the international monetary reserves of lenders. Generally, Fund policy is to limit total borrowings to 50 percent of total quotas. As of April 30, 1985, the total outstanding borrowings and unused lines of the credit of the Fund amounted to SDR 32.7 billion, equivalent to 37 percent of total Fund quotas. Thus, unlike the World Bank, the IMF does not use the equivalent of capital to create the creditworthiness needed to make possible borrowing from private sources but, instead, uses these contributed resources to help fund its financial operations.

The Fund holds about 100 million fine ounces of gold, valued at about SDR 3.5 billion on the basis of SDR 35 per ounce. This is, of course, only a small fraction of the market value of this gold. At market prices, this gold stock amounts to something more like $30 billion or more. However, although gold is an asset in the Fund's balance sheet and financial statements, it is not regarded as an immediately usable resource and is not used in the Fund's operations and transactions. However, this gold stock is bound to strengthen the Fund as a borrower, especially from private sources.

In contrast to gold, the Fund's holdings of SDRs in its General Resources Account constitute a readily usable asset. Members are required to pay charges (equivalent to interest) in SDRs and can also pay 25 percent of the payments for quota increases in SDRs. The SDRs are used extensively in financial transactions with members, but the Fund limits its holdings of SDRs to a small fraction of its total assets. As noted earlier, most of the assets of the Fund are held in national currencies. The Fund can legally ask members to convert these currencies into other needed currencies when they are sold to members, but Fund policy is not to do so in the case of currency holdings of members that are indebted to the Fund or are in balance-of-payments difficulties. Thus, during the present period of financial disturbances, much of the Fund's reserve became unusable. For example, the Mexican peso was usable at one time, but not after 1982. The Fund sells only the currencies of members that are in strong balance-of-payments and international monetary reserve positions.

The sale of currency to a member obtaining financial assistance from the Fund reduces the Fund's holdings of that currency. It thereby increases the ability of the issuing member (that is, the member whose currency is sold) to obtain credits from the Fund, if necessary. This sale of its currency automatically increases a country's ability to receive assistance from the Fund in the future. If its currency holdings are reduced below specified levels, the member gets automatic drawing rights, called a *reserve position*.

Against these liquid assets, comprising usable currencies and SDRs, the Fund has immediate, or liquid, liabilities consisting of members' claims on the Fund. Claims come from members' reserve positions in the Fund, undrawn balances under so-called standby or extended arrangements, and lenders' claims on the Fund. Fund liquidity is also importantly affected by repurchases (repayments) by members. Since the Fund is a revolving pool of currencies, repurchase is of critical importance. In itself, it creates a limit on the maturity of Fund credit. The longer the average maturity of Fund credit, and the consequent lower probability of early repurchases, the lower is the availability of new resources for fresh lending out of repurchases.

Use of IMF Resources

The Fund's financial resources are made available to members through a varied range of policies and facilities. These differ mainly in the type of balance-of-payments need they seek to address and in the degree of conditionality—that is, conditions for lending—attached to them.

The rules governing access to the Fund's resources apply uniformly to all members. However, certain facilities, though open to all members, are designed and intended to be of special help to developing countries. These include the compensatory financing facility for shortfalls in export earnings or additional cost of cereal imports, the buffer stock financing facility, and a new structural adjustment facility. The compensating financing facility assists members with balance-of-payments difficulties caused by declines in export earnings or increases in the price of food imports. The buffer stock financing facility helps finance the building of stocks of commodities acquired in international commodity agreements to help stabilize their prices. The structural adjustment facility is intended to provide balance-of-payments support for joint programs with the World Bank to help countries with medium-term (3 years) financing to meet developmental needs.

The Fund's guidelines for use of its resources are related to the economic indicators of the external payments position of a country. The Fund assesses both the balance-of-payments need of a member country and the adequacy of measures to correct the underlying balance-of-payments disequilibrium. These measures constitute what is commonly referred to as the *adjustment program*. A country's need to use the Fund's resources is judged in light of the country's overall balance of payments, excluding so-called compensating borrowing—that is, official borrowing by a member country primarily to avoid use of its international reserves. Thus, the Fund focuses on the entire external financial position of a country, rather than on any part of it. In this process, judgmental factors are unavoidable. In addition, Fund policies, under particular facilities, set forth requirements concerning particular causes of balance-of-payments need. For instance, the use of the compensatory financing facility is restricted to balance-of-payments deficits arising out of export shortfalls or increased costs of specified cereal imports. The structural adjustment facility provides medium-term assistance for structural balance-of-payments difficulties of economies characterized by slow growth.

The Fund encourages members to have early resort to the Fund when they are experiencing balance-of-payments difficulties. Once need has been determined and eligibility to use a facility has been established, purchases—or drawings—are subject to specified terms and conditions of use that are summed up in the word *conditionality*. The aim of conditionality is to ensure that an adequate adjustment program is undertaken by the borrowing member. There are no fixed standards of conditionality; they vary with individual programs. Conditionality aims at achieving a sustainable balance-of-payments position—that is, a current account deficit financed by normal capital inflows, at a level and on terms consistent with satisfactory growth and development prospects. The severity of conditionality increases as members increase their use of Fund credit.

The amount of financial assistance to members is determined according to guidelines periodically adopted by the Fund.

In practice, the Fund has tended to increase substantially the amounts of credit a member can obtain, not merely by increasing the total size of the Fund (the Fund is now about ten times its original size) but also by increasing the size of drawings (credit) in relation to a member's share in the Fund—that is, its quota.

A member may make outright purchase of foreign exchange from the Fund, but usually it operates through standby or extended arrangements, which are analogous to lines of credit extended by banks to their customers. These Fund arrangements usually are from 12 to 24 months (standby) or up to 36 months (extended arrangements). Terms and conditions embody macroeconomic elements, such as economic performance criteria—for example, budgetary and credit ceilings, exchange and interest rate actions, and limits on amount and maturity of new short- and medium-term external debt. The credits made available by the Fund are phased over time (sometimes years) to ensure observance of the performance criteria. The nonobservance of performance criteria interrupts the right of members to make further purchases—that is, to use their credit lines. The Fund charges (interest) on these credits are levied periodically and reflect the sources of the Fund's financing. Credits based on the Fund's quota resources are charged about 7 percent per annum, which is well below market rates. Credits based on resources borrowed by the Fund are related to the cost of borrowings, except that low-income countries receive subsidies on the charges they pay for credits financed by the Fund with borrowed funds.

SDRs require some separate explanation. The SDR is an interest-bearing international monetary reserve asset created by the Fund, since 1970, as a supplement to existing reserve assets. The aim was to create an international reserve asset that could substitute, over time, for gold or for the U.S. dollar. The SDR is an asset to its holder but—unlike a currency—it is no country's liability. The U.S. dollar, for example, is a reserve asset if held by the Bank of England but a liability of the United States. An SDR held by the Bank of England is an asset but no country's liability. The SDR can be held by, and traded among, only member country participants and prescribed official entities. Thus, the Fund can create this form of unconditional international liquidity and can allocate SDRs to participant members. In its decision on SDR allocations, the Fund is required to take into account the long-term global need to supplement existing international reserve assets and the Fund's objective of making the SDR the principal reserve asset in the international monetary system.

The Fund has been cautious in exercising this power and has created only about SDR 21 billion of this reserve asset. This compares with total world reserves of about $450 billion. Allocations of SDRs are a uniform percentage of a member's quotas. Thus, the countries with the largest quotas, such as the United States and Germany, receive the largest shares of SDR creations. The value of the SDR is defined by decisions of the Fund, and the Fund has decided to value the SDR in terms of a "basket" of five major currencies—the U.S. dollar, the German deutsche mark, the British pound sterling, the French franc, and the Japanese yen. Because currency values fluctuate, SDR values also change in terms of foreign currencies. These currencies do not fluctuate uniformly, and they often offset each other. Thus, the SDR as a unit is relatively stable compared with any single national currency. The Fund publishes, daily, the exchange rates for a wide range of currencies in terms of the SDR. The SDR can be, and is, used by its holders in wide range of international transactions, including obtaining an equivalent amount of other members' currencies and settlement of financial obligations. However, it has not yet become a major factor in international finance or gained strong acceptance.

Because of its various characteristics, the SDR has frequently been described as "paper gold" created by the IMF. It remains a potential source of major increases in international liquidity. The fact that the international community did not resort to this mechanism during recent years reflects, in part, the fact that developed countries have not had shortages of international liquidity. The reserves of the industrial countries, which include only liquid holdings of official agencies, rose, even during the troubled 1980s, from about $180 billion at the end of 1979 to over $250 billion in 1985. In addition, equivalent or greater amounts of U.S. dollar assets have been acquired by countries and are held by their private citizens or are in maturities or forms that are not counted as monetary assets.

Developed countries have not had to follow deflationary domestic policies because of foreign exchange shortages. Such policies have resulted, rather, from their eagerness to reduce inflation, improve productivity, and strengthen their international competitiveness. In contrast, the developing countries have suffered severely from a shortage of international liquidity. Deflation has been forced by this illiquidity. However, the international community has not regarded SDR creation as an appropriate way to deal with the widespread illiquidity of developing countries. Developed countries have been concerned with the inflationary impact of large-scale SDR creation on developing countries already experiencing strong inflation. Developing countries, in any case, obtain only a small share of total SDR creations, because their quotas in the Fund are small in relation to total quotas. Thus, Brazil and India, two of the largest developing countries, each have quotas that are less than 3 percent of total quotas. Yet the SDR mechanism can be used to create international liquidity for developed and developing countries if the international community, organized through the Fund, wishes to use its authority to do so. In considering the financial crisis that began in 1982, it is important to keep in mind that it has not been a general crisis of worldwide illiquidity. Rather, it has been a crisis of developing countries. The SDR was not intended to be a mechanism to defend development although its use for this purpose has been advocated since the beginning of the 1970s. It could be so used if the international community decided to do so, but this course of action seems unlikely. Other ways to defend development, such as increased resources obtained with the help of the multilateral development banks, would seem preferable, but the SDR may be used because better alternatives are not available.

International Capital Markets for Debt and Equity

Debt: Old and New Forms

This book is principally concerned with the international financial system as it applies to developing countries. Therefore, debt capital obtained from banks is the primary focus of attention. It is necessary, however, to have an overview of international capital markets other than bank loans, though they mostly serve the developed countries. Such an overview is useful because it gives perspective to our understanding of the system as it functions in relation to developing countries. Moreover, solutions to current problems of these countries may well be found in using mechanisms that exist in international capital markets at present, but are used almost exclusively for industrial countries, OPEC countries, or international development agencies. Attention to capital markets is necessary in assessing the adequacy of the international financial system of our integrated, interdependent world economy.

The term *international capital markets* usually refers to markets in international bonds, medium-term (over 1 year) and long-term bank loans, foreign loans from sources other than banks, and a recent category labeled "other international facilities," which encompasses a wide and rapidly growing range of innovative mechanisms and debt instruments that are traded in financial markets but are not long-term fixed instruments like bonds. It includes floating rate notes and Eurocommercial paper of maturities similar to bank loans but issued as securities sold to investors and traded in the financial markets.

International bonds consist of foreign and Eurocurrency bonds. *Foreign bonds* are issued by a borrower that is of a nationality different from the country in which the bonds are issued. Such issues are underwritten and sold by a group of banks of the market country and are denominated in that country's currency. In contrast, *Eurocurrency bonds* are those underwritten and sold in various national markets simultaneously, usually through international syndicates of financial institutions of several countries. Eurobonds are denominated in a currency that need not be any of the currencies of the market countries.

Debt instruments are issued, bought, and sold. These transactions take place in true markets. Bank loans, with very few exceptions, are not bought or sold—that is, they are not traded in a market. The issuers in capital markets can be governments, corporations, parastatals, or multilateral institutions. In issuing debt instruments for sale in markets, underwriters of such issues may or may not commit themselves to the issuers to assure sale of such instruments at agreed prices. All sorts of varieties exist. The borrower faces open competition for funds, and its creditworthiness is reflected in market quotations for its "paper" (the debt instrument issued by it). Other factors, such as yields, also influence market pricing and trading. At all times, the debt is worth what the market says it is worth; buyers match sellers of credit, while the original issuer, the debtor, is bound by the terms at which the debt instrument was issued. Unlike a bank loan, the debt instrument can be traded in markets at a discount or premium.

If all bank credit to developing countries were refinanced into capital market instruments, much of what is now regarded as the debt problem would disappear. Repudiation would clearly be seen as an unusable option. Banks would no longer be holders of unwanted assets. The market would find the price at which the debts were held by willing investors (who automatically become lenders as long as they hold the debt instruments). Moratoriums, or threats of moratoriums, by a country would drive down the prices of debt instruments of such a country to levels attractive to some investors. Automatically, increased perceptions of risk would translate into higher yields for the investor/lender because of the reduced price for the debt instrument. No debt restructuring is needed. The discount on debt paper could fall, reflecting market price based on a speculative future worth. Yet even so, the buyer would be a willing speculator, unless no buyers could be found and the last purchasers of the instruments automatically became and remained the lenders—a risk taken by the investor when it purchased this instrument.

In practice, marketability of debt, with all its consequences, mostly divides capital markets rather than maturity of debt. A traded floating rate note may have a maturity of only a few months. It may even be used to help finance international trade, but if it is traded in markets, it is considered herein as distinctly different from bank loans, which, whatever the maturities, have contractually agreed lenders and borrowers. Bank loans have begun to be bought and sold, but not in true markets and only exceptionally. Such beginnings may, however, be harbingers of future developments. In their very different forms, capital markets for traded debt instruments may again become major; indeed, they may become the most important sources of external funds for developing countries.

International capital markets tend to be concentrated in relatively few financial centers—New York, London, Paris, Zurich, Luxembourg, Frankfurt, Tokyo, and a few other cities. To these centers come funds from all over the world and seekers of funds from all over the world. It is this coming together of lenders, borrowers, and investors from different countries for lending and borrowing in currencies other than the currency of the country in which the capital market is found that essentially makes the markets international. The Eurodollar bond in London is a major example. In addition, reflecting nationality diversity, different national laws or regulations may apply differently to such international transactions than to domestic transactions. Authorities of a country in which an international capital market is found will not feel the same degree of responsibility for transactions in such markets as in truly domestic markets in domestic currencies. Rules of business conduct exist and are enforced, but domestic financial systems are regulated or supervised more closely. The great variety and pricing of loans can often outcompete their national counterparts dealing in these currencies. Borrowers often go to London to get Japanese yen and to Zurich to get sterling.

These markets are highly efficient in their interlinking. Instant global communication exists on a 24-hour, around-the-globe basis. Markets are highly integrated; even great differences in time zones are overcome. Their centers are, in turn, linked instantaneously with other cities around the world. A borrower or investor need not go to an international capital market institution to handle its needs. Its local bank or financial firm, or even a nonfinancial entity, can access any open market anywhere in the world instantaneously. Virtually any need for capital, however novel and exotic, can be met. Innovation grows like flowers in a hothouse. New debt and equity (or combined) instruments are created daily and, if a need exists without a corresponding instrument, an instrument can be created *de novo* for this purpose. Its creation then creates further demand for it. Finance has never been more inventive. The complexities are so great that subdivisions of expertise prevail, like debt instruments of governments that have subdivisions and sub-subdivisions; for example, there are experts in marketing school board bonds within cities, which also issue bonds in states, which also issue bonds in the nation and, finally, in international markets. All have specialized markets and entities. The attraction of quasi-equity instruments is that their servicing depends on the performance of the borrowing entity.

The developing countries have paid a high price for the bond defaults of a number of countries, such as Argentina in the 1930s. Investors, by choice or regulation, have avoided buying their bonds when offered. Most developing countries have only limited access to the international capital markets; they are mostly confined to medium- and long-term bank loans. This restriction has prevailed for the last half-century. In the United States, for example, state laws have severely limited the right of insurance companies to invest in foreign bonds. The World Bank and then the Inter-American and Asian Development Banks and, currently, the African Development Bank have had to seek and obtain acceptance by state legislatures for purchases of their bonds by such state-incorporated entities. Only a few entities in developing countries have been able to float bonds in the international capital markets. Investors in bond markets, as a group, are the most cautious of international lenders, making funds available at long term on fixed interest rates. Ironically, Mexico was one of the few developing countries whose entities met the credit standards of the bond markets—ironic in view of the disrepute experienced by Mexico in the 1980s after its major mistake of permitting its balance of payments to deteriorate to the degree that it required a moratorium on servicing of external debt. By 1980, U.S. insurance companies were prepared to consider lending to more developing countries. Events of 1981–82 brought this hopeful development to an abrupt halt, perhaps for decades, in the traditional forms of capital markets. However, as mentioned earlier, nontraditional forms of borrowing may become of major importance for developing countries.

World capital markets have grown at a rapid pace in the postwar period. Including medium- and long-term bank loans, total funds raised in international markets increased from about $20 billion in 1972 to over $240 billion in 1985. Bonds continued to increase steadily, rising to about $162 billion in 1985.

Banks may choose to withdraw from international lending, but the process of lending is not likely to diminish or cease. The 1980s saw a major change in the composition of the capital markets. Whereas in 1980, bank loans accounted for about 67 percent of total lending and bonds for 32 percent, in 1985, banks accounted for only about 16 percent and bonds for about 67 percent, with the new innovations accounting for about another 15 percent. It is too early to say that this change is structural, but it suggests, again, that future international lending to developing countries may be very different from the past. It is more likely that new techniques will be used that are more flexible and more adaptable to changing conditions in capital importing and capital exporting countries. Banks themselves can change their roles. Instead of being lenders, they can become underwriters, whose responsibilities as lenders are very temporary and limited. Countries may try to access capital markets—not necessarily with fixed interest, long-term bonds that have AA or AAA ratings but with floating rate notes at the most favorable yields that their investment bankers can arrange. Borrowing countries will have the options of fixing schedules of interest and amortization payments or letting markets determine yields. Once these potentials are open—and they could prove to be a Pandora's box if not done carefully—the future prospects of international lending to developing countries will change dramatically.

It would be useful, perhaps, to emphasize that by far the largest borrowers from the international capital markets are found in the industrial countries. In 1981, when OPEC and some borrowers in non-OPEC developing countries were able to borrow, about two-thirds of total borrowing was done by entities in the OECD area. In 1985, as the OPEC countries lost their prior standings, the OECD area accounted for about 80 percent of total borrowing; much of the remainder was borrowing by the World Bank and other multilateral institutions.

Another major development in the international capital markets is the growing use of floating interest rates in both bonds and bank loans. For example, in 1974, only 1 percent of all issued international bonds carried floating rate coupons; in 1985, over 35 percent had floating interest rates. Commercial bank lending is almost entirely done on a floating interest rate basis. As bond markets become more acceptive of floating interest rates, their willingness to lend to developing countries will become greater. Prime or strongest borrowers have tended to be favored by lenders when they choose to invest in fixed interest debt. Persistent inflation, however, brings a major element of uncertainty into fixed interest lending, which can be offset by the credit strength of the borrower. A borrower in a developing country is unlikely, however, to have a strong credit standing. A floating rate, by reducing the interest rate risk, makes a lender less concerned about other risks, which is a desirable state of affairs for borrowers with weaker credit standing. As inflation rates declined in 1985–86, fixed interest bonds became even more attractive. In the future, a mixture of both fixed and floating rate instruments is likely to be available to creditworthy borrowers.

It is questionable, however, whether new innovations in the capital markets can quickly reverse the recent unfavorable trends for developing countries. In the late 1970s, the flow of funds shifted in the direction of developing countries. In 1979, these countries, including OPEC members, accounted for over 40 percent of all borrowings in international markets. Over the 4-year period from 1979 to 1982, the non-oil developing countries as a group borrowed $155 billion, or 25 percent of total funds raised, and the OPEC members an additional $32 billion, or 5 percent—over 90 percent of this borrowing being in bank loans, with bonds of minor importance. As noted earlier, by 1985, this trend had been completely reversed: non-oil developing countries and OPEC combined accounted for only 12 percent of the total.

New instruments have quickly become important, while traditional forms of borrowing in bonds and bank loans are declining. However, these new instruments have been used mostly by industrial country borrowers. In these countries, commercial banks are becoming investment bankers, mobilizing different sources of finance. "Packaging" is the new game, rather than syndication. In packaging, financiers bring together different kinds of finance from widely varying sources. In syndications, banks bring in other banks.

This trend reflects a clear preference of investors and lenders in securitized forms of financing—that is, the use of instruments which can be traded. In 1982, securitized forms of financing accounted for about 44 percent of borrowings in capital markets, as bank loans predominated. In 1985, securitized forms of financing accounted for close to 80 percent. Loans were the only form of financing that declined during these years.

In periods of chronic uncertainty and country risk, securitization meets investors' demands for greater international diversification of their portfolios, as well as providing a better matching of the preferences of both investors and borrowers in terms of liquidity and flexibility. In a world of global markets, trading in securities becomes increasingly sophisticated, and previous magnitudes of capital flows are dwarfed as new sources of funds and new borrowers of funds come into these markets. Domestic capital markets are becoming parts of the mechanisms of the international capital market. These markets match the concerns of lenders and investors to reduce risk and obtain attractive risk/reward ratios. With the concerns of borrowers to reduce costs and secure more sources of supply as available markets shrink or disappear, borrowers must become more expert in these new innovations and in the possibilities of creating instruments that are tailor-made for their needs. The proliferation of identified new financial products include zero coupon bonds, revolving underwriting facilities, and "swaps"—either currency or interest rate swaps—to match the differing views of investors regarding the attractiveness for their portfolios of different kinds of maturities, earnings, currencies, and countries.

In response to such trends, and assisting them, deregulation movements have taken place in large markets, such as the United States, Germany, the United Kingdom, Japan, and others. With deregulation, innovation can be accelerated and broadened. Borrowers considered virtually unacceptable for traditional forms of lending can now find new ways, *but* they must be prepared to accept market evaluations and responses to their borrowing needs and demands. Politics, statesmanship, and assistance all go by the board. The markets are impersonal, but they are available at a price. Borrowers who choose to go this route will have to ensure that their usage of borrowed funds is for high returns in improved productivity, output, and competitiveness. Artificial, nonmarket pricing and controls in borrowing countries would make the use of these new market-oriented facilities too costly and unwise, whereas high-return usage based on realistic pricing in the domestic economy would make such foreign funds relatively attractive.

Private Direct Investment and Equity

For developing countries, foreign direct investment has provided needed capital, technical know-how, and managerial expertise for a long time. The 1970s was the decade of commercial bank lending; the 1980s has seen a revived interest in foreign private investment as a means of development finance. (Private direct investment consists of both new equity capital and reinvested earnings, plus borrowing from the parent company and its affiliates. Reinvested earnings account for over half of the measured flows of direct investment in developing countries.)

The share of foreign private direct investment in the total net flow of financial resources from developed to developing countries, which had been as high as 50 percent in the early 1960s, declined from an average of about 22 percent at the beginning of the 1970s to 13 percent in the early 1980s. As the 1980s have progressed, that share of total financing has tended to increase only because private lending has declined even more drastically.

Direct investment has been highly concentrated in relatively few developing countries. Like commercial bank lending, it has gone mainly to the higher-income countries in Asia and Latin America, such as Brazil, Mexico, and Singapore. The largest borrowing countries also have the largest stock of foreign private investment, reflecting the relatively high opinion of these countries in private business circles abroad. The United States and the United Kingdom have been the major suppliers. More recently, Germany and Japan have gained importance. Together, these four industrialized countries have supplied over 75 percent of total direct investment for developing countries. British and German firms have concentrated heavily in the manufacturing sector, while Japanese and U.S. investments are more evenly spread across resource-based industries, manufacturing, and the service sector. Generally, the overall host country policies for traditional forms of foreign private direct investment deteriorated during the 1970s. Expropriations were rare, but government policies—such as limitations on the degree of foreign participation or prohibitions on entry into industries deemed especially sensitive—reduced the expected profitability of investments. Reservation of key industries for state ownership also reduced the scope or attractiveness of foreign private investment.

In general, it can be said that there are considerable complementarities between foreign private direct investment and other financial flow. There is substitutability between debt and equity finance. Much can be done to encourage more direct investment. An outstanding example is the proposal for the establishment of the Multilateral Investment Guarantee Agency (MIGA), with a projected initial capital of $1 billion, initiated by the World Bank. The MIGA would issue guarantees against noncommercial risks.

Closely related to innovations in the capital markets for debt are the innovations in the equity markets. From a financial viewpoint, far too much of the capital imported into Latin America and other developing countries has been in the form of loans rather than equity. Loans have to be serviced; equity does not.

Borrowing countries should encourage more mobilization and domestic usage of equity capital or quasi-equity-debt instruments that have many of the characteristics of equity. This is the opposite of capital flight. It will take a high degree of confidence in a country's economic and political management as well as profits attractive enough to outcompete unproductive domestic uses or capital flight. Many developing countries can hope to meet these requirements, especially as new technologies that are adaptable to local conditions become commercialized by private sector enterprises. Opportunities for relatively "small" investments—in the millions and tens of millions of dollars per investment—are growing rapidly. Joint enterprises can readily be formed. As a consequence, venture capital is becoming involved in financing technology transfers to such countries—sometimes domestic venture capital in the developing countries, sometimes foreign venture capital, sometimes a combination of the two. Official institutions are often eager to join, providing debt or equity or both. Quite feasible are highly complex "packages" of debt and equity from a wide variety of sources. On the micro level, they represent the meshing of official and private institutions for international purposes, which has become commonplace in the domestic markets, especially those of industrial countries. The different element for international finance is the presence of multilateral sources of financing—such as the IMF, the World Bank, and the regional development banks—which, in the future, can play an important role in mobilizing debt and equity capital.

In addition to the international capital markets, and more akin to the packaging of debt and equity finance, is the recent globalization of equity markets. This development is occurring much later than the globalization of debt markets, but it is already important and it has implications for future flows of funds to developing countries.

More and more companies have equity securities that are actively trading outside their home markets. As much as 20 percent to 30 percent of the securities of such companies are traded abroad. Liquid assets are available for investments in such shares or stocks. Companies with outstanding reputations find this a true option for raising capital instead of increased debt. There are many usages, including using securities to facilitate foreign mergers and acquisitions. Multimarket offerings in various countries are coming into vogue. Institutional investors dominate the world's equity markets. Institutions around the world wish to invest a certain portion of their portfolios in foreign countries to increase earnings and diversify risks, high among which are currency and country risks. Pension funds available for investments are in the tens of billions of dollars and can rise in the next five years or so to hundreds of billions. As multinational firms become multinational in business activities, it becomes logical to managers and shareholders to spread their shareholding to approximate the spread of business activities more closely. The demand for such equity is fueled by the pent-up demand for equity reflected in stock markets around the world. Moreover, companies can raise equity on the international market within a period of weeks or even days. This process has become institutionalized and has been made more efficient by the formation of truly international syndicates of banks and brokers, capable of quickly placing a line of stocks for the major multinational firms. Companies can obtain good prices for their shares, reportedly at ever-decreasing margins. The presence of banks large enough to absorb huge amounts of risk capital is creating a potentially huge primary issuer market for equity.

These equity market developments are still in their early stages of development. However, they hold out the promise of another way to obtain the external finance needed by developing countries. The mechanisms probably cannot yield relatively large, attractive opportunities in most developing countries—but Brazil, Mexico, Argentina, Venezuela, and Korea are big enough economies to be interesting, and they have domestic firms with international reputations.

The use of equity markets implies a willingness to share ownership—a hard step for firms to take, even in advanced industrialized countries. The use of international equity markets implies sharing ownership with foreigners, which is a sensitive, even explosive, issue in developing countries. The relative importance of equity flows adds to the significance of the withdrawal of commercial banks from lending. The private sectors, however, are potentially more important as they offer potentially attractive opportunities for foreign investors. These firms and their governments face the choice of broadening foreign ownership and obtaining capital on a debt-free basis or continuing to try to borrow or reduce the growth of the national economy. It is impossible to predict which course different countries will choose. There are visible signs that a number are choosing to share equity ownership with foreigners to obtain technology, markets, management, and foreign exchange. Much will depend on the availability of the sources of finance. What seems clear is that equity sharing can be a major source of finance for the most highly indebted countries and is, therefore, a major option open for their consideration and acceptance or rejection.

Official Development Assistance: Bilateral and Multilateral Aid

The international financial system cannot be described nor its functioning understood without noting the presence of what is commonly called foreign aid—bilateral and multilateral—and is more formally called official development assistance (ODA).

Bilateral Aid

Bilateral development assistance started in the 1950s essentially as an emergency, temporary measure. It has since become a well-established and accepted part of the international financial system.

Hundreds of books and thousands of articles have described the various national aid programs and multilateral development efforts. There have been as many official reports as private and personal analyses, and there is probably a conference or official meeting on this subject somewhere every day of the year. Fortunately, the involved national agencies issue lengthy, authoritative studies and report on their activities and on development issues. The aid activities of governments are coordinated in the Development Assistance Committee (DAC) of the Organization for Economic Cooperation and Development (OECD), which gives leadership to the national aid programs—usually referred to as bilateral aid. The DAC also issues very useful reports, including its annual reports. For the interested reader, particular attention is drawn to the 1985 DAC report, which marked the twenty-fifth anniversary of the DAC and reviewed the entire period of DAC's existence. The multilateral development banks also issue reviews, studies, reports, and the like, and bring facts and views together in their annual reports and periodic surveys. These documents are highly recommended to those who have a deep interest in international finance or in developing countries and who have the time for serious study.

Development assistance is different from other areas of international finance. It is clearly socially and politically motivated—it is not neutral. It is to be judged by its political and social purposes and achievements, although its mechanisms are economic and financial. Its catchwords are *economic and social progress*, and its origin was the United Nations Charter in 1945.

From a financial perspective, the foreign aid programs have been predicated on the assumption that social and economic progress could be accelerated by providing funds from official sources, on terms more favorable to the borrower (or grant receiver) than could be obtained from commercial sources. The economic test has essentially been per capita rates of growth in industry and agriculture; the social tests have been literacy, health, and life expectancy. The aims were to achieve more rapid progress than the industrialized countries had experienced in their history or were experiencing currently. By these tests, the foreign aid programs have been successes. The main conclusion, which can be amply documented, is that development in various countries in all regions of the world has been greatly accelerated over at least a generation. To cite just a few figures for the most comprehensive indicators of human progress—between 1950 and 1980, average life expectancy in all developing countries rose about 40 percent, from 42 to 59 years, and infant mortality among children aged 1 to 4 declined from twenty eight per thousand to twelve per thousand, a reduction of more than 50 percent. To achieve this accelerated progress, the governments in the OECD undertook to provide resources through bilateral arrangements (with recipient countries) or multilateral cooperation.

In the entire period since World War II, three major periods in official development assistance can be distinguished. The first period was during the 1950s and early 1960s, which saw a rapid buildup of economic assistance. The United States alone accounted for about half of total economic assistance, France for about 30 percent, and the United Kingdom for about 10 percent. During the 1950s, assistance from the United States consisted mainly of nonproject assistance to a group of countries stretching from Greece to South Korea along the borders of what was then known as the Sino-Soviet bloc. Aid from France concentrated on its former colonies in Francophone Africa. Aid from the United Kingdom was directed toward the newly independent Commonwealth countries, mostly in Asia and Africa—for example, India and Pakistan.

In the early 1960s, the U.S. program was broadened geographically. In these years, the United States continued to provide the leadership in development assistance. In 1960, the United States provided 58 percent of total economic assistance to developing countries. All regions were included: India and Pakistan in Asia, the Alliance for Progress in Latin America, and increased aid to Africa. The United States was also a major donor of food aid, reflecting both its domestic surpluses and the food crises in the South Asian subcontinent (mostly India). France and the United Kingdom, as well as Australia and Canada, expanded their programs, and Germany and Japan launched major programs.

The second major period was from the mid-1960s to the early 1970s. This period witnessed relative stability in aggregate levels of aid from DAC countries as a group. A downward drift in U.S. aid was offset by increases in aid from the newer donors, which now included Kuwait, Denmark, Norway, Sweden, and the Netherlands. Paradoxically, this decade of aggregate stagnation was proclaimed by the United Nations as the "Development Decade." The United States reduced its relative share of development assistance, but by the early 1970s it was still roughly one-third of total aid to developing countries. In 1970–71, the United States provided (in 1983 prices and exchange rates) about $7 billion of the total DAC assistance of about $18 billion. It continued to be, by far, the largest single source of official assistance.

The third period was the mid-1970s to the present. This period has seen rapid increases in DAC aid in response to new, pressing developing country needs resulting from the oil price shocks and a variety of other adverse developments, including accelerating inflation, climbing interest rates, the effects of world economic recession, the widening external debt crises, and the African disasters. Total DAC assistance in 1983–84 rose to over $28 billion, of which the United States provided about $8 billion (of which about 50 percent was politically oriented), further reducing the U.S. share to about 22 percent, compared with almost 30 percent in 1970-71. Very large increases were registered by Germany, Japan, and Saudi Arabia, and Italy became an important contributor as strong parliamentary and public concern with hunger and malnutrition were expressed.

Regarding the recipients of ODA, India has remained the largest single recipient, although its percentage of total ODA declined from 16.8 percent in 1960–61 to 6.3 percent in 1982–83. In terms of regions, official development assistance (measured as a percentage of GNP) has been most important for Africa. For understanding the international financial system, it is noteworthy that in Asia as a whole, ODA amounted to less than 1 percent (0.8 percent) of GNP in 1982–83. Pakistan was relatively high, with 2.4 percent. In sub-Sahara Africa, it amounted to 4.5 percent but it was much higher for the Sahel group, Tanzania, Sudan, and others. In Egypt, it amounted to nearly 5 percent. In these countries, domestic savings would amount to about 15 percent to 20 percent of GNP. External funds provided about one-fifth or one-fourth of investable funds. Most investable funds in almost all developing countries come from their own domestic savings.

Multilateral Aid: World Bank, Regional Development Banks, and Others

The role of the multilateral development banks, like the IMF's role, is alluded to repeatedly in this volume. Details are given in later chapters, but at this point it may be helpful to discuss them very briefly in the context of sources of international development assistance and the totality of international finance.

The principal multilateral institution is the International Bank for Reconstruction and Development (IBRD), known as the World Bank. It was one of two outcomes of the 1944 Bretton Woods Conference, the other being the International Monetary Fund. The World Bank has steadily grown in membership and now has about 150 members. (The Soviet Union is not a member.) Its capital of about $60 billion is provided by sale of shares to governments, and voting power is proportionate to share ownership. The United States is the largest shareholder, and the majority of shares is owned by developed countries. Originally, the World Bank was intended to provide guarantees for foreign borrowers in international capital markets. Instead, it evolved quickly into a direct lender, mostly for public sector projects in developing countries. In 1960 came the establishment of the International Development Association (IDA) as a "soft-loan" affiliate of the World Bank. The developed countries preferred this to the alternative proposal of a special fund of the United Nations, because the structure of the World Bank ensured weighted voting in their favor.

Shortly before the creation of the IDA, the Inter-American Development Bank (IDB) was formed. The IDA and the IDB provided a model for other regions of the developing world, such as Africa and Asia, and the African and Asian Development Banks were formed in the 1960s. Other multilateral institutions were formed— for example, those of the European Economic Community (EEC)— but the World Bank, the IDA, and the regional banks have been the most important and are the central elements of the system of official international development finance.

In 1984, DAC members contributed nearly $9 billion to the multilateral development agencies and their associated funds, compared with less than $1 billion on average in 1965–66. About $5 billion went to financial institutions—over 90 percent to the World Bank, the IDA, and the regional development banks. This $5 billion was about seven times the average for 1965–66 and five times the average for 1971–72. The most spectacular increase was in contributions to the IDA. The sixth replenishment of the IDA for the 1981–83 period amounted to $12 billion followed by a seventh replenishment of $9 billion. The member countries of the IMF and the World Bank continue to consider ways to increase the financial resources and scope of these institutions. For example, in 1985, the World Bank established a special facility for sub-Saharan Africa in order to support economic recovery and policy reforms in the region.

In terms of disbursements from the multilateral agencies, the story is about the same. In 1984, the multilateral institutions, including new institutions formed by OPEC countries, disbursed about $16 billion in one year. The World Bank group—that is, the World Bank, the IDA, and the International Finance Corporation (IFC), the "private arm" of the World Bank—was the largest single source. In 1984 and 1985, the World Bank group entered into loan and credit commitments of over $14 billion, of which about $3 billion was from the IDA.

These figures are impressive, and resource flows financed by the multilateral agencies are important. They are, however, still a small fraction of total resource flows to developing countries, and they are much less than the resources from private sources. Resource flows from all sources totaled over $92 billion in 1984, after reaching nearly $118 billion in 1983; most of the decline was in private sources of finance. Bilateral sources of official development assistance accounted for about 30 percent, having reached over $27 billion—$20 billion from DAC countries and nearly $4 billion from OPEC countries. Private sources of finance accounted for $34 billion in 1984 and over $62 billion in 1983.

Since multilateral finance is only a small fraction of the total finance for resource flows to the developing countries, the importance of the multilateral institutions lies more in their leadership and coordination of international assistance. However, the significance of their relatively small size cannot be overlooked in considering future needs and policies. The multilateral development banks have played only a relatively minor role in coping with the crisis conditions of the 1980s. They could do much more, but their role in providing financial resources would have to be greatly enhanced. Greatly broadened functions for these institutions is a major component of the program suggested herein for modernizing the international financial system, restoring creditworthiness, and reestablishing a major role for private sources of finance.

Export Credit Agencies

Thus far, we have explored some of the main private and official sources of financing open to debtor countries. Another main source is export credit extended by official agencies or insured, in large part, by officially supported insurance schemes.

Export credit flows are vital for the smooth functioning of the international trade system, and they can be extended by commercial banks without the benefit of insurance schemes to cover possible losses. Guaranteed credits have become an important source of financing. Trade credits, extended or guaranteed by official creditors to developing countries, amounted to roughly one-fourth of their external debt by the end of 1983, or the equivalent of about 40 percent of nonguaranteed commercial bank credits.

Export credits are a major factor in international competition, especially in capital goods, as financial costs are a significant element of total costs. Governments have used public funds to enable exporters to provide cheaper credits to their customers than their foreign competitors can provide.

Since before World War II, industrial countries have established mechanisms for giving official support to export credits as a means of promoting their exports. Essentially, such support is given in two ways: official export credit agencies like the Export-Import Bank of the United States lend directly to finance international trade and export credit agencies like the Export Credits Guarantee Department (ECGD) of the United Kingdom insure loans by private lenders, covering total funds. Equivalent institutions are found in virtually all industrial countries—for example, COFACE in France and HERMES in Germany. Although some of their practices differ, they all belong to the International Union of Credit and Investment Insurers, more popularly known as the Berne Union. The Berne Union set guidelines—for example, minimum terms and interest rates—for all its members to avoid acrimonious and disruptive competitive practices. The tendency is for these agencies to try to keep interest rates relatively low to help the competitive position of their exporters.

These export credit agencies try to make profits and avoid losses. However, a large proportion of insured export credit has been subject to rescheduling. These debt reschedulings and the attendant heavy claims payments by the export credit agencies caused unprecedented deterioration in the agencies' financial positions. In the 1980s, the flow of such credits to developing countries contracted, as did total bank lending—and similar factors were operative. In addition, export credits are generally used to finance imports of capital goods, which were directly affected by the declines in investment that resulted from austerity programs. The agencies became more cautious in extending insurance coverage. Payment delays were the major deciding factor in taking restrictive action. The agencies also tended to raise interest rates to be more in line with those in capital markets, thus striving to defend their financial positions.

Two notable policy exceptions have been the maintenance of short-term credit flows and the provision of export credit assistance to countries undertaking appropriate adjustment programs endorsed by the IMF. All the agencies have shown a willingness to maintain short-term credit cover for rescheduling countries to ensure financing for essential imports, provided that conditions are met. Rescheduling of short-term debt is avoided.

The export credit agencies have not seen export credit financing as an appropriate tool for balance of payments support and have resisted providing credits on exceptional "soft" terms. In evaluating the significance of these export credit agencies, it is notable that debt rescheduling has led to the suspension of insurance coverage for medium- and long-term credits.

It is also notable that the export credit agencies have had a better record of servicing debt owed or guaranteed by public sector borrowers than debt owed by private sector borrowers. That is, governments have taken care of their own creditworthiness first. In restoring the creditworthiness of private borrowers that are not guaranteed by governments, lenders will keep this experience in mind. Governments of borrowing countries will have to take steps to assure lenders that they will not repeat the practice of giving themselves preferred positions in allocations of foreign exchange to service debt if they wish to achieve satisfactory inflows of capital. This assurance can take the form of general policy and practice. It can also take the form of special contractual deals involving a central bank, borrowers, and lenders, in which the lender is protected from the borrower being discriminated against by the government. This past experience also gives weight to greater use of external or third-country guarantors for specific transactions and other forms of collateral requirements, such as tying the provision of coverage to the retention of foreign exchange earned by the project through escrow accounts.

All in all, the experience of the export credit agencies has indicated that they are sensitive to their own financial credit and that they try to protect themselves, as private banks did, by reducing troubled exposure, thus limiting risk and minimizing claims payments. At the same time, so long as claims were not high, competitive pressures compelled these agencies to provide coverage even when signals of the medium-term outlook were becoming unfavorable. In the event of uncertainties, extending the claims waiting period can buy time through deferring payments of claims. Agencies can reduce the percentage covered by the insurance, but there is a limit in practice to the proportion of risk exporters are willing to bear. Experience indicates that agencies can reduce the percentage covered, in steps, from a normal 90 to 95 percent down to as low as 70 percent. Beyond 70 percent, the required degree of self-insurance by exporters is reportedly prohibitively expensive.

The export credit agencies have a strong interest in playing a more dynamic role in the restoration of creditworthiness. They wish to help their exporters compete successfully in export markets. Since debt reschedulings are taken as signs of difficulties and result in suspension of export coverage, these agencies are thus failing to support their exporters. This is another example of the harmful effects of rescheduling compared with programs to restore creditworthiness. Programs to restore creditworthiness would facilitate, not constrain, the expansion of the activities of the export credit agencies. In the meantime, it is suggested that they develop more independent country risk assessment mechanisms that would enable them to act independently. Risks are not homogeneous to all lenders, nor are the benefits of insurance homogeneous to all insurers. These agencies have gotten into the mode of seeking common lender or insurer behavior to countries that are, or may be, in difficulties. This uniform approach gives priority to the "slowest boat in the convoy," thus resulting in a degree of caution by all agencies that is not warranted for most. The consequence might well be to discourage extension of export credits beyond what the lender or insurer would do separately in an environment of clear, individual responsibility for lending or insuring decisions.

The use of guarantees points to one of the ways to help restore creditworthiness. Banks can be used as the mechanisms to extend credits, and they can use their credit mechanisms to evaluate risks other than country risks—what may be called business risks. Country risk can be reduced to acceptable levels by the presence of official lenders. Cofinancing by official and private lenders is one form of guarantee. Another form is to have multilateral agencies insure all or part of export credits that are not insured by a national agency—in effect, another form of cofinancing. This could be done by the World Bank or by a regional development bank. The multilateral insurance scheme to cover noncommercial risk is now being advanced by the World Bank. As country risk diminishes, the willingness to pay for such insurance diminishes and lending eventually returns to commercial terms. It is important to take steps to avoid such schemes that encourage nonproductive borrowing.

The International Debt Problem

6

Origins of the Debt Crisis of the 1980s

Setting and Theme

The international debt problem has suffered from repeated inadequate or erroneous approaches, which have obscured the real problems and have hampered the finding of durable, practical solutions. This has happened despite the extraordinarily large amount of time and effort devoted to this problem by first-rate professionals, as well as amateurs, throughout the world. Probably no subject in international economics has received comparable attention in the post–World War II period, with the possible exception of the oil price increases. Discussions of this subject tend to address two basic questions: Did the commercial banks unwisely lend too much to the developing countries? Did these developing countries unwisely borrow too much? The taken-for-granted answers to both questions are yes. The easy and general acceptance of these answers reflects widespread misunderstanding, which hampers the finding of viable solutions.

The immediate roots of the misunderstandings of the 1980s are found in the 1970s, when analyses of the subject of international lending to developing countries were first bedeviled by the popular explanation of international lending as petrodollar recycling. The huge price increases of the OPEC cartel in 1973–74 had greatly increased the export earnings of the oil-exporting nations, whether they belonged to the OPEC cartel—like Indonesia, Kuwait, Nigeria, Saudi Arabia, and Venezuela—or were non-OPEC countries that could take advantage of the monopoly prices established by OPEC—like Mexico and the United Kingdom. Despite huge increases in their expenditures for imports of everything from luxury consumer goods to public utilities and manufacturing plants, their foreign trade surpluses were measured in the tens of billions of U.S. dollars and accumulated to hundreds of billions of dollars.

This condition led to an easy acceptance of the explanation of the expansion of international commercial lending in the 1970s to the developing countries—that it was the result of a flood of petrodollars coming into the banks and that the banks were vigorously, and often stupidly, pushing loans on developing countries in their eagerness to "recycle" petrodollars. The surpluses of the oil-exporting countries did add to world savings. They acted like a tax on oil consumption, transferring revenues from oil users to oil providers (producers, shippers, brokers, transporters, developers, insurance companies, and so forth). Oil users in developed countries, such as Japan, Germany, and the United States, as well as in developing countries, such as Brazil and India, had to find the U.S. dollar funds to pay for these imports. Nearly all borrowed for this purpose as well as using some of their accumulated international monetary reserves. Among the borrowings were foreign exchange purchases from the International Monetary Fund and other special international official financial facilities established for this purpose.

The essential point is that the increase in international lending was demand-driven, not supply-driven, as I repeatedly noted at the time. There was a supply capability, made possible partly by the inflow of petrodollars but also by the monetary policy of the United States. This supply created the possibility of a very large increase in international lending and borrowing, but the demand occurred because oil importers did not find it feasible to reduce their demands for nonoil imports or to increase export earnings sufficiently to counteract the increased cost of oil imports. Developed countries experienced their worst growth/employment conditions since World War II and chose to borrow to avoid the even deeper recessions necessary to bring down oil imports further. Fortunately, these countries, such as Japan and Germany, had strong credit standings based on their strong economies. Creditworthy developing countries, such as Brazil, could also borrow. The United States could pay for oil in its own national currency, the U.S. dollar. Countries that did not have acceptable credit standings did not have access to the same commercial banks that were receiving deposits from oil-exporting countries. The ability of banks to make loans did not mean that loans were made to all countries desiring to borrow. It was in this period that country risk analysis and management was seriously introduced into international banking. It was a period not of lowering standards for risk analysis or management but of raising standards. The banks did not lend to countries that were considered likely to lose their credit standing in international financial markets. At that time, the banking regulators and controllers were worried about Italy, not Brazil. Korea and Indonesia were questioned by many in financial circles because of the possible repercussions for them of the outcome of the war in Vietnam, not because of the large oil deficits in Korea. Italy was questioned not because of its oil deficit but because of its continued unstable political situation. Eurocommunism was still seen as a threat to the existing economic, political, and social order. However, because of the obsession with petrodollar recycling as the explanation of expanded lending and borrowing, banks quickly panicked when difficulties occurred in 1982. They easily accepted the view that the countries had overborrowed and that they had overlent. The banks reacted, and financial difficulties were transformed into crises.

The fact that lending to borrowing countries is demand-driven is critical for understanding the crises of the 1980s. Countries that borrow heavily are not seen simply as overborrowing or as mismanaged. They are seen, at least in part, as countries that are determined to sustain their growth and employment—usually with an emphasis on export promotion. If necessary, they had no difficulties in the 1970s in having their domestic policies endorsed by the International Monetary Fund. No one viewed these countries as perfectly managed, but the scorecard was favorable. Korea is a current example. Banks do not overlend, but loans made sensibly can prove to be nonperforming in the future.

The 1970s demonstrated the importance of developing countries being able to borrow sufficiently to maintain a flow of needed imports. These countries know about debt servicing. They had been reared on debt service ratios, but imports were essential for social stability and economic progress. To cut imports is to court social disruption and economic stagnation. With this perspective, borrowing developing countries are not expected to refrain from external borrowing and increasing their total levels of external debt in the future. A total lowering of external debt can happen, but if it does, the economy of the borrowing country is likely to be seriously hurt, and foreign lenders will have even more difficulties. It may be argued, however, that banks will not wish to lend.

Some commercial banks have defensive strategies for reducing their loans to a country if conditions become worrisome. Usually, such strategies distinguish among kinds of loans—trade financing; interbank credit lines; short-term loans to governments for general purposes; medium- and long-term loans to private firms, government agencies, and government-owned firms; and so forth. A cautious, thoughtful bank aims at having a portfolio that is capable of being reduced quickly, in total, if conditions and outlooks become unfavorable. Some banks did take this precaution in the 1970s. However, the prerequisite for success in this maneuver is to be prepared to withdraw before governments in borrowing countries are compelled to prevent such actions.

As noted earlier, individual loans are likely to be repaid. Total external debt, however, is likely to increase. A developing country can only hope to maintain its ability to service accumulated external debt if it continues to be able to borrow externally. Direct private investment, very largely driven by risk/reward ratios, is not likely to be a significant offset to loss of debt funds for some years. Indeed, direct investment is also likely to be constrained. Of course, official lending can substitute for commercial bank lending and has done so to a limited extent, mainly through the financial operations of the International Monetary Fund. However, the Fund has to defend its own liquidity. It has only limited resources—not enough to meet a situation of general balance-of-payments difficulties, such as the result of the oil price increases and the recessions of 1974–75 and 1981–83.

The size of external debt servicing obligations measures the potential for trouble if creditworthiness is lost. Even selectively, small debt servicing obligations become a serious burden if a borrowing country loses its ability to obtain new funds. For some time, the country can try to do with less foreign exchange by using stocks of imported goods, finding domestic substitutes, and simply doing without, but these expedients are temporary. They must be followed by resumed borrowings or by drastic changes in domestic policies and conditions—whether the debt service burden is relatively large or small.

Larger debt accumulations mean that the countries have been well regarded in financial circles. If this reputation is carefully defended, as in the case of Korea and Singapore, the country can continue to be a net borrower, even in difficult international circumstances. Thus, its adjustment to adverse events becomes much more manageable. If the reputation that made possible the accumulation of the large external debt is not defended, retribution and punishment are swift and drastic. Signs of health in earlier periods, such as ability to borrow abroad, become signs of incompetence and folly after creditworthiness is lost. As has often happened, governments frequently choose folly over wisdom. The key error made by lenders in the 1970s was the assumption that intelligent, rational managers of borrowing countries would behave intelligently in times of adversities—that is, that needed adjustments to changed conditions could be made in timely fashion by the very lenders that, for years, had shown the ability to act wisely and quickly in the interests of their countries. This assumption of rational behavior proved wrong in Argentina, Brazil, Mexico, Nigeria, Venezuela, and elsewhere. Unfortunately, if rational behavior by rational borrowers cannot be assumed by financial decision makers, uncertainty and risk become intolerably great for lenders. Past careful decisions are seen, in a new light, as excessively optimistic and wrong. Paralyzing uncertainty then dominates decision making. In these circumstances, the need for international credit remains, but the suppliers of credit are reluctant, irrespective of their general financial capability to make more loans. The monetary policy of the United States was quite liberal during the recession years of 1982–83. Banks had the funds to lend, just as they had petrodollars in earlier years, yet they did not lend internationally to developing countries because of their pessimistic assessment of country risk. Borrowing countries had to turn to sources of external funds that were less concerned with country risk, such as the IMF and the World Bank, and commercial banks focused on restructuring the stock of accumulated external assets in developing countries (their debts) rather than on new lending.

Had borrowers not been misled by all the talk of petrodollar recycling and of the pushing of loans by lenders—that is, by a supply view of international lending—they might well have paid more attention to the need to follow policies for defending their creditworthiness. The complacency I found in some of the monetary authorities of Brazil and Mexico in the late 1970s and in 1980–81 might have been easier to combat. It was hard to convince central bank governors and ministers of finance, taught to believe that lenders were eager to lend to them under almost any circumstances, that they should react more effectively and quickly to the effects of the second round of oil price increases in the late 1970s, combined with such other adverse developments as accelerating global inflation, rapidly rising interest rates, the possibility of increased protectionism, the spreading of the deep world recession, and the nearly inevitable loss of confidence of their own residents in their government's economic policies, especially the frequently found policies of keeping exchange rates overvalued. The massive capital flight that took place was not a new phenomenon in any of these countries; the dangers of capital flight were known before 1982. The likelihood of its recurrence was not a vague concern. It was, and remains, an ever-present threat, irrespective of any efforts of governments to prevent it by administrative actions. The international financial crises of the early 1980s would have been avoidable if borrowing countries—that is, their managers—had been convinced that they could lose their creditworthiness and that their very large but manageable external debts could be transformed into unmanageable debt burdens. The origin of the nonsense that lenders were so eager to lend that they ignored risks was part of the petrodollar mythology—that is, that banks were so overloaded with oil-earned surpluses that they irresponsibly made loans to noncreditworthy borrowers. The myth still lives.

Similarly, the focus on external debt restructuring when difficulties arose in the 1970s and 1980s also diverted efforts from defending or reestablishing creditworthiness—and it still does. Restructuring was not based on the view that the ability to service past debt depends on being creditworthy for new money. The circumstance that borrowing countries had accumulated arrears in debt servicing and might conceivably repudiate debt or be declared in default by lenders dominated the thinking in lending institutions. Borrowing countries were not urged to follow policies that would restore their previous creditworthiness in international credit markets. Programs endorsed by the Fund helped get banks to restructure some of a country's external debt, but the incentive to succeed in restoring creditworthiness was weak. Countries should have followed domestic policies that would have enabled them to sustain satisfactory growth rates and avoid increases in unemployment and consequent social instability. Adjustment programs had to be growth programs, because only growth programs can endure in developing countries. Instead, austerity became the watchword. As seen repeatedly in the Far East and in Southeast Asia, these adjustment policies need not have been austerity programs; rather, they could have been growth-oriented programs based on policies that would give confidence to foreign lenders. The focal points would have been the underlying economic strength and longer outlook of countries, rather than policies designed to bring about quick balance-of-payments improvement. Again, this point was made repeatedly during these years, but debt restructuring and IMF help in this process was the method chosen to deal with the deepening crises.

The need remains the same—that is, to reestablish the creditworthiness of developing countries with the principal sources of external finance. This book has been written in the conviction that the developing countries can handle their external debt problem only by raising net inflows of resources and capital. Short of repudiation, they cannot, by their own actions, significantly reduce their past accumulated debt. Their debt will increase, although the relative importance of lenders may change. The principal lenders for such countries as Brazil, Mexico, and Korea will probably be private, but different institutions and mechanisms may be used. In economically weaker countries, however, private lenders may want the presence, in some form, of creditworthy entities to reinforce the weaker standings of borrowing countries. These techniques are available and can be readily expanded. The policies followed by developing countries will reflect their social and political, as well as economic, conditions. Growth objectives will be paramount for the indefinite future. What is commonplace in domestic finance but is still esoteric in international finance will be adapted to international conditions in manners acceptable to lenders and borrowers.

Historical Experience with Lending and Crises

The early 1980s were hardly the first period in modern times in which the world was threatened by financial crisis. The 1930s were marked by a series of such crises, as the Great Depression made it practically impossible for borrowers—including sovereign governments—to honor their debts. The 1930s witnessed the failure of nations to pay World War I reparations and war debts, the widespread resort to higher tariffs and severe trade restrictions, frequent unilateral changes in exchange rates to gain unfair competitive advantages, and the near collapse of the international financial system. These

adversities resulted in defaults on debt servicing and created a legacy
of skepticism about international lending that is still strong.

The frightening experience of the 1930s encouraged the leaders
of the Allied powers to make extraordinary efforts during and after
World War II to provide an environment in which international
flows of money, goods, and services could take place smoothly while
countries strove to recover from the devastation of the war. One of
the most important features of the wartime U.S. Lend-Lease program was that it avoided huge war debts for the Allies of the United
States. Moreover, reparations were kept small and, after intense negotiations over nearly three years, the Bretton Woods Agreement of
1944 established new institutions—the International Bank for Reconstruction and Development (known as the World Bank) and the
International Monetary Fund (IMF). This agreement committed sig-
natory nations to what was, in effect, a set of rules to ensure that the
cooperating countries would dismantle and later avoid international
payments restrictions while maintaining stable exchange rates or
changing them only with international concurrence. National currencies were to be made freely convertible into one another and thus
were usable around the world for trade and finance. The purposes
of the World Bank were clearly expressed in its formal name. Unfortunately, from the beginning, the funds provided to the two institutions were too small to fulfill their purposes. The World Bank
was too small to finance reconstruction of worldwide war damage,
and the IMF was too small to finance the return to convertibility,
free exchange markets, and withdrawal of the widespread restrictions on international payments. The IMF did not have the authority
or influence to cause its member countries to introduce realistic exchange rates, thus aggravating the difficulties in moving to a multilateral payments system.

Those early postwar weaknesses were offset to an important extent by the Marshall Plan, which, after 1947, provided substantial
financing for reconstruction and recovery in Europe on a grant—not
loan—basis. The grants, provided principally by the United States,
were meant primarily to achieve the quickest possible European recovery and to encourage European collaboration, and they suc-
ceeded remarkably well. In only a few years—by about 1950—Europe was back on its feet economically and on its way to 20 years of
exceptional growth and prosperity, together with Japan, Canada,
and the United States.

In the early postwar years, such new institutions as NATO, the Common Market, and the OECD overshadowed the Bretton Woods institutions, although the IMF and the World Bank continued their work with their available resources. In the euphoria of the 1950s and 1960s, however, the Bretton Woods institutions were expanded and, as noted earlier, regional official organizations were formed—notably, the Inter-American, African, and Asian Development Banks. These, too, bore the imprint of a concern with avoiding excessive external debts, and they provided international funds to their borrowers at below-market cost. Many developing countries received near grants from the International Development Association, a part of the World Bank, and from the "soft loan windows" of the regional development banks.

This international cooperation, spurred by the fearful experience of the 1930s and 1940s, set the stage for a renaissance of international private lending in the 1950s and 1960s. Modern banking and other credit mechanisms spread within industrial countries and, more slowly, within developing countries. All sectors of economic activity were involved, as modernization was experienced in traditional activities and industries, such as agriculture, textiles, and domestic trade, as well as in newer industries, such as automobile and consumer durables. These structural changes increased the demands for domestic and international credit. The efficiency and scope of financial markets expanded and were linked together in a world of instantaneous communication. National savings streams became part of a worldwide network of savings that could be channeled to creditworthy borrowers. Such borrowing was done in private credit markets on a competitive basis. The interest rates charged were based on prevailing rates in the major financial centers, especially the United States and the Eurocurrency market in London. Despite the rising trend in interest rates in the 1960s and 1970s, these rates were attractive to borrowers in developing countries. The burden of paying interest was of little concern, since external borrowing was available to cover such payments as well as others, while inflation eroded the real value of debt. Thus, while international measures were being taken to avoid a recurrence of the debt problems of the 1930s, creditworthy countries began to increase their external debt borrowing from private bank lenders and continued to do so until the external debt problem of the late 1970s and early 1980s was created, largely with commercial banks.

The reconstruction of Europe and Japan, within the framework of the Bretton Woods system, sparked record growth in national economies and world trade throughout the 1950s. Toward the end of the 1950s, the currencies of the major European countries became widely convertible, as the U.S. dollar already was. This was accomplished by the removal of governmental restrictions on international payments for goods and services—that is, "current" transactions. Foreign currencies could be purchased freely for such purposes, although restrictions on trade, such as quotas, continued to exist. The removal of these administrative restrictions on the exchange of currencies created the preconditions for the establishment of foreign exchange markets around the world. It set the stage for a huge expansion of private international credit to complement the lending between governments that dominated international lending until the 1960s. The move to the convertibility of the more important European currencies and the Japanese yen was led by the IMF. It was the major achievement of the IMF in this period of its history.

In addition to the demand for credit from the recovering industrial countries, the ongoing economic, political, and social transformation in the developing countries that constituted the majority of the world's population generated a growing demand for capital that markedly changed the nature of international lending. As one colonial area after another gained independence, scores of new governments around the world committed themselves to modernizing their emerging economies, substantially improving the standard of living of their people as rapidly as possible, and creating opportunities for social mobility. By the early 1960s, the world financial system faced a large and growing demand for credit by developing countries, many of them new national entities whose needs for resources greatly exceeded their domestic savings. These countries were low in output and poor in income, but their vast potential for economic growth was widely appreciated. In the 1950s and into the 1960s, the principal response to this increasing demand for external funds was in the form of official assistance—mostly bilateral but increasingly multilateral. The U.S. aid program, together with the activities of the Export-Import Bank and supplemented by the World Bank, was typical in the industrial countries.

In the 1960s, spurred by the recovery of Europe and Japan and the development efforts of Third World countries, international trade expanded dramatically. Commercial banks financed international trade and thus automatically expanded such lending. In addition, internationally oriented private commercial banks became an increasingly important source of development finance. They began to provide finance for purposes other than short-term trade financing, thus supplementing the flow of capital that had been generated largely by governments acting individually or collectively, through the IMF, the World Bank, and the regional development banks. Commercial banks in the United States, Europe, and Japan established larger networks of branches abroad. As modern and efficiently functioning international financial markets grew in size and depth during the 1960s, the market instruments used, such as syndicated loans, increased in number and complexity.

Private bank lending to developing countries was steadily and warmly endorsed by foreign supporters of those countries. When the United States, because of its balance-of-payments deficits—a chronic problem—placed constraints on private international lending by its banks in the 1950s, exceptions were made for borrowing by developing countries. The United States was committed on a bipartisan basis to help developing countries accelerate their economic and social development. The commitment had begun with President Truman, was continued by President Eisenhower, and was enthusiastically expanded by President Kennedy. Although the extraordinary sense of statesmanship exemplified by the Marshall Plan—with its avoidance of debt and its building of European institutions—did not survive, U.S. foreign aid for developing countries was gradually expanded in the 1950s and 1960s. These net inflows of capital helped the borrowing developing countries to achieve and sustain very high growth rates—exceeding the rates in most industrial countries—thus making dreams of material improvement in living standards a reality, despite the concurrent population explosion. The notion of stagnating poverty was replaced by the dynamics of rising expectations. In the process, concerns about external debt were felt, but not strongly. Arguments in favor of concessional lending (at below-market costs) and grants emphasized that such sources of finance resulted in larger net resource inflows for the borrowing developing countries compared to financing on commercial terms. Concessional finances made possible higher levels of both consumption and investment. Concerns about external debts were expressed and debts to official creditors were renegotiated at times, but the debt problem as such was not considered a major general worry. In the expanding postwar world economy, the ability of developing countries to service external debt, much of which was extended on concessional terms, seemed easy to achieve and sustain.

At the same time, storm clouds—such as disruption in capital flows and exchange rate instability—had been gathering on the horizon of the world's financial system during the 1960s. The environment of economic and financial growth of the 1950s and 1960s had not been entirely trouble-free. The most important potentially disturbing signs were the continued U.S. balance-of-payments deficit and the uneven rates of inflation among countries that were, in fact, part of the persistent inflation gaining hold throughout the world economy.

During the 1950s and 1960s, the international flows of goods, services, and capital had been helped by a relatively stable exchange rate pattern. The pound sterling of the United Kingdom showed repeated weaknesses in the 1960s, but changes in the sterling exchange rate were few and infrequent. European currencies were linked to each other in the European Monetary System that evolved in these years and continue to be so linked. The Bretton Woods system functioned reasonably well during the 20 years from 1950 to 1970. However, the uneven global inflation, which was tightening its grip during these years, eroded existing exchange rate patterns. In addition, the large deficits in the U.S. balance of payments and corresponding increases in foreign holdings of U.S. dollars resulted, in the 1960s, in revaluations of a number of currencies against the U.S. dollar—the price of which was fixed to the price of gold. Large speculative capital outflows of dollars from the United States to Europe became commonplace in the late 1960s as speculators anticipated devaluations of the U.S. dollar. Eurocurrency markets, not subject to government restrictions on credit, started in the 1950s and grew rapidly in the 1960s as a result of a growing demand for international credit by governments and multinational corporations. These markets proved efficient both in financing international trade and in financing international speculation in currencies. Because their deposits were not subject to reserve requirements, their loans could be cheaper than those in other creditor countries.

The basic causes of the international monetary instability evidenced in the late 1960s—the worldwide persistent inflation, the U.S. balance-of-payments deficits, and the rigidly fixed $35-per-ounce price for gold—were not tackled successfully. Accelerating global inflation, which was evident in the late 1960s, was largely neglected by governments, especially the United States. Many refused to accept the intractability of global inflation. The U.S. dollar, which had been the linchpin of the international financial system, had weakened in the latter part of the 1960s. The United States had maintained the value of the U.S. dollar in terms of gold at $35 per ounce since pre-World War II years, but in the 1960s, the dollar holdings of foreign central banks greatly exceeded the gold holdings of the United States. The United States was thus unable to fulfill its declared policy of selling gold at the official price. Its policy depended on the willingness of foreign central banks to refrain voluntarily from exchanging their dollars into gold. Whereas U.S. dollar holdings could be invested in interest-earning securities, gold could not. This stabilized the situation until it became evident that a major change in the price of gold was likely, more than offsetting revenues earned from holding dollars. Yet the United States insisted, in the 1960s, that any change in the official price of gold was out of the question. It continued to rely on the assumption that foreign governments and central banks would not request that the United States convert their dollar holdings into gold.

This vulnerability was observed by many, and the result was widespread expectation of a devaluation of the dollar in some form. Speculation against the dollar in the late 1960s and early 1970s, in favor of strong European currencies like the German mark and the Swiss franc, was perceived as a virtually riskless source of profit. Interest rates in the United States were low in real terms. Something had to give—the price of gold, the stable exchange rate system, the convertibility of currencies, or the low real interest rates.

In 1971, President Nixon introduced his new economic policy, breaking the official link between the U.S. dollar and gold. Non-U.S. monetary authorities no longer were able to convert their U.S. dollar holdings into gold at a fixed price of $35 per ounce. The system of stable and internationally approved exchange rates, frequently called the Bretton Woods system, ceased to exist. Inflation rates, interest rates, and exchange rates all became unpredictable after 1971.

Consequently, the world economy was already reeling when it was hit by the major oil price increase of 1973–74. The recession of 1974–75 was the deepest up to that time in the postwar period. The world economy was rocked again in 1979–80 by a second round of large oil price increases. Throughout the period from 1974 to 1980, persistent inflation thwarted attempts to regain satisfactory levels of growth and employment, as governments fought inflation unsuccessfully essentially with strict monetary policies and weak budgetary policies. National economic behavior diverged. Business cycles of industrial countries were linked but varied, while key commodity prices plunged and the growth of international trade—excluding oil—slowed. Currency instability gradually worsened, and speculative capital flows dominated exchange markets. The floating rate system that followed the collapse of the Bretton Woods system did not bring to an end the large balance-of-payments deficits of the United States, nor did it automatically correct mistakes in the pattern of exchange rates. Confidence in the international monetary system remained low in the 1970s. The optimism and euphoria of the 1950s and 1960s gave way to the pessimism and widespread fears of the 1970s. The expansion in international lending in the 1970s did not take place in an atmosphere of easy confidence or optimism, as is sometimes stated or inferred—quite the contrary. It was the willingness of lenders to judge differences in country risks among borrowers and to lend to those deemed creditworthy despite the worldwide difficulties that distinguished the 1970s from the 1980s. The 1970s were years of cautious risk-taking; the 1980s were years of risk avoidance.

The storm that burst in the early 1970s, with the end of the system of fixed exchange rates and the acceleration of world inflation, eventually redefined the size and nature of private international finance. The official international institutions that had been established in the previous three decades could not prevent the gradual reemergence of the external debt problem. They did not have the resources or modes of operation to enable countries to achieve their economic and social targets without large-scale use of commercial sources of credit. Drastic changes in such targets did not appear warranted in countries where, despite all kinds of difficulties and shocks, high growth rates and substantial expansion in exports were being maintained or oil was being found, produced, and exported. Brazil, Korea, Mexico, and Nigeria exemplified countries that continued to do well despite the global conditions. The events of the 1970s created the need and demand for much more international credit; official sources were inadequate, however, and private sources took up the slack for creditworthy borrowers. Borrowers and lenders believed in the ability of such borrowers to continue to borrow on acceptable terms and to service debt. It took a series of shocks, extending over the whole decade from the early 1970s to the early 1980s, to replace excessive optimism with excessive pessimism—that is, for lenders to move from a willingness to judge country risk on a disaggregated (country-by-country) basis to judging virtually all developing countries as high and mostly unacceptable country risks.

Commercial Bank Lending amid the Shocks of the 1970s

The expansion of the international financial system through the 1960s, including its commercial bank element, proved to be of critical importance in the ability of the world community to weather the economic and financial shocks of the 1970s.

The developing countries that imported oil, such as Brazil and Korea, were the hardest hit by the shocks of the 1970s. At the same time, however, their governments were unwilling to abandon their objectives of continued strong economic growth and development, enhanced social mobility, and further improvement of the standard of living of their populations. People and countries were confident that the cyclical downturn of 1974–75 would be short-lived, and that the world economy would again expand. It did so, though not at the rate of the 1960s. The recovery in the world economy helped borrowing countries maintain their creditworthiness with the private banks, even during and after the second round of oil price increases in 1978–79. Most important, however, was the management of the economies of the major borrowers, especially the nonoil borrowers. They acted effectively and impressed foreign lenders with their management capability. The adjustment process for developing countries was also eased in the 1970s by increases in the financial resources of the IMF, which had a rebirth of influence, laying the basis for its greatly enhanced role in the early 1980s. The experience of the 1970s was that private international lending was not necessarily cyclical. It could be sustained and even expanded during adverse phases in the business cycle. It depended on achieving high rates of price-competitive output and exports, avoidance of restrictions on international payments, and avoidance of arrears on external payments. Indeed, even high rates of domestic inflation were not necessarily destructive of external creditworthiness if exchange and interest rates were kept realistic.

It was against the background of persistent global inflation, oil price increases, international monetary uncertainty, and firm adherence by modernizing developing countries to goals of economic growth and development that private international bank lending expanded rapidly in the 1970s, despite the secular rise in U.S. interest rates. The key was case-by-case judgments on country creditworthiness. The banks usually did not lend to borrowers in countries they did not regard as creditworthy, except for self-liquidating short-term trade credits. Private banks were able to respond quickly and with the desired, often very large, amounts to the demands of creditworthy borrowers. The Bank for International Settlements (BIS) has estimated that total international lending by banks in major industrial countries increased from about $125 billion at the end of 1970, to $893 billion at the end of 1978, to $1,550 billion at the end of 1981, and to $1,754 billion at the end of 1983. These loans did much to prevent a drastic deterioration in the economies of the borrowing countries, which would have resulted in lower growth rates; more unemployment, inflation, and sociopolitical distress in developing countries; reduced international trade; and a strengthening of domestic forces, favoring autarkic, protectionist policies. Argentina, for example, consciously and deliberately chose to resist estimated protectionist forces strongly, in favor of an open economy. This was greatly helped by its access to foreign credit. By assisting major developing countries as well as developed countries, the international flows of private bank capital played an important role in preventing further deterioration in the world economy during the difficult period from 1974 to 1980.

Many doubts were expressed in the 1970s about the feasibility and wisdom of the greatly expanded international lending by commercial banks. Experts had exaggerated views on how big the surpluses of the oil exporters and the corresponding deficits of oil importers would be and how long they would last. Such surpluses, it was declared, would soon disrupt the international financial system. Oil-importing borrowing countries were seen as unable to cope with their oil-induced problems. Banks lending to them were described as being nearly irresponsible in discounting the risks involved. Defaults were thought to be inevitable. Individual lending banks would be greatly damaged, and international lending would come to a crushing halt. This view gained credence through its expression by authorities in multilateral institutions and central banks, by ministers of finance, by private banks, and by commentators, journalists, and academicians. Many urged a slowdown in international lending by commercial banks, such as took place in the 1980s.

Some argued that private bank lending would discourage governments from providing more concessional assistance. Given the poverty and low output of the developing countries, many in developed and developing countries favored concessional forms of financing. Instead of commercial lending being seen as offsetting the shortfalls resulting from the limited willingness of governments to provide more official assistance, it was seen as weakening the case for concessional lending. Borrowing countries, it was argued, were not in a position to use effectively any funds obtained from commercial sources. They needed the technical assistance and discipline provided by official lenders. In addition, official financing more efficiently served the needs of a developing country for long-term capital on a long-term, fixed-interest basis or grants—for uses with long gestation periods and low financial returns, though possibly high social returns. For some, the debt servicing aspects were also important.

These views strengthened a long-existing tendency of those who advocated more external assistance to developing countries to emphasize various shortcomings of these countries, such as their political instability and social weaknesses. Commercial lenders made judgments in favor of borrowing countries that seemed opposite from the views of well-wishers of these countries. Given the fact of expanded lending by commercial banks, it was a small step to argue that the banks were hard at work "selling" loans to unsophisticated borrowers, or that borrowers were misguided, unsophisticated, or motivated by personal greed rather than by a sense of national responsibility. Throughout the late 1970s—long before the much larger debt figures of the early 1980s were experienced—predictions were repeatedly and widely circulated that individual lending banks were flirting with bankruptcy because of their lending to developing countries.

A lesson for future lending is that large-scale international lending by commercial banks does not require either a generally favorable world economic climate or a general agreement among experts and practitioners that such lending is warranted by analyses of country conditions. Country risk assessments are judgmental and are likely to remain so. Lenders may well have individual judgments that are quite contrary to the views of others. Therefore, they provide credits to borrowers on terms that are acceptable to them as lenders. Commercial banks, operating as credit market makers, reflect their own country risk judgments in interest rates and other financial terms.

The banks were constantly sensitive to the popular views of risks in lending to developing countries, often propounded in media the banks considered friendly. The banks continued to lend because of their favorable experience with international lending to countries they regarded as creditworthy. Credits extended to developing countries in the 1970s usually performed (were serviced) at least as well as domestic credits. Nonperforming loans remained at acceptable levels—that is, very small fractions of total lending. International loans provided sources of attractive earnings for banks without actually causing excessive offsetting losses for the lenders. The fact that creditworthy borrowers in the 1970s lost their creditworthiness in the 1980s does not demonstrate that bad decisions were made in the 1970s. Rather, it points to the central importance of creditworthiness and why it can be lost.

With a growing body of experience and knowledge, banks improved their ability to assess and manage country risk. International exposures in the late 1970s were already large for some banks, but most banks in the United States and elsewhere still did not have large international exposures. Lending domestically and to other industrialized countries accounted for most of their loan portfolios. International lending to developed countries greatly exceeded lending to developing countries. The desire for profitable, risk-acceptable portfolio diversification made international lending to developing countries attractive in the 1970s. The fact that banks could join with other respected banks in loan syndications added to the feeling of comfort within the lending institutions. Such considerations continue to be major factors in loan decision making.

Individual cases of debt difficulties—such as Zaire, Peru, Turkey, Jamaica, and even Poland—were handled on a case-by-case basis. They were seen by some as threatening the international banking system, but not by the great majority of banks. These experiences did not significantly inhibit international lending, although they made lenders more cautious. Their main impact was to come somewhat later, in the early 1980s, when these cases became part of the thinking that was strongly, and more widely, averse to lending to developing countries. Individual problem countries in the 1970s, such as Peru, demonstrated that their situations could be improved quickly and that their difficulties need not snowball into general crises.

Although the 1970s were difficult years, with repeated major shocks to the world economy and the global financial system, there was still confidence in the ability of the major borrowing countries to manage their affairs effectively and in the ability of banks to select good credits. Credits that did not work out as originally expected were seen as exceptions to the rule. In hindsight, what proved excessively optimistic was the belief that well-managed economies would continue to be well managed and that banks would continue to be willing to make their own judgments on country risk, select their borrowers, and not be dominated by general thinking and uniform approaches.

Repeated references were made in the 1970s to the high ratios or leveraging of bank assets and liabilities to capital, frequently twenty to one or even higher. By the late 1970s, the highly leveraged bank had been typical for many years. Banks defended their own liquidity by maintaining their own creditworthiness—that is, their ability to borrow through careful and prudent management of their assets and liabilities as well as the recording of reasonable profits. Capital ceased to be the first or even second line of defense of a bank's financial viability. A bank that had to slice into any of its capital would be in very serious straits. Lending criteria were designed to avoid significant losses and to maintain satisfactory profitability. The risk/reward ratio was a clear guide to portfolio management. The geographic distribution of assets was significant, but more in terms of avoiding portfolio concentrations than in relation to capital structure. With a twenty-to-one ratio of assets to capital for all significant categories of loans—correspondent banks, industries, countries, and even individual borrowers—any category or group of loans could soon add up to a frightening proportion of capital. Banks had to avoid losses by focusing on the quality of their assets and on avoidance of concentration. Sharp declines in bank earnings because of loan losses could destroy a bank's own creditworthiness and, therefore, its ability to fund its lending, even if it had not significantly impaired its capital.

In the 1970s, the luxury of debate over the importance of various factors in a bank's financial standing could well be afforded. Expert banking opinion frequently questioned the traditional importance attached to capital. Nevertheless, it was a factor of major importance that, throughout the 1970s, many continued to emphasize the need for more capital to defend the banks against possible losses. At the same time, many regarded international lending not as a collection of individual loans and credits with differing credit and country risks, but rather as a lump sum of loans to countries—mostly governments in the case of all the borrowing entities within a developing country. The stage was being set for aggregating the international debt of a developing country irrespective of the varying quality of individual borrowers, maturities, lenders, usage, guarantors, and so forth. The total loans of a bank in a particular country were then compared with its capital as if the loan portfolio were homogeneous. The logic for this approach, as noted earlier, was that a country in balance-of-payments difficulties would not be able to service all its loans and might well treat all debt servicing obligations the same, although experience had indicated that countries often did not give equal treatment to all debts.

If all debts were treated the same, the probability was that some portion of the debt servicing could be maintained for all debt. A country had to be in the most unlikely dire straits not to be able to meet any significant portion of its total debt servicing obligations. For example, a country in difficulties might decide to postpone amortization payments on all debt except preferred creditors but still would be able to pay interest in whole or in part. It might service its trade-related short-term debt but ask to renegotiate longer-term project financing. The lure of simple ratios aggregating everything was too attractive to avoid. Unfortunately, simple ratios lend themselves to oversimplified analyses and oversimplified solutions.

Dramatic statements can be made about all loans to a single country being equal to, or exceeding, or doubling, or tripling all of a bank's capital—as if this would be surprising when the total assets of the bank are more than ten or twenty times its capital. By aggregating loans in a relatively large country, such as Brazil or Mexico, and then assuming repudiation or default of the entire debt, it is easy to demonstrate the dangers of devastating effects on a bank's capital and reserves. Any significant grouping of assets soon yields multiples of capital. Because banks are highly leveraged in their capital/

assets ratios, the avoidance of concentrations by borrowing entities is a well-established portfolio and regulatory practice. Commercial banks must be chronically worried about nonperforming loans. These concerns are reflected in their buildup of capital and reserves and, more important, in their lending practices that avoid excessive amounts of poorly performing loans and that avoid concentrations. The regulators must evaluate such systems. In the final analysis, if a bank does experience intolerable losses, whether it should be "rescued" by government may well become an issue. Such rescues are much more acceptable and more in the public interest if the bank's lending criteria and management process have been scrutinized and well regarded by supervisors. Loan losses then reflect the functioning of the entire economic system, not just bank management.

Thus, although the 1970s saw a huge expansion in private bank lending to developing countries and a mounting confidence by bankers in their ability to function in a world of risk, other forces were at work that would eventually erode this self-confidence. When a banker loses confidence in his ability to assess and manage risk, he loses the professional poise needed to function efficiently, and all of the bank's assets become at risk, wherever they are located. Assessing and managing risk is the essence of banking.

The Onset of the Current Crisis: What Went Wrong?

In the 1970s, private bank lending played a predominant external financing role in many of the nonoil developing countries, especially those in Latin America. The growth of concessional official development assistance was constrained by domestic budgetary difficulties in the donor countries. Private flows of financial resources to all developing countries began to exceed official flows as early as 1975.

As might be expected, the constraints on official assistance were applied mostly on the higher-income countries, such as Argentina and Brazil, which were known to be able to borrow from private sources. Even the largest official multilateral bank, the World Bank, began to reduce the relative importance of these countries in its 1970s lending. These countries turned to the commercial banks and found them able to provide them much larger sums than could be provided by official institutions. Private banks are wired into the world savings and credit-creating mechanism, and the deficits of a developing country are always small in relation to this global mechanism.

At the margin, a foreign borrower may be competing with another borrower but can do so if the borrower and its country are regarded as creditworthy. In the early 1980s, well-managed developing countries faced new, severe challenges to their ability to manage and retain their creditworthiness. Developing countries faced a combination of factors that decreased their foreign exchange income drastically. Commodity prices fell further, and markets for manufactured exports weakened and became more competitive. Protectionism increased, threats of more protectionism were heard increasingly, and persistent world inflation sustained high import prices for manufactured goods. Although oil prices fell, oil import bills were still very high for such importing countries as Brazil and Korea. At the same time, oil exporters, such as Mexico, Nigeria, and Venezuela, had adjusted their economies to the higher revenues from oil exports and expected them to remain high. Instead, they did not benefit from the expected strong markets for oil, and they experienced severe balance-of-payments difficulties as their imports reflected their now-dwindling oil prosperity. Interest rates fell, but not as much as rates of inflation, so that real interest rates remained extraordinarily high. Capital flight, in such countries as Mexico, the Philippines, and Argentina, added to the demand for foreign exchange as citizens voted with their bank deposits and other assets against their governments' policies.

As always, the maintenance of overvalued exchange rates, however rationalized, played havoc with domestic and external economic and financial management. Nearly all of the Latin American large borrowing countries had chronic problems of inflation. Virtually continuous devaluation of their currencies was the means of keeping their products internationally competitive. Nevertheless, sophisticated financial authorities in developing countries were favorably impressed, at times, with the argument often heard in continental Europe and the United States—that overvalued exchange rates helped fight inflation. Import prices were kept down, and more resources were available to the inflating economy. Balance-of-payments deficits became larger, but creditworthy countries could finance such deficits. Financial authorities in developing countries virtually ignored the obvious fact that industrial countries have ways and means of financing balance-of-payments deficits that are not available to developing countries. The outstanding example is the United States, which can finance its external deficits in its own national currency. If Germany, Japan, Switzerland, the United Kingdom, and so on, have external deficits, they must finance them mostly in U.S. dollars, but their creditworthiness is so strong that borrowing in dollars is a true option so long as they are prepared to pay market rates of interest. In this sense, they can afford the luxury of using overvalued exchange rates to fight inflation. Developing countries do not have this option. Yet virtually every country that became a major external debt problem went through a period of trying to maintain an overvalued exchange rate, resulting in damages that lasted for years. Among the examples are Argentina, Brazil, Mexico, and Nigeria.

Capital flight is endemic in many developing countries. Assets or investments in foreign countries, such as the United States and Germany, are attractive for many different reasons at most times. Creditworthy countries are nevertheless likely to have only a manageable or tolerable level of such capital flight, whereas an overvalued exchange rate guarantees large and unmanageable capital flight. Capital controls can only change the form of the flight; they cannot prevent it. The incentives are too strong, as huge capital gains are made with very little risk to the speculator. Capital flight proved to be the straw that broke the camel's back. At first, countries borrowed heavily to finance the capital flight; but as banks perceived the errors of these countries in economic management, they lost their creditworthiness. Normal external payments fell into arrears, and creditworthiness with banks was lost. The borrowing countries declared moratoriums on debt servicing, and the lending banks went into shock. Thus, the early 1980s saw dramatic changes in the pattern of international lending. Opposite to what happened in the 1970s, official lending had to substitute for private lending. The IMF, which had been formed to be countercyclical—to provide international funds during depressions—greatly expanded its lending. Similarly, official export credit insurance institutions grew in relative importance to help troubled export industries. The commercial banks became increasingly cautious as the recession proved to be deeper and more protracted than earlier recessions had been. Domestic assets of the banks, as well as international assets, were feeling the adverse impact of what became a world depression, combined with the structural transformation of world manufacturing, which continued during the depression. For countries like those in Latin America, which had become dependent on commercial bank credit for external financing, the increasing cautiousness of commercial banks was of decisive importance in intensifying their difficulties in managing their balance of payments.

The 1980s seem destined to be very difficult. The sharp U.S. recovery in 1983–84 was not followed by similar recoveries in Europe, and primary product prices remained low. Inflation rates lowered, but inflation was not eliminated. The U.S. recovery faltered, and budgetary deficits prevailed in the United States and elsewhere. Protectionism increased, and exchange rates were clearly out of line with economic conditions in the major countries. International trade declined, and external problems multiplied rapidly. Even the major oil surplus countries became part of the world recession, they had become the symbols of financial wealth and strength. The United States became, more than ever, the safe and profitable haven for funds, creating the deep problem of an overvalued dollar as the global economic recession intensified and persisted.

In the meantime, private lenders had been growing increasingly uneasy about the growing list of creditworthy developing and Eastern European nations that had accumulated strikingly large external debts, in absolute and relative terms, if these countries were to lose their creditworthiness. This possibility was no longer regarded as remote. The rapid increase in external debt had resulted in large debt service obligations for many developing countries. Total debt service payments of developing countries to all lenders reached an estimated $109 billion in 1981 and $130 billion in 1982, compared with $11 billion in 1971. Much attention was again given to so-called debt service ratios. Although a number of borrowing countries had had high debt service ratios for many years, the generally expanding world economy, combined with the continued availability of external credit, had kept the high ratios from becoming a cause for concern. The high ratios eventually did become worrisome in the late 1970s and early 1980s, but only after borrowers were in danger of losing their creditworthiness, thereby losing an essential ingredient of their ability to continue servicing their debts. This lesson of the need to maintain creditworthiness is of critical importance to countries that are still creditworthy, such as Korea.

In the summer of 1982, fears of widespread repudiations and defaults by major borrowing countries became widespread. Arrears on interest payments had already become commonplace. The prospect increased that more loans in continuous arrears would have to be classified by bank comptrollers and regulators as "nonperforming." The stage was set for the great debt crisis that began in 1982 and remained unsolved in 1986.

In commercial banking, loans are regarded as income-earning even during the intervals between servicing payments. Such income is regarded as being accrued and is reflected in banks' financial statements in the same way as actual income. If loans are declared nonperforming, any income accrued before the due date has to be subtracted from current income accounts. If the amount is substantial, this can transform a healthy financial picture into a weak one. If delinquency in servicing continues, the bank eventually is compelled to regard such loans as losses and must charge them off against reserves accumulated for such purposes. Future income has to be used to rebuild reserves, thus, in effect, reducing future income. Nonperforming loans are usually a very small fraction of total loans—3 to 4 percent would be quite high by normal standards. Charge-offs to reserves are much less frequent, even during difficult periods. Nonperformance means loss of earnings, which can affect a bank's own credit standing. This is a repeated experience in banking, and it is not serious unless the magnitudes are large or the losses reflect on the caliber of management. The latter consideration weighs heavily with bank managers, depositors, shareholders, and the public.

The vulnerability of a commercial bank lies, as noted earlier, in its potential loss of its own creditworthiness. The bank's borrowings take many forms: deposits from other banks, demand and time deposits from the public, notes issued to the public, certificates of deposit, and so forth. A bank's loss of any noticeable amount of its capital is assiduously avoided as a sign of deep trouble. The bank must retain its creditworthiness to meet its obligations, including deposits resulting from its own loans. Since many of its liabilities are demand liabilities and its assets are not demand assets, a bank cannot expect to hold enough liquid assets to meet sudden demands from its own creditors. The bank cannot expect that its borrowers will be as strong as the bank has to be as a borrower; this is a built-in asymmetry in banking. A U.S. bank can turn to the Federal Reserve System and borrow against its assets, and a bank in another country can turn to its central bank, but the scale of such actions is limited. If the bank cannot borrow sufficiently against its assets, it may find itself threatened with illiquidity or even insolvency. Individual banks have experienced this scenario even during postwar decades, when general financial crises or panics have not been present. This vulnerability is experienced by all commercial banks. It gives great weight to profitability after deductions, if any, for loan losses. Profitability is the best single test of good bank management. After deductions, if any, for loan losses, banks must stress avoidance of drastic declines in income resulting from too many poorly performing loans.

In fact, the developing countries as a group serviced their loans in 1982 and into 1983 about as well as domestic loans were serviced. Nonperforming loans were a small proportion of international loans or of banks' total loan portfolios. Charge-offs against reserves were small and exceptional. Nevertheless, continuous references to global debt figures, or comparisons of a bank's total loans to a country with the bank's capital, created "what if" fears. Worst-case scenarios were discussed as though they were likely to occur. Such fears did not materialize, however. Banks withdrew from lending to many countries, and such countries became increasingly unable to service their external debts to commercial banks. By 1984–85, banks were experiencing serious losses from their loans to developing countries, despite repeated and more generous debt restructuring, which avoid loans from being regarded as losses, at least temporarily.

To the extent that such developing countries as Korea, Malaysia, Thailand, and Singapore moved quickly to adjust to the new, more adverse global conditions, they were able to keep their creditworthiness. In effect, this meant that the commercial banks continued to lend to them on a commercial basis. The experience of these countries demonstrated that countries could maintain their creditworthiness with private lenders during major cyclical adversities. It was a lesson that the Latin American countries had to learn with great pain, which could have been less if they had not failed to defend their creditworthiness.

Such countries as India and Pakistan also did well during these cyclical adversities. Their external obligations were relatively small because they were financed externally, mostly by long-term concessional funds from official institutions. In addition, they adjusted their policies well to the changed world conditions and found their commercial creditworthiness strengthened. It was mostly Latin American and African countries that lost their creditworthiness. These countries moved reluctantly and often too slowly to make domestic policy adjustments to the difficult world economic situation.

They often found it hard to accept the view that the cyclical downturn would be deep and lengthy. Their delays made the needed adjustments all the more severe. Unfortunately, in many quarters in Latin America, belt-tightening was seen as a choice that could be avoided. In fact, the only alternative to adjustment was massive official or noncommercial balance-of-payments support, which simply was not available. Real wages and real incomes had to fall because of world conditions, and delayed adjustments meant that they had to fall by more than they would have fallen if adjustments had been made soon enough to avoid loss of creditworthiness and the consequent loss of commercial sources of external credit. External borrowing is not a practical or sufficient alternative to domestic adjustments in consumption and investment in the public and private sectors. Nevertheless, such borrowing reduces the need to constrain consumption and investment and reduce growth rates as much. Developing countries can even strengthen their economies during periods of world recessions if they are assisted by appropriate external finance combined with economically rational domestic policies.

The damage to creditworthiness in Latin America and other regions was profound, and the road back to creditworthiness is not easy. It involves major, painful changes in domestic policies and a strengthening of the entire fabric of international finance in light of the needs of a continually evolving world economy. It cannot be a simple return to the past nor a move to a known or certain future, for the future must be unknown or uncertain. The reformed international financial system must be flexible, adaptable, and financially adequate. It must apply imagination to experience. Important changes will be needed, but they can be made.

7

Responses to the Crisis

External Debt

To review briefly, the external debt of nonoil developing countries increased more than fourfold between 1973 and 1981—an annual increase of about 20 percent per annum. The share of private financial institutions in the net external financing of these countries rose from about 40 percent in 1973 to an average of 61 percent during 1980–81. There was also a significant change in the forms and terms of private flows, reflecting the trend toward more extensive use of syndicated bank loans at variable interest rates and away from more traditional types of private finance, such as bonds, supplier credits, and direct investments. In addition, the increased global integration of banks—for example, the global interbank market—facilitated a rapid expansion·in the short-term debt of these countries. Debt service payments of nonoil developing countries increased fivefold between 1973 and 1981—more than the increase in total debt—reflecting the expanded use of variable interest rates, combined with the steep rise in nominal international interest rates in the late 1970s.

The impact of the financial crisis was seen in a sharp contraction of lending to developing countries. The growth in external debt owed to private creditors during 1982–84 fell to an annual average rate of 7 percent—only one-third of that experienced during 1978-81. Of this increase, about 40 percent was lending to Latin American countries as part of the concerted lending by creditor banks that was related to debt restructuring, not to banks' views on the creditworthiness of the borrowing countries for truly voluntary or spontaneous lending. During this period, moreover, developing countries were substantially increasing their deposits with the international banking system, which rose by more than $50 billion in 1983–84.

As a consequence, a long trend of increasing net liabilities of developing countries to international banks was reversed by $10 billion in 1984.

The sharp reversal in international lending to developing countries was clearly evident in the debt service payments recorded in 1985. In that year, debt service payments by developing countries exceeded new borrowings by an estimated $22 billion, still more than the $14 billion recorded in 1984. Even during the crisis years of 1982 and 1983, net transfers had been positive to the developing countries, although they had fallen to $16 billion and $4 billion in 1982 and 1983, respectively, compared with $34 billion in 1981. Thus, the estimated swing from 1981 through 1985 was about $56 billion. In brief, in 1985, the banks were still trying to reduce their exposure to developing countries. Although the developing countries were reducing their current account deficits from over $105 billion in 1981 to about $38 billion in 1985, the decline in deficits was at least partly due to the inability of countries to obtain from the banks the credits they needed to finance a larger volume of imports.

The banks' reluctance to lend meant that the total debt of developing countries continued to grow slowly in 1985, at 4.6 percent per annum. The World Bank projected that the 1986 growth rate would be not much higher, at 6.3 percent. By the end of 1986, developing country debt is expected to be about $1,010 billion, of which long-term debt will account for $815 billion (including the use of IMF credit). Of the $815 billion, official sources account for $299 billion and private sources for $516 billion. Long-term debt has been growing faster than the overall rate because of reschedulings of short-term debt into longer maturities.

The trend away from new bank lending has been influenced by the growth of securities markets. Top-quality borrowers are increasingly going to nonbank lenders rather than to banks, and some banks have been selling loans in the secondary market.

The amount of bank debt restructured in 1985 is estimated at $87 billion by private creditors and $6 billion by official lenders. In addition, the amount of short-term debt rolled over, or converted, into medium-term loans under arrangements concluded in the context of debt restructurings is estimated at $28 billion in 1983 and $36 billion in 1984. In 1983–84, ten IMF member countries reached agreements with banks in so-called concerted lending packages. Approval of a country's economic adjustment program by the Fund depended on the prior commitment of a "critical mass" of lending by the private banks involved in the debt restructuring. In 1983, this concerted lending for eight countries amounted to $13.9 billion, or 40 percent of new external commitments to developing countries; the amounts in 1984 were higher. This concerted lending was concentrated, however, in the Western Hemisphere and Yugoslavia.

Mexico and Brazil

An important immediate cause of the widespread feeling of impending worldwide financial crisis in 1982 was the severe difficulties of the two largest and strongest developing country borrowers, Brazil and Mexico. I do not intend here to describe their situation in detail. It may be sufficient to note that these two countries had the largest international debts of any of the developing countries; that U.S. banks and banks in other countries had substantial exposures in these countries by any portfolio criteria; that by any ratios or criteria they were heavily indebted; and that if conditions had become such that their loans became nonperforming and would have had to be charged off or defaulted, some individual major banks would have suffered serious losses, threatening their own creditworthiness and viability. Similar statements could be made about Venezuela, Argentina, and Korea, but Brazil and Mexico had special importance.

Brazil was the new economic Eldorado, and Mexico the new major producer and exporter of liquid gold—oil. Brazil and Mexico were the largest borrowers from the commercial banks around the world because they were thought to be the strongest economically and financially and to have acceptable stability—socially and politically. They were not newcomers to international finance. Some of their entities had enjoyed access to the world's capital markets for decades. Their banks had enviable domestic and international reputations. Their industries were cited as examples of the benefits of desirable structural transformation of developing countries. They had vigorous and innovative private sectors. Their state enterprises were among the most efficient in the world. They maintained high economic growth rates. Brazil had managed the problem of being dependent on foreign oil without sacrificing its growth targets. A new category of developing countries—newly industrializing countries (NICs)—was invented to reflect their modernization and capitalization. Brazil had a chronic inflation problem, but widespread cost of living indexation had prevented the usual social disruptions caused by inflation, at least temporarily. Mexico also had inflation, but it was not as strong, because an influential central bank—the Bank of Mexico—had continuing great authority in government policymaking.

The financial leaders of Brazil and Mexico were lauded by the world press and governments. Their private entrepreneurs competed successfully with entrepreneurs anywhere. The most sophisticated and experienced foreign firms sought to expand their manufacturing and export operations in these countries. Academic analysts and other experts cited these two countries as being exceptionally well managed, diversified, and geographically well placed; as offering large returns with minimum risks; and as involving virtually no country risk to lenders and equity investors. These countries had had sizable debt servicing obligations for decades, but their large debts were seen, in the 1970s, as signs of strength, not weakness, reflecting their strong standing in financial markets.

Was this foolishness, wishful thinking, or blindness? To gain perspective, it is necessary to see these countries as of the end of the 1970s, before the world became convinced that the era of prosperity was over and that an era of recession and contraction had set in. Brazil had a phenomenal growth record. Despite an incredible population expansion, it had substantially increased its real income per capita in the 1970s, the decade of shocks and surprises, with its huge increases in oil import costs. Exports in manufactures had grown even more. Although coffee exports were still important, the country no longer depended on primary products for its foreign exchange earnings. Its problems were massive—huge urbanization, large-scale unemployment or hidden unemployment, endemic inflation, and very wide disparities in income and wealth—but the country was clearly bounding forward. Investments were for infrastructure and productive private activities. Brazil's economic and financial institutions were strong, and it had demonstrated the benefits of a well-managed growth strategy. By the end of the 1970s, Brazil was emerging as one of the industrial giants of the world. It borrowed at interest rates and maturities comparable to those obtained by strong industrial countries.

There were clouds on the horizon—misgivings about the ability to move from a military to a civilian government, the reluctance of the government to devalue the currency as Brazilian inflation exceeded world inflation, and the continued existence of large budgetary deficits. No Brazilian leaders was unmindful of these negatives. The balance, however, seemed clearly favorable to Brazil, which had repeatedly confounded pessimistic observers and commentators.

Unfortunately, Brazil did not comprehend how quickly it could change from one of the strongest, most favored borrowers to a weak, shunned borrower. Because the Brazilians underestimated the difficulties for them in the changed world climate of 1980–82, they postponed adjustments. They also did not appreciate that Brazil's external credit could be weakened by the actions of other borrowers, particularly Mexico. This mistake compounded Brazil's problems. For commercial lenders, Brazil, like Mexico, was a traumatic experience in 1982 when the financial crisis arose. If the most promising, strongest, most resilient, brilliantly managed country could not service its obligations fully and promptly, what could they think of the others?

Mexico went through a similar metamorphosis. Like Brazil, it had profound economic and social structural problems—such as rural poverty and too rapid urbanization in only a few centers—that obviously could not be solved quickly. At the same time, it seemed certain to benefit, in coming years, from the previous 50 years of political stability, social progress, rising living standards, modernization of manufacturing and other sectors, improvements in education and health, and its huge oil-producing and export capacity. The future belonged to Mexico. Its leaders in business and finance were widely praised—and for good reasons. The fact that President Portillo had refused to adjust fiscal expenditures in his last years of office was judged unfortunate, but not fatal. It had happened before. Exchange rate adjustment had also been delayed; but, at first, this did not arouse deep fears. When the delays in exchange rate adjustment continued and it became clear that the falling oil prices would not rebound quickly, massive capital flight set in and blew the house down. Mexico weakened its creditworthiness in the latter part of 1981 and destroyed it in the first half of 1982. With Mexico's capital flight and loss of creditworthiness, concerns turned to fears and then to panic. In the spring of 1982, Mexico suspended payments on its external debts. The international rescue operation for Mexico, led by the United States, was considered a great success. However, when not everything went as expected, pessimism regarding Mexico in 1985 and 1986 was greater than ever.

Arguments used to mobilize emergency external assistance for Mexico fanned the flames. Existing institutions and resources were too weak and small to bring the liquidity crisis to an end soon. Instead, emergency funds had to be mobilized, and Mexico became a cause celèbre. If Mexico and then Brazil, why not Venezuela, Chile, Argentina, Peru, Nigeria, and others? Mexico was to the international financial situation in 1982 what the failure of the Austrian Kredit Anstalt was to the international credit system in 1931. Yet in 1981, Mexico was not overborrowed or overlent. Its economy had many of the weaknesses of rapid expansion, not depression. It needed reorganization and adjustments to the new, worsened world situation, but it did not need to lose its creditworthiness to accomplish this needed reorganization and adaptation. In 1981, the stubborn, mistaken persistence of President Portillo—against the advice of his financial experts—to maintain an overvalued exchange rate triggered the massive capital flight. Capital flight is financed from existing international monetary reserves of the country or is borrowed externally. Usually, it is mostly borrowed. Mexico's external debt increased sharply in 1981 and early 1982. In 1981, many were reluctant to regard Mexico's problems as being overwhelmingly serious. By 1982, Mexico had greatly weakened its reputation. When it declared its inability to service debt in May 1982, the curtain on Mexico's creditworthiness came down. The damage would take years, if not decades, to repair.

Borrowing Countries and Banks

It is instructive to note that the debt crisis of the early 1980s was not marked by the action that caused such lasting damage and long-term loss of creditworthiness in the 1930s—namely, outright debt repudiation by debtor countries. No country refused to make an effort to reschedule its outstanding debt, even when the debtor's inability to pay had been primarily due to factors beyond its control, such as a recession in export markets, a drop in commodity prices, or a natural disaster such as a drought. Moreover, as noted earlier, debt restructuring has, in effect, been made conditional on reaching economic and financial policy agreements with the IMF that unlock the door to IMF financing. At most, such countries as Peru and Nigeria have indicated that only a specified portion of their foreign exchange income could be directed to meeting obligations or past debts. This qualification could spread, but it is far from repudiation, since the amounts mentioned as available for debt obligations are substantial, not mere token payments.

Debtor countries have no viable alternative to trying to make difficult adjustments in their economies—adjustments made more difficult by the loss of creditworthiness. These adjustments include reducing their balance-of-payments deficits, lowering inflation, creating market incentives to produce and increase exports, reducing fiscal deficits, rationalizing public investments, and closely managing their external payments on the basis of economic criteria. The policy instruments to achieve these goals include exchange rate adjustments, changes in interest rates, taxation, pricing policies, subsidization, and so forth. The choice of policy mixes, however, is often socially disturbing and politically controversial.

These borrowing developing countries face a common fundamental problem that is behind the debt crisis—namely, a decline in, or loss of, creditworthiness. It is the lack of sufficient fresh financial resources, resulting from reduced or lost creditworthiness, that has bred the environment of uncertainty and fear. Without sufficient net inflows of external resources, debtor countries cannot hope to meet their development objectives, their social commitments, and their debt service obligations. The difficulties facing developing countries and their vulnerabilities have been widely appreciated for many years, but the length and intensity of the recession-turned-depression of the early 1980s were totally unexpected. Governments, lenders, and many borrowers failed to discern, at an early stage, the need for major economic adjustments. In 1980, most managers of developing country economies that had already established their external creditworthiness with commercial banks were confident of their ability to weather crises with the help of official bilateral and multilateral creditors and commercial banks. These lenders repeatedly gave borrowers reasons to believe that they, as lenders, had come to feel that these sovereign government borrowers required careful, continuous scrutiny but were essentially creditworthy.

As the recession of the early 1980s took hold, many borrowing countries, including Brazil and Mexico, took what had become the fairly traditional wait-and-see attitude toward what was thought to be yet another cyclical downturn in the world economy. They strongly hoped that by making minimal adjustments to the souring domestic and world economic situation, they could weather the latest storm and avoid politically and socially difficult adjustments, such as drastic cuts in imports and incomes. The cyclical upturn was awaited. The oil and larger nonoil exporting countries—Brazil and Korea, in particular—trusted that because they were among the most competitive exporting nations in the world, their conditions were bound to improve in the short run—in a year or 18 months at most. It was on the basis of that strength and the accepted view of short-term cyclical fluctuations in economic activity that lenders and others maintained an optimistic attitude toward the ability of borrowing nations to service their external debts. Borrowing countries continued to be creditworthy for borrowing. Liquidity crises were generally avoided in the early years of the recession of 1980–83.

With the surprising lengthening of the downswing in the business cycle in 1981–82 and the onset of the worst world economic conditions since the Great Depression, optimism about continued creditworthiness—particularly of Mexico, Brazil, and Argentina—turned to fear. The underestimation of the recession was accompanied by a questioning of the resiliency of developing economies, especially those with heavy debt obligations. Strong borrowers lost their creditworthiness with commercial lenders. Without adequate available substitutes, liquidity crises in borrowing countries became inevitable—and these circumstances may well recur in the future. As noted repeatedly in this book, Mexico, Venezuela, and Nigeria demonstrated that even strong oil-exporting developing countries could encounter very serious balance-of-payments difficulties if they lost their creditworthiness with external lenders.

During the 1980s, banks began to experience a significant increase in the number of nonperforming loans in developing countries. Since the countries involved in debt crises were the largest borrowers—not relatively small ones, such as Zaire or Jamaica—it was obvious that many banks had total exposures in these countries that were a substantial portion of their primary capital or even exceeded their capital. Many proceeded from this line of analysis to the "obvious" conclusion that a number of major banks faced bankruptcy in the foreseeable future. Uncertainty became "certainty" of excessive risk in lending to Latin American and other developing countries. The resulting general loss of creditworthiness had not been anticipated in earlier years. It had not been a factor in judging individual country risk. Rationally handled, this widespread loss of creditworthiness need not have occurred or could have been overcome quickly before causing deep and lasting damage. The world-wide depression caused great external payments difficulties for countries, but the loss of creditworthiness, which heightened these difficulties, was not inevitable.

Mechanisms existed for offsetting the fears of lenders. The IMF was capable of quick visible financing to mitigate crises, and special drawing rights (SDRs) by the IMF could have been created to avoid liquidity crises. Adjustment programs endorsed by the IMF—together with the support of the multilateral development banks—could have been adopted in time. The difficulties of 1981–82 need not have led to the widespread crises of 1982 and thereafter. These crises were avoidable. Capital flight in anticipation of exchange rate devaluations or intensive restrictions on international trade and payments could have been avoided. This capital flight was a major cause of the debt crises in 1982–84, but it was not inevitable. It is not a question of assessing blame—a bootless exercise, at best—but of understanding the system and why it failed. If we see failures in mechanisms, we look to technology for improvements. If we see that the failures are human, we look to people and their actions (or policies) to achieve improvements. Both mechanisms and people were involved, but the human errors were more important in explaining the loss of creditworthiness in the 1980s.

In a more immediate and direct sense, the loss of creditworthiness resulted from a combination of deterioration in the management of the borrowing countries, frequent delays in debt servicing, and the adverse reactions of the commercial bank lenders. These banks operated, as noted earlier, in an environment of virulent pessimism, echoed and reechoed whenever experts and bankers met or spoke with one another. Daily predictions were made of impending disasters, and less gloomy views were set aside as not worthy of repetition. Within banks, international lending to developing countries—especially Argentina, Brazil, and Mexico—lost its constituency. Bank lending to these countries became involuntary, urged by outsiders such as the IMF or government and monetary officials. Conferences on the external debt problem became daily occurrences. Paradoxically, the very acts of "crisis management" by those eager to assist the borrowing countries, by reducing their magnitudes of debt servicing or by mobilizing emergency credits, fanned the fears. Advocates of such special measures had to draw vivid pictures of the catastrophes ahead, which urgently required their advocated measures. For the Latin American countries, the inadequacies of their own adjustments, their delays, the skittishness of their creditors, the limitations of the official national and international entities, and the loud, ill-informed public discussions combined to convert difficulties into disasters. The disasters could have been avoided. The borrowing countries need not have had as much damage done to their creditworthiness as actually occurred. The road back to creditworthiness could have been easier and quicker. The past is past, however. What is important now is to see how countries can avoid repetition of such crises in the future and, in the process, restore their creditworthiness.

As of 1986, individual commercial banks did not get into serious troubles because of lending to developing countries, and the international banking system did not collapse. Southeast Asian and Far Eastern countries became favored borrowers instead of the Latin American countries. The experience of the early 1980s was painful for the banks, however. In time, it could prove devastating for developing countries. Commercial banking is a major source of the international credits needed for development. No adequate substitute is even being seriously contemplated. The developing countries and the world economy were handicapped for decades by the damage done to international capital flows by the defaults of the 1930s; so will serious damage to the creditworthiness of Latin American countries now handicap their development for years or decades to come. Not surprisingly, Brazil has demonstrated more capacity to recover than other countries—more like a developed country, which it is rapidly becoming. Brazil's experience shows how a country, even with a huge debt, can move to restore creditworthiness. Its return to a high growth rate based on export growth is quite impressive.

There was a global economic recovery in 1983–84, but the recovery was relatively weak and uneven. Oil prices remained depressed and weakening. Exports of manufactures continued to be undermined by growing trade barriers and the continued low demand for imports in industrial countries besides the United States. Investment and production in developing countries responded to the economic recovery in the industrial countries, but the gains were not sufficient to offset the setbacks of earlier years. The adjustment programs endorsed by the Fund had proved remarkably successful in reducing balance-of-payments deficits—probably more than many had expected—but growth was poor, and the countries remained in balance-of-payments difficulties because they did not recover their creditworthiness. Developing countries in Latin America and elsewhere will be in balance-of-payments difficulties so long as they do not have creditworthiness with lenders, irrespective of their reduced balance-of-payments deficits.

Commercial banks continued to be reluctant to resume lending to Latin American countries, even when the conditions in borrowing countries had clearly begun to improve. It was not until well into 1984 that banks showed a serious willingness to consider making fresh voluntary credit available to Brazil or Mexico, despite Mexico's praised adjustment measures. This heightened confidence proved fragile and short-lived. By 1985, Mexico was again a poor credit risk; it was indeed paying a high price for the foolish policies of President Portillo. Asian countries continued to be clearly preferred to African and Latin American countries as borrowers. Fear, rather than cautious professional analysis, seemed the dominant feature of evaluations of developing countries. As history has repeatedly demonstrated, confidence in international lending is easily destroyed and is difficult to rebuild. Those who quickly accepted debt restructuring as their approach to handling external payments difficulties did not seem to realize that they were institutionalizing loss of confidence in the borrowing countries involved.

The Spread of Debt Restructuring

The experience of 1981–83 convinced the world that the largest borrowers could get into payments difficulties and that lenders to them could suffer significant losses. Renegotiation and restructuring of outstanding debts become the main response. Official and private lenders have traditionally kept a close eye on developments in borrowing countries, and debt rescheduling—usually a stretching out of the original repayment schedule—was resorted to often in the postwar period. Through the 1960s and early 1970s, most rescheduling involved debt to official agencies and was handled on a multilateral basis, mostly under the so-called Paris Club arrangements first agreed to in 1956. By the end of 1982, some sixty multilateral debt renegotiations, involving twenty countries, had been held under the aegis of the Paris Club. The IMF and the World Bank were part of this process, providing their assessments of country conditions. By the late 1970s, however, debt to commercial banks had increasingly become the subject of renegotiations, usually involving the debtor country and a group of banks representing all the banks with outstanding loans to that debtor country. In the 1970s, these renegotiations were still exceptional, but they were occurring with increasing frequency. Many of the policies and practices that still guide reschedulings were established in those years.

In the mid-1970s, Zaire was the first major rescheduling case that importantly involved the commercial banks, as distinct from government lenders. Because it was the first case, a number of decisions had to be made that were novel and precedent-setting. The precedents established in the Zaire case included collective actions of the creditor banks vis-à-vis the debtor country, instead of separate bank negotiations and restructuring of debt; relating debt restructuring and new credits to improved economic management; linking use of new credits to use of IMF resources resulting from programs agreed with the IMF; and the willingness to restructure debts and avoid default declarations so long as a debtor recognized its obligations and paid interest due.

The emphasis in the Zaire case, however, was on the reestablishment of creditworthiness—that is, the willingness of commercial banks to lend to Zaire on a voluntary basis, reflecting the lending criteria of the individual banks without the guidance or influence of creditor governments. Zaire did not, however, restore good economic management that could meet the criteria of private lenders. The initial emphasis in the Zaire case on reestablishing creditworthiness gave way to an emphasis on restructuring accumulated debt. This shift in emphasis crippled international lending for years. It gave more importance to uniform action by all creditor banks—no longer competing for acceptable international business but viewed as common victims of past policies.

Zaire was seen as a country that had been a strong borrower but had not adjusted to the sharp decline in copper prices, its principal export, and had not made needed reforms in its foreign exchange management—all curable ills, not calling for pushing panic buttons. The experience of strong borrowers getting into difficulties happened repeatedly in banking. Banking was not a no-risk, no-pain activity. In the case of Zaire, banks had been encouraged, at first, to demonstrate renewed creditworthiness by providing new credits in differing magnitudes deemed appropriate by the individual banks. Debt rescheduling was part of the mechanism to restore normal banking relations. New, voluntary credits were to be the signs of restored creditworthiness, and each bank would decide that for itself in light of its own country risk criteria and portfolio policies. No panic buttons were pushed by the banks, though commentators quickly made the most gloomy forecasts in line with what had become popular during the 1973 oil price increase period. Without realizing it, Zaire let down the entire developing world. Zaire had the objective conditions to restore its creditworthiness. Despite the depressed prices for copper, its entire balance of payments was viable. It could service its debts. It could not, however, administer its economy and therefore lost the confidence and cooperation of the business community at home and abroad.

By shifting the emphasis to debt restructuring, the presumptions and processes of international lending became uncertain and often confused. In the debt reschedulings that followed, banks agreed to uniform actions even in extending credits, an extraordinary procedure for banks with separate ownership, management, profit goals, and so forth, and often in competition with each other. Peru, Turkey, and Jamaica followed Zaire. At the end of the 1970s, Poland was the case that linked this period of occasional or exceptional reschedulings to the latest period, when many—including the largest debtors—have become involved in commercial loan rescheduling. The external debt problem and the use of the rescheduling techniques were transformed into global concerns. By 1983, more than thirty debtor countries had found it appropriate to renegotiate their external debts. The external debt problem became an ingredient in all discussions, analyses, and commentaries on the international political, as well as economic, situation. International lending to Latin America and Africa on a voluntary basis largely ceased. The question was when, if ever, it would resume. The external debt problem was no longer the problem of isolated countries but was part of the widespread balance-of-payments difficulties resulting from the world depression of the 1980s and the inadequate national responses to these adversities. It became an international political issue of first-order magnitude.

As noted elsewhere in some detail, the spread of serious debt servicing difficulties posed a threat to the economies of the countries affected and also to the international financial system. It resulted in a coordinated effort by the debtor countries, official and bank creditors, and international financial institutions. The desire was to support debtor country policies that were designed to regain viable external positions and help restore sustained economic growth. This was to be done in such a way as to result in "equitable burden sharing" among creditors. The context was usually a Fund-supported economic adjustment program. As negotiations proceeded on such adjustment programs, authorities in financial markets, such as the United States and the Bank for International Settlements (BIS), helped obtain immediate temporary financing support through bridging loans.

Official debt reschedulings typically have covered both principal and interest payments in medium-term and long-term loans. In private restructuring cases, an advisory group or steering committee of bankers has been established to assist liaison with all bank creditors to discuss the coverage and terms of the restructuring and, where required, to coordinate the maintenance of short-term bank exposure and the provision of new financing. The Fund has participated in these meetings.

Financial packages arranged with bank creditors have generally consisted of debt restructuring covering only amortization payments, together with an arrangement necessary to ensure the maintenance of short-term credit lines. In some cases, "new money" or concerted lending was also included in the package. At first, the rescheduling covered debt servicing falling due during a year—the so-called consolidation period—with postponement of amortization payments for short periods. Among other disadvantages to this approach, in addition to the sheer effort needed for each exercise, was the tendency to create bunching of amortizations. The combination of one-year consolidations and relatively short-term maturities meant that servicing was merely postponed and added to later maturities of the same debt. As experience has been gained, debtor countries and banks have negotiated multiyear debt restructuring agreements (MYRAs) with longer consolidation periods of even more than 5 years and extended repayment periods of over 10 years. Thus, for the borrowing country, debt servicing was considerably eased for a number of years. For the lenders, it helped avoid unfavorable loan classifications if the borrower continued to pay interest. The banks, however, remained involuntary holders of these restructured assets and, if anything, the transformation of short-term assets into longer maturities often hampered the extension of new credits on a voluntary basis. The restructured loans remained unwanted risk assets in troubled countries.

The Changed Role of the International Monetary Fund

Beginning in the 1970s, both Paris Club and commercial bank debt renegotiations increasingly involved the International Monetary Fund. The Fund became a vital link in the country risk management system of the banks.

Fortunately, the shift in emphasis in the Zaire case from reestablishing creditworthiness to debt restructuring did not result in eliminating the notion of the need for an economic reform program endorsed by the Fund as part of the exercise. Official and private creditors required that countries requesting debt restructuring have an economic and financial adjustment program, officially supported by the IMF, in place before the restructuring agreement could become effective. The need for debt restructuring indicated that the country had greatly weakened or lost its creditworthiness with commercial bank lenders. The country risk assessment by a bank had presumably been made, and the country had been found to be an excessive risk for further loans. However, the need to reschedule compelled the bank to make a modified lending decision. Debts (or loans) already contracted were renegotiated and, in effect, replaced with new loans. The magnitudes of exposures remained the same, but the maturities and interest rates were usually changed. Maturities were usually greatly lengthened from months to years. Restructuring thus means, at least, a change in the international portfolio maturity mix.

In restructuring debt, a bank's ordinary lending criteria are ambiguous guides to decision making. The bank can simply proceed to restructuring, but it wants the country to achieve conditions that will enable it again to service its external debts fully and promptly. The banks turned to the IMF to help achieve this objective. The IMF was a natural selection because it focused on the very factors that the banks employed in their own country risk evaluations— namely, balance-of-payments behavior and the pursuit of policies needed to achieve manageable balance-of-payments conditions that made possible servicing of external debt. Since the IMF membership of more than 150 countries includes debtor and creditor governments, and since its staff is international, its judgments are regarded as impartial and expert. The IMF gives what is, in effect, an official international stamp of approval to a debtor country's economic and financial policies, thereby paving the way for a debt restructuring. This approach became standard. The adjustment programs endorsed by the Fund are based on decades of experience and relations with members. At some time or another over the past 30 years, nearly every member country of the Fund has experienced balance-of-payments difficulties requiring changes in government policies that have been discussed with the Fund as part of the country's normal relations with the Fund. Agreeing with countries on an IMF-sponsored program was not a new activity for the Fund; rather, it was the application, in the late 1970s and 1980s, of established activities and practices to a new usage—dealing with the external debt obligations of members to commercial banks.

By the 1980s, the Fund prescriptions for dealing with balance-of-payments difficulties had evolved and had been tested over decades. The causes or ingredients of the difficulties had usually been excessive monetary expansion, unbalanced budgets, public sector deficits, unrealistic exchange rates, excessive protectionism, and poorly managed state enterprises, combined with price and other administrative controls—such as ceilings on interest rates, commitments to adjust wages to price increases (indexation), subsidization of consumption, and capital flight. The Fund experience had been that policies were available to reduce balance-of-payments deficits rather quickly, though exchange rate adjustments by themselves were not adequate. A combination, or package, of coordinated policies was necessary. Success might well not be lasting if the adjustment policies were not sustained. This was often the case in developing countries where economic policies were severely constrained by social and political conditions. Nevertheless, these policies, by emphasizing reductions in balance-of-payments deficits and means of achieving such reductions, came closest to dealing with the immediate conditions that had resulted in the need for debt restructuring.

The IMF-endorsed programs are frequently difficult for debtor countries to implement, but the IMF typically supports a program by making its own financial resources available. The available IMF financing may be phased over 1 to 3 years in so-called tranches. Each additional tranche of IMF credit is made contingent upon the observance, by the borrower, of more stringent agreed conditions that usually call for a realistic exchange rate, an anti-inflation program consisting of limitations on credit expansion, small fiscal deficits, removal of price controls—or at least more realistic pricing—and restraints on wage increases, while encouraging a transfer of resources to the export-producing sector. The aim of an IMF-supported program is to improve the borrowing country's balance-of-payments position, thereby enabling it to finance more imports, to service its debt on a timely basis, and to maintain as liberal and nonrestrictive a system of international trade and payments as possible.

In becoming central to the external debt problems of commercial banks, the Fund modified its modes of activities to relate to nongovernmental entities. Its role in the private debt problem became of paramount importance to the Fund and to the international community in the 1980s. For the Fund, it was a major departure from the previous course of activities, which were nearly entirely with governments and central banks. Secrecy and quiet diplomacy had been characteristic. Problems of member countries were not discussed with public media. Fund visits to countries were not publicized, and Fund staff working on countries were anonymous. Fund-recommended programs or domestic policies were essentially advisory. Governments took clear and full responsibility for their policies. There were no Fund programs as such, but rather country programs endorsed by the Fund, if the question was raised. Fund-endorsed programs were often seen as imperfect—part of a continuing process of member relations and based on the recognition that governments are virtually incapable of following optimum economic policies but work and live with policies that are economically suboptimal but politically and socially feasible. Fund endorsement was not given to policies that would not improve the balance of payments, but it did not require that policies achieve immediate improvement. Nor did the Fund question the willingness of governments to fulfill their stated objectives. The Fund was part of a country's political process—its link with the world in monetary matters.

The internal debt problems not only expanded but significantly changed the role of the Fund and the Fund's relations with its members. The banks turned to the Fund to provide assessments of country conditions to guide their debt restructuring activities. Thus, in effect, country risk evaluations for countries requiring restructuring moved from the individual banks to the IMF.

In the 1980s, the Fund has performed the dual role of being monitor of and catalyst for commercial as well as official financing, while being the largest source of anticyclical balance-of-payments financing. The developing countries were those in greatest need of such financing and, among these, the debt restructuring countries were those with the most acute problems. The combination gave the Fund great influence and leadership in dealing with the external debt crises of its developing country members. The Fund's influence was felt most directly in the criteria used to judge a country's economic management. Fund conditionality (its conditions for use of its financial resources) became the conditionality of the private banks. Aside from the Fund's use of its own resources, the restructuring by the banks was the most important external action in dealing with the external financial problems of the borrowing developing countries in difficulties. By its direct control over its own resources and its influence over the banks in debt restructuring, the Fund became, by far, the most important element in dealing with the international financial problems of developing countries in the 1980s. It had become much more than a lender of last resort. It was the authority on acceptable economic management.

All in all, the debt restructuring has been done in an organized and orderly fashion by the banks, acting collectively. The banks have had to agree on the content of the actual restructuring and, in some cases—as urged by the Fund—on providing new, incremental loans to the country whose past debt was being restructured. Given the large number of banks involved in each rescheduling (usually in the hundreds or even over a thousand worldwide), these negotiations and agreements have not been easy to arrange. Nevertheless, the most difficult part of the process has been getting the debtor country to agree to adopt and pursue policies that meet the conditionality of the IMF for the use of its resources. The banks could readily follow the IMF's lead; it was the borrowing countries that repeatedly declared that they could not implement the degree of austerity required under the IMF's criteria. Despite such difficulties and frequent delays, agreements with countries were eventually reached in virtually all cases. In some cases, such as Venezuela, countries adopted programs that had the same content as an IMF-endorsed program but without a request for a separate arrangement with the Fund in the usual form of a standby arrangement.

Expanded Lending by the International Monetary Fund

As private sources of credit virtually dried up for many developing countries in the early 1980s, the International Monetary Fund wisely stepped into the gap as best it could. IMF lending reached record levels in the early 1980s, as debtor countries turned to the IMF, some reluctantly and as a last resort, and agreed to have adjustment programs that met the criteria of IMF conditionality. The Fund became the only significant substitute for the reduced lending of the commercial banks. The IMF had little or no choice but to require the adoption of painful, deflationary adjustment measures by its borrowers. The Fund had been established to promote "prosperity," not recession. However, it could not fulfill this primary function in the 1980s. The IMF's resources were not sufficiently large to support programs that could achieve satisfactory balance-of-payments positions and strong economic growth at the same time. A simple test would be the ability to maintain satisfactory growth and employment levels—without the need to resort to exchange and trade restrictions to reduce imports because of foreign exchange shortages. The IMF's creditor member countries were experiencing recession and had introduced austerity programs because they had not discovered how to fight persistent inflation except with persistent deflation. Persistent inflation was being fought by drastic reductions in growth rates and high levels of unemployment. Easy credit, originating in fiscal deficits, was seen as the primary cause of inflation and external payments difficulties. Fiscal deficits proved intractable, and strict monetary policies were used instead. The result was widespread deflation.

For developing countries, large external deficits had to be financed if severe deflation was to be avoided. The IMF's resources were large enough to help prevent disasters and collapses in the developing countries but not to avoid the need for austerity adjustments, and surely not enough to be able to urge growth policies as the alternatives to deflation. IMF quotas were increased, and member governments lent large sums to the IMF for its own lending operations with developing country members, but still the Fund remained relatively poor in resources.

The IMF was thus limited in its ability to be a more effective instrument in the pursuit of noninflationary growth policies. An IMF that could provide very large amounts of financial resources to its members, some argued, could discourage countries from taking needed adjustment measures. Moreover, the IMF had to assure itself, its own creditors, and borrowing countries' creditors that the IMF's credit would be repaid on schedule. The arguments for a modest Fund role gave insufficient attention to the key purpose of the Fund—to help avoid deep and prolonged world recessions and, instead, to promote world prosperity. Nevertheless, the Fund did play an important role in meeting the external financial needs of its members, even if such financial assistance fell short of what could have been gainfully used. The Fund was able to provide only a small fraction of what countries were able to borrow before 1982 and only a small fraction of what they needed in 1983 and to the present.

Medium-term debts to the Fund took the place of medium-term debts to the banks. Debts to the Fund, however, were not open to renegotiation, as debts to banks were. The IMF is a revolving fund. Unless it is given much greater easy access to credit itself, the Fund has to be repaid to protect its own liquidity and solvency. The Fund is not a credit-creating institution like a bank. It depends on contributions from governments in the form of quotas, and it has borrowed extensively from some governments. Thus far, it has not seen fit to borrow from private sources. Moreover, some creditor countries have believed that an IMF with limited resources would be more likely to enforce needed austerity policies than an IMF with very large resources. Thus, the IMF had to be a lending institution with rather rigid lending limits and had to insist on being repaid fully and promptly.

Under the conditions of the early 1980s, IMF member countries had little or no choice but to cut imports severely in order to make essential improvements in their external payments positions. There was no room to plan for a reduced, though protracted, balance-of-payments deficit that was still large enough for satisfactory growth rates. The painful adjustments in the member countries' economies had already been dangerously postponed. In those circumstances, it was not surprising that private creditors and debtors alike viewed the economic adjustment process with dread and pessimism. In many countries, enforced austerity came as a very unwelcome shock, as people had come to believe in the possibility of raising real living standards steadily, despite high rates of population growth. Opponents and proponents within countries that had austerity measures blamed the IMF for the need to introduce them. The IMF did not have sufficient resources to ease the pain of delayed adjustment, and it seemed that private sources of capital were following the Fund's leads. International lending became increasingly politicized. The Fund was an international political organization, and its willingness or reluctance to act in individual cases, as well as generally, was widely interpreted to reflect the wishes of its economically stronger members, especially the United States, Germany, Japan, France, and the United Kingdom. By using the IMF as their crutch in judging country creditworthiness and deciding on new lending, the banks were, in effect, involving their governments deeply in their own lending and debt restructuring decisions—a major change from previous policies and practices. The politicization resulted not from the IMF's involvement as such, but rather from the failure of the banks to continue to rely on their own judgments in making lending and restructuring decisions.

Other financial institutions did not play a major role in dealing with the crises of the 1980s, though moves were made in that direction by the multilateral development banks, especially after 1984. These steps are covered in subsequent chapters, which deal with the restoration of creditworthiness and its preconditions.

Ending the Crisis

8

Restoration of Creditworthiness: Implications of the Current Crisis

The Need for Other Approaches

Before discussing how the international financial system can be strengthened and the debt crisis can be ended, it would be useful to bring together, briefly, the various major threads of recent events to interpret how they relate to each other and to suggest what significance to attach to them, especially the implications for the restoration of creditworthiness.

The key developments have been the changed role of private banks, the drastic loss of creditworthiness of the Latin American countries, the new functions of the International Monetary Fund, the widespread renegotiation and restructuring of the external debt of many developing countries, and the adjustment policies of the borrowing countries—all in an environment of world recession or incomplete and weak recoveries in many industrial countries.

The temporary moratorium declared by Mexico in May 1982 may be regarded as the beginning of the crisis. Signs of difficulties were increasingly present in Mexico in 1980–82. During these years, however, the banks did not shut down the lending windows for Brazil and Mexico or for other countries in Latin America. So long as new lending took place and arrears in debt servicing were not long enough to cause loans to be classified as nonperforming by banks' controllers and official regulators or were limited to relatively few countries, there was no international financial crisis. The summer of 1982 saw the end of an era begun in the late 1960s, when banks and official authorities in the United States and elsewhere welcomed expansion of commercial bank lending to developing countries, especially in Latin America. In trying to understand what happened in the years from 1982 to 1986, it cannot be overemphasized that Brazil and Mexico were among the highest regarded developing or industrializing economies in the world in the 1970s and, in many respects, into the 1980s. Indeed, despite their loss of creditworthiness, the lead roles of these two countries continue. The restoration of their creditworthiness would go a long way toward restoring the creditworthiness of almost all countries in Latin America and would greatly facilitate borrowing by developing countries in other regions.

At first, many of those involved believed that the Mexican moratorium action, followed by the Brazilian action, would prove short-lived. It was thought that adjustments in exchange rates—reinforced by feasible monetary, fiscal, and wage policies—would remedy the external positions of these two giant economies among developing countries. The impact of the world recession was not given enough weight, especially its effect in bringing down oil prices and dampening world trade. Exports were encouraged, but world markets became weaker than expected, and protectionism in industrial countries became a much greater threat and disincentive to investments for export promotion.

The focus of attention was on the lending banks, rather than on the borrowing countries. High interest rates, though beginning to decline in 1982 and 1983, obscured the more fundamental point— that even at lower rates of interest, borrowing countries could not service interest payments unless they had a net inflow of capital larger than the interest payments, and this depended on restoration of creditworthiness or the availability of substitute sources of finance, such as the IMF. Such sources were obviously not large enough to substitute for the banks. The solution was seen in retrenchment and exchange rate adjustments. World markets were the area in which shortages of foreign exchange for many countries were to be overcome, despite the worldwide recession.

Many had great confidence that with these adjustment measures, countries would soon enough create the basis for reducing balance-of-payments deficits and resuming satisfactory growth. The interrelations between expanding exports and domestic growth were well understood. The limitations imposed by the world economy did not discourage those who believed that borrowing countries, such as Brazil and Mexico, could sharply reduce or eliminate their balance-of-payments deficits and still have acceptable income and employment conditions after a short spell. They argued that higher domestic savings rates would substitute for smaller imported savings in enabling the resumption of investment, especially in the export industries. Export-led growth would result. Such views were overly optimistic in judging how much austerity in consumption was acceptable and how soon such austerity would result in sufficient export promotion to overcome large balance-of-payments deficits and expand the export-promoting economies. Drastic austerity was urgently necessary, and improvements came slowly. Shifting resources into export industries was a slow process, even under favorable world conditions.

Balance-of-payments deficits declined dramatically, and countries slowed down growth rates. Austerity worked, but in some countries, the progress of decades was lost in a few years. Political strains multiplied. In many countries, growth became negative. In other countries, profound changes were made in domestic policies.

Thus, the crisis was only partially a crisis of international lending and borrowing. It was more profoundly a crisis of development. The entire postwar strategy of accelerating development by governmental policies and investments focused on the public sectors, including large borrowing from abroad, came into question. Accommodation to a world recession would, in any case, have been difficult and painful. Simultaneous accommodation to a world recession and to the loss of a major source of external resources was too much for existing institutions and policies. Self-correcting mechanisms need time to work in any case, but what was needed was adjustments not to a self-correcting market mechanism but to major changes in the role of governments. In the 1970s, the Brazilian government and the governments of many other developing countries could obtain large amounts of foreign resources, which were a major tool of economic management. When this tool broke, or at least shrank to a small size, governments in borrowing countries had to cope with the adverse domestic conditions resulting from the world recession with crippled tools.

The implications were practical, visible, and great. Leaving aside the economic wisdom of its policies, Brazil's social and political viability had been maintained through the use of such policies. With large net capital inflows, wages in Brazil could be adjusted to inflation by indexation, even though this increased domestic demand and therefore increased demand for imports. Part of the imports could be paid for with borrowed funds. Food consumption could be subsidized and more food could be imported so long as borrowed funds were available. Public investment programs, with long-term payoffs, could be afforded. Such investments absorbed domestic resources that could have been employed in current output and, by raising income, instead created more demand for imports and reduced export capability without adequate increases in current output of goods and services. Private sectors flourished under conditions of rapid real growth and rising real incomes, though wages and other costs rose; but this private sector growth depended on a net inflow of foreign funds.

The crisis begun in 1982 stressed reductions in balance-of-payments deficits and continued payment of interest to the lending banks. Unfortunately, even if this were achieved, it would not restore the creditworthiness of borrowing countries once that creditworthiness was lost, even though it might have been sufficient to prevent the loss of creditworthiness if it had been done earlier. Without this restoration, the process of adjustment had run head on into the walls of social and political conditions. For decades, these countries had achieved substantial material improvement, made feasible by net inflows of capital or, as in the cases of Mexico and Venezuela, by windfall foreign exchange earnings created by the oil cartel—a situation not very different in many respects from inflows of capital. Without the net inflows of revenues from borrowing or monopoly prices, aspirations could not be fulfilled, even in part. The economic foundation of social and political stability was cracked and was threatened with destruction. Nevertheless, many financial and political lenders continued to hope that the adjustment process would soon restore more normal conditions.

As adjustments did not quickly restore ability to service debt, the banks became more convinced than ever that their decision to withdraw from lending to many developing countries was correct. Countries were not restoring their creditworthiness; for many, their economic conditions and financial standing worsened.

The International Monetary Fund stepped into the breach. It provided financial resources in unprecedented amounts. It used its own resources and borrowed more from governments that were able to lend, such as Saudi Arabia. It could cushion the combined impacts of the world recession and loss of creditworthiness, though only in part. It did not have the resources to have, as its lending criteria, the maintenance of high levels of employment and income and the avoidance of measures destructive of international prosperity—its purposes under its own Articles of Agreement. Instead, it had no true choice except to insist on the need for austerity to reduce balance-of-payments deficits. Where these adjustments were simply too severe even to be attempted, it could insist that more external funds were necessary from the banks if the agreed austerity programs were to have any chance of success. Under these pressures, banks lent to countries that they did not regard as creditworthy—an unstable condition and a temporary action at most.

The Fund could have performed its role of defending world prosperity if it had had the resources. It even had the necessary mechanism in the creation of special drawing rights (SDRs), but the international community chose austerity, reduced external deficits, and debt restructuring. This meant less demand on the budgets of the developed countries. At the same time, these developed countries were following slow growth policies to fight inflation and to deal with large budgetary deficits. Their governments were besieged by demands for protection or export subsidization in competing with the developing countries. All wished for speedy recovery in the developing countries but were unable or unwilling to act to bring it about.

For some, it was a question of their philosophy of economic management—countries should learn to live within their means. Austerity conformed to this principle. Admittedly, developing countries had been encouraged for decades to accelerate domestic development and achieve living standards beyond their means with the help of foreign resources. Now that the time of troubles had come, this philosophy had to be abandoned. Whatever else may be said, a more unfavorable time to do so would be hard to imagine. For an oil-exporting country such as Nigeria or Venezuela, it had been possible to argue that it could live within its means because the "means" had included earnings from the high monopoly price for oil. For countries without such extraordinary foreign exchange receipts, the application of this philosophy clashed with social and political realities within the countries and with the objectives of the industrial countries themselves. Governments of developing countries could undertake austerity programs reflecting this philosophy, but it was predictable that such programs could not endure long enough to obtain the desired benefits to bring countries back to tolerable growth paths and the levels of employment necessary for social and political viability.

The Fund was applauded for its willingness to insist on the need for difficult adjustments. It could provide resources to reduce the level of pain, but it could not provide the necessary resources to restore satisfactory growth conditions in the troubled developing countries. Instead, it often became the scapegoat of those who were unable or unwilling to see that the fault was not in the Fund but in the lack of options it had as an international financial institution with resources much too small for its responsibilities. Long before the 1982 crisis, I had proposed a greatly expanded IMF because the world needed a Fund large enough to defend world prosperity. The international community did not agree to this, but it did agree to a Fund large enough to influence developing countries, which were desperately short of foreign exchange, to try to adjust by austerity. This set the stage for the Fund to be criticized by some for being too insistent on austerity and by others for not succeeding in having successful austerity programs adopted and implemented. Unfortunately for the Fund's reputation, these programs were labeled "Fund programs," as though they represented what the Fund might have counseled as proper economic management if sufficient external resources were available to finance productive, noninflationary growth.

The Latin American debtor countries focused on their debts rather than on the fundamental causes of their loss of creditworthiness. The need to service external debts was regarded as the primary cause of difficulties. Reduction of debt servicing obligations became the cure-all for Latin American ailments. Latin American debt was considered "excessive," and the accepted formula was to reduce the debt in total, or reduce the interest servicing burden—and Latin America could breathe easily again. The lending banks had to share the burdens of adjustment—clearly they had lent too much! Latin American spokesmen emphasized the foreign exchange costs of high interest rates. Although many of the borrowings had been arranged when interest rates were at their highest levels (1980–81), they were on a floating rate basis, so these countries benefited from the declining rates in the 1980s. The Latin American spokesmen noted that Latin America had high debt service rates—higher than could be handled with foreign exchange needed for debt servicing, amounting to half or more of all foreign exchange receipts. They agreed that they had borrowed "excessively"—but then, the banks had been willing to lend. Austerity was necessary, but the burden of servicing debt was too great.

Latin America joined the world in making the debt problem the central issue in international finance and on the world economic scene, rather than the need for noninflationary growth. Latin America withdrew from its defense of rapid growth and development. It apologized for developing its resources and for trying to achieve higher living standards for its people. It apologized for its active private sector. It did not insist on focusing on the central issue—the need for accelerated growth mechanisms for achieving social stability and political order. Is austerity a viable option for a Latin American country if the causes are not temporary and largely self-correcting in the short run? How could Latin America again obtain access to the world's financial markets on a voluntary basis, not dependent on extraordinary political pressures or involuntary concerted action? What could be done to get the world economy back on a growth path, with expanding international markets for all kinds of goods? How could Latin America cope with protectionist measures in developed countries in agriculture as well as manufactures? How could it achieve a stable, realistic exchange rate system? How could it deal with cyclical changes with mechanisms for defending development? How could it create a system of capital movements that would not be disrupted by cyclical movements or unexpected shocks? The Latin American countries did not focus on such fundamental questions. They did not insist on the need for growth, which is not possible without a net inflow of resources. They did not insist that the issue was not the magnitudes of interest payments but the inability to finance even lower rates of interest unless net capital inflows were available. They did not ask why they had lost their creditworthiness and what was necessary to restore it. Instead of growth issues, such as inducements for productive investments and increasing profitability for private sector production, the emphasis was on balance-of-payments items, especially the service items for debts.

Latin America needed to restore its creditworthiness. Instead, by emphasizing debt management, it convinced others of its weak creditworthiness and lost the basis of its past creditworthiness—its devotion to modernization, growth, and export competitiveness. Instead of concentrating on domestic economic performance and the composition and magnitudes of exports, the size of the external deficits became the criterion of success or failure—as though a slow-growth, highly inflationary economy could hope to regain the confidence of world lenders because it was reducing its external deficit. How long would it be before inflation would undermine growth and competitiveness by scaring officials into abortive attempts to slow down currency devaluations?

The practice of debt restructuring reinforced these trends. Debts—not new loans—were the subject matter of debt rescheduling. Debt restructuring was a response to immediate needs and dangers—repudiations and defaults. Debt servicing was reduced. Acute financial crises and collapses were prevented. From the 1970s, the process strengthened a link to the IMF. Debt rescheduling was a benefit to the debtor country as maturities were lengthened. For many banks, their loan portfolios in a country being restructured because of payments difficulties were transformed from short- or medium-term loan portfolios to medium- or long-term portfolios. This was paradoxical, because banks generally considered longer-term maturities more suitable for stronger borrowers. Debt restructuring may well mean that weaker borrowers are given longer terms than stronger borrowers.

In addition, interest rates on restructured debt only partially reflected the decline in creditworthiness. Debt restructuring was the result of negotiation and bargaining by the collective group of lenders—usually hundreds of banks—with a borrowing country government, not with individual borrowers. Outside forces, such as governments and multilateral agencies, were also present—again, entities that were not part of the market mechanism. The private bank lenders were aware of markets. They had no choice because they, themselves, were borrowers from markets. Their shareholders were also market-oriented, but the debt negotiating process was not market-oriented or market-driven. A foreseeable consequence was that debtors would go on, as they did, to suggest interest rates for the restructured debt that were not related to markets. For a number of years, the general practice was that the interest rates would be something above the cost of money to the lending bank. LIBOR—an interest rate quoted in the London market—was a frequent reference basis. The lending bank did not get a risk premium that equated its risk assessment with return on the loans, but it got some return or profit from the restructured loan. A new chapter was possibly opened when some Latin American countries suggested that the banks accept interest rates below the cost of funds to the banks. Banks can take losses, but this completely changes the character of debt restructuring by making restructuring no longer a device to avoid losses and achieve earnings but, rather, a device to limit losses. This development was logical in a process in which debt restructuring was a mechanism for dealing with past debts, not part of a mechanism for restoring creditworthiness. Once a debtor country perceives that it is not likely to restore its creditworthiness, the bargaining process with its creditors is entirely altered. If this happens (it has not happened yet), the creditor loses its strongest card—that is, resumption of lending. The debtor has little to lose beyond what it has already lost.

The presence of the IMF did not, by itself, keep the process from being focused on debt restructuring instead of on restoration of creditworthiness. The Fund emphasis was on reducing balance-of-payments deficits; growth was a consequence. The IMF had a mutually advantageous relationship with the banks. The banks' insistence on a Fund program as a prerequisite for debt restructuring and, at times, involuntary lending by the banks to the debtor country, reinforced the influence of the Fund. It even gave many the impression that the Fund managed these countries, or could do so, if it chose to! On the other hand, the banks could hope that the debtor would see the advantage in debt restructuring as part of a parcel of actions that resulted in new money from the Fund.

The missing card was the restoration of creditworthiness. The economic precondition for creditworthiness was economic management designed to achieve sustained, noninflationary, adequate growth. The Fund could not promise a country that fulfillment of a Fund program would restore true creditworthiness with other lenders. At most, it would mean the rather short-term relief coming from reduced amortization on past debts. It could not even promise relief from interest payments. It could not keep a cynical debtor from concluding that the presence of the Fund did not help it get a better deal with the banks. The trade-off was clear—Fund conditionality versus Fund financial assistance. Fund assistance was only a fraction of a country's need if it were to follow a growth strategy requiring more external resources. If these conditions necessitated a basic rethinking and reshaping of development strategy and priorities, why not go all the way to a growth strategy based on no net capital inflows except from governmental sources not affected by the debtor's relations with the banks? Repudiation was an extreme, but in between were various positions, such as below-market interest rates or unilateral limits on total debt servicing to some fraction of exchange earnings before negotiating with the bank. Because the Fund was not part of a process of restoration of creditworthiness, it could not prevent the deterioration in relations between debtors and private sources of external finance.

Debt restructuring has not been limited to Latin America. It is also fashionable in Africa. In these countries, also, debt restructuring has not been a step toward the restoration of creditworthiness, even though a Fund program is part of the mechanism. This is not to argue that debt restructuring cannot be part of the procedure for restoring creditworthiness. Indeed, it is probably a necessary, though not sufficient, part. Some settlement of past debt is necessary. Whatever is accomplished will probably be attained by negotiation, as in debt restructuring, not unilaterally by debtors or creditors.

In the future, however, the process of facilitating debt servicing must include what is necessary to restore creditworthiness. It must not end with debt restructuring. It must include the conditions that must be met to reestablish true creditworthiness. Fund advice and approval should be sought for these conditions. (Perhaps Fund approval will be joined by approval of other agencies, such as the World Bank and the regional development banks.) Fund resources—in much larger magnitudes, it is hoped—should be available if needed.

The test of success in restoring creditworthiness will be new money from lending sources not involved in debt restructuring or in magnitudes not related to past debt accumulations. Past lenders would not be pressured to be part of the new lending. All lending would be voluntary; lenders would be induced to lend because of their assessments of profitability and risk. The emphasis in judging economic management would shift from short- to medium-term balance-of-payments management to the factors that make countries eligible for new money that must be repaid in the medium to longer term. The ability to create conditions for social and political stability would rate high. High priorities would also be given to maintenance or improvement of productive facilities, avoidance of new uneconomic public sector projects, encouragement of more savings and attracting them by public policies into productive investments, strengthened export competitiveness, and continuation of efforts to sustain and improve human resources ("human capital"). These would be the earmarks of good economic management. Successful fiscal and monetary management to overcome inflation and end incentives to capital flight would give convincing evidence that the troubled country's economic management was prepared to have a new assessment or rating of its creditworthiness by private lenders. Successful growth, instead of successful austerity, would be the fundamental objective and test.

IMF programs related to debt restructuring have involved more than thirty countries, mainly in Latin America and Africa. A number of these programs have had to be revised a number of times, as agreed programs could not be implemented successfully. Such programs, their financing, and relations with other lenders, especially private banks, became prime activities of the IMF. The center of gravity of Fund activity and influence moved from the developed countries to the developing countries in external payments difficulties. Developing countries that did not seek debt restructuring or important use of IMF resources in the credit tranches received the attention given to all members of the IMF, but the role of the Fund was primarily to assist in the crisis management of troubled countries. What the Fund did quietly with other less troubled countries was taken for granted. Instead, the Fund became widely known as a center of controversies over the adjustment processes in troubled countries.

Similarly, banking experiences in troubled countries dominated banks' managements. Developing countries with strong and untroubled debt servicing records were regarded with much more caution regarding their country creditworthiness. The banks publicly deprecated their ability to manage international lending. Instead of assessing their entire experience with international lending for the 1970s and 1980s, the banks permitted the events in Latin America after 1981 to dominate their management decisions. International divisions of banks were slashed, and market positions abroad were given up to others. Instead, banks insisted that any new funds be available on a collective, shared basis, as in the debt restructuring. As a consequence, new lending to Brazil and Mexico, for example, under Fund sponsorship and creditor government support, was not a decisive step in the restoration of creditworthiness. The banks lost confidence in their own business judgments and practices. They were glad to dance to tunes composed and played by the IMF. The banks neither defended nor explained what had happened in their international lending, and their acquiescence implied agreement with the negative criticism of others. This passive acceptance of criticism reinforced convictions of the wisdom of avoiding voluntary lending to developing countries and, if possible, achieving reductions in exposures. Stretching out maturities through restructuring became an easily acceptable route.

Implications of the Spread of Crisis

The spread of the 1982 crisis in individual countries transformed the situation from individual and separate country problems into a crisis of the international financial system. The scope for actions was narrowed, not only strengthening fears of the future for debtors and creditors but also limiting options. Arrangements reached in one country situation became precedents for others, including those still not foreseen. Issues such as the debts considered eligible for restructuring, the treatment of interest rates, maturity stretch-outs, the role of the International Monetary Fund, the availability of new money, and the shares of participating lender banks in debt restructuring and provision of new monies could not be considered separately, even though each troubled country was handled separately on a country-by-country basis. This was particularly true as the private banks gave an official, public character to the process. With the banks operating as a collective bargaining unit, with the ties to programs endorsed by the Fund, with the debtor negotiating partner being the government of the country acting on behalf of myriad individual debts, with the front-page, worldwide publicity on the course of negotiation, with the interventions of creditor governments, and with the more open role of bank regulators and central banks, the process was transformed. It was negotiating on the front lawn with everyone looking on. Despite these handicaps, the financial mechanisms operated rather smoothly, but they operated within many constraints not usually found in relationships between a lending bank and a borrower having payments difficulties. These mechanisms, by themselves, do not operate to restore the creditworthiness of borrowing countries.

The process of debt restructuring transformed the arena of action for the International Monetary Fund and the World Bank, especially the IMF. The Fund had long had a central bank tradition—confidential, forthright, private, patient, technical, nonpolitical, and nonpolemical. The Fund staff often found itself disagreeing with the policies and practices of a member country, but the world never knew. Central banking relies heavily on mystique (not being fully understood), magic, and awe to gain public support—that is, noninterference. Effectiveness and experience are the advocates. Thus, in many cases in which I participated, disagreements with national policies were clearly expressed, but the Fund's relationship with the member remained unbroken—there was always the future. Members of the Fund were not clients or customers of the Fund; they were part of the Fund family. The Fund staff worked for them. To embarrass a country was to embarrass the Fund. Every situation could be handled individually. General policies of the Fund acted as guidelines—for example, the amounts, terms, and purposes of financial assistance to a country—but if a member country did not qualify, no one needed to know but the country and, sometimes, the executive directors of the Fund. Leaks to the press were unforgivable sins. Discretion and flexibility were highly prized.

The new role of the Fund is very different. It is seen by many as polemical and political—and surely not quiet. Whereas the discretion of member countries was the counterpart to Fund secrecy, open criticism of the Fund by government officials is the counterpart to the new role of the Fund. By accepting the responsibility for judging country performance on behalf of the banks and, incidentally, keeping banks informed of country developments, the Fund became much more important in authority and influence. At the same time, as is so often true, this authority and power have inhibited its flexibility. Again, the process of relating bank restructuring to IMF programs with the borrowing countries involved worked reasonably well. However, the process, did not work to restore the creditworthiness of countries. Failures to implement IMF programs became highly publicized and further eroded confidence in the Fund in borrowing countries. An announcement that a country was undertaking to have an adjustment program agreed to by the Fund in order to make possible a debt restructuring was an obvious signal of trouble, not of overcoming troubles. Fund member countries became bargainers negotiating at arms length with the Fund, instead of troubled members of a family coming to the family hearth for help.

Thus, despite many Fund programs, the international debt crisis persisted, both on the individual country level and in general. The Fund used its resources with great deliberation and courage. It took the lead in international statesmanship, but it could not lead countries back to creditworthiness. Its lending criteria were keyed to improvements in balance of payments. To be effective in helping to end the international debt crisis, country programs would have to deal with growth, employment, income distribution, social equity, expectations of living standards, and so forth. In addition, the Fund would have to have programs that were regarded as politically and socially feasible and sustainable. The restoration of creditworthiness needed a developmental dimension, and the multilateral development banks were better placed to provide this need.

The debt crisis is by no means the only crucial preoccupation of the Fund. In its role as the actual manager of the international monetary system, other matters are of critical importance—business cycles, money supply management, U.S. dollar exchange rates with major currencies, interest rates, capital movements, and protectionism are all on the Fund's crowded agenda. These matters are subjects for commentary in other chapters of this book, and they are all worthy of separate detailed analyses.

9

Preconditions for the Restoration of Creditworthiness

Optimal and Minimal Conditions

The restoration of creditworthiness cannot await the achievement of optimal conditions, yet it is useful to identify them as goals or standards. These optimal conditions would be noninflationary—a world economy growing at a rate of, say, 4 percent to 5 percent per annum in real terms; international trade expanding more rapidly; currency stability; and savings increased and funneled into productive investments. The optimal conditions also include free and efficient private international capital flows, liberal international trading systems, adequate grantlike assistance to poor developing countries, effective economic management within developing countries, domestic investment compatible with available external capital inflows, efficient government administration, and an effective private sector.

All these conditions cannot be presumed to prevail in the foreseeable future. The world economy is likely to be growing slowly, with cyclical swings. Many developing countries will have strong inflation, with inadequate fiscal, monetary, and exchange rate policies. Industrial countries will have large budgetary deficits and high degrees of government intervention and ownership of enterprises, even if privitization has marked successes. The United States will be trying to cope with a two-layer economy—services and manufactures—in a way that will result in a growth rate that reduces unemployment and encourages savings and productive investment but does not succeed in doing so steadily. Protectionism in the United

States and elsewhere will be stronger. Currency instability, centered on the U.S. dollar, is likely to endure, although the overvaluation of the dollar is ceasing and may even give way to undervaluation. High real interest rates cannot be wished away, although nominal interest rates may well decline markedly because of expectations of lower rates of inflation than in the past. Expansion of international trade will continue to be hampered by exchange rates that are not able to serve the function of encouraging economies to expand on their focus on comparative advantages and consequent expanding international trade. Unrealistic commercial policies that continue to focus on bilateral balances—for example, the United States and Japan—are likely to continue, even though focusing on bilateral behavior is wrong because the world economy is highly integrated, international business is multinational, and the world economy is well served by the multilateral character of world trade and payments. Population explosion and rising expectations of improvements in living standards, combined with social and political conditions, will create a strong demand for expanding output and trade, but existing institutions are not likely to be able to transform this incipient demand into sufficient effective economic demand without rekindling inflationary expectations globally and strong inflation in many developing countries.

Therefore, the question arises of what the minimal or essential threshold conditions are for the return to creditworthiness. The starting points are the conditions in the borrowing countries. However inadequate or faulty the international financial system may be judged, the ability to lend by far outstrips the ability to borrow.

An essential prerequisite is a clear view by a borrowing country of the benefits it can derive from borrowing from private sources. Borrowing is often a reactive process. Lenders judge country risk and credit risk in light of their own institutional objectives and standards, especially their criteria and procedures for portfolio management. If they find that a country is risk acceptable, and if a requested credit meets their lending criteria, they than become seekers of acceptable risk assets. Their business is making profitable loans. At this point, the warning of caveat emptor becomes crucial. If governments and state enterprises are borrowers, their standards for usage of borrowed funds may not be carefully articulated or implemented. Financial terms may be judged by comparisons with other borrowers, instead of the economics of the usage of the borrowed funds.

Funds obtained at "bargain" costs at the time of borrowing may be judged attractive and irresistible. The market price for foreign funds does not, however, automatically result in efficient or economic usage by a particular borrowing firm or country. Usage must be analyzed, and returns must be compared with costs. If nothing else, borrowed funds are likely to be cheap by comparison with domestic funds or returns on investments, unless there are governmental ceilings on domestic interest rates. Because of their relative cheapness, their use may be attractive but not necessarily efficient economically.

Benefits from a loan must at least exceed costs. Costs must also be seen in terms of opportunity costs—that is, the use of borrowed funds for one purpose as against an other. Borrowing is not without limits. Borrowing for one purpose is likely to be at the expense of borrowing for some other purpose currently or in the future. Precise calculations of relative benefit/cost ratios are not practical, but the borrower can avoid serious mistakes by being conscious of this aspect when borrowing. Another aspect of opportunity cost is the impact of particular borrowings on other lenders. For example, if countries are seen to be borrowing for nonproductive purposes or for capital flight financing, other lenders may refrain from lending for productive purposes. Borrowers that borrow thoughtfully, carefully, and professionally will be preferred by lenders. They will find it easier both to maintain their creditworthiness and to restore it when it has been seriously damaged or destroyed.

Calculations of costs and benefits are difficult and complex, however simple the concept may seem. This is particularly true for governments, whether they are borrowing directly, from external sources or via state-owned enterprises, or indirectly and contingently as guarantors. Knowledge of the intent of lenders is imperfect; even knowledge of the entities that might be lenders is imperfect. Moreover, as loans are made for longer periods, future conditions are not predictable. They can be anticipated but not clearly foreseen. Governments are not profit-maximizing, but they compete for funds with entities that are profit-maximizing. The borrowing criteria of governments are very mixed. They have primary responsibility for orderly conditions in their countries, and political and social order overshadows financial criteria. Short-run governmental needs often dominate economic decisions. What seems to observers to be ignorance, stupidity, cupidity, and even corruption, finds its rationale in the process of government as it exists in the borrowing country. Governments eagerly latch on to such concepts as "shadow prices" and "social benefits" for reasons other than those of the economic analyst. These benefits cannot be calculated, even though numbers can be assigned to them for analytical purposes. They help governments convince themselves and others that they are borrowing rationally, from their viewpoints, for purposes and on terms that seem reasonable to them but cannot meet the calculus of financial analysis and criteria. The private lender is in a quandary.

The private lender cannot escape this quandary solely by using macroeconomic analysis of a borrowing country's domestic and international conditions, policies, and outlooks. Such analysis may well be necessary, however, for preliminary judgments on the ability of a country to generate foreign exchange to meet its international payments, but it is a far cry from judging the risks involved in particular lending operations. A judgment on the ability to muster foreign exchange for all international payments provides, at most, only the framework for judging whether payments for external debt will be made and, within that segment, whether particular loans will be serviced. An analogy can be seen in the servicing of debt to the official multilateral development banks and the International Monetary Fund. For various reasons, these institutions are generally accepted as preferred creditors—a brilliant stroke of financial management on the part of the original managers of these financial institutions. Because of their preferred position, even countries that need (or desire) to renegotiate or restructure their external debt with other official lenders, and often with private lenders, continue to consider payments due to the multilateral development banks and the IMF as not subject to lengthy postponements or restructuring. Indeed, when it is known that some borrowing countries are falling behind in servicing debts to these international lenders, the financial community regards the borrower as being in the most dire straits and the international institutions as faulty in their management.

The private lender is often reluctant to proceed beyond narrow macroeconomic analysis in judging country risk, even though failure to do so may lead to wrong decisions. In using macroeconomic analysis, the lender has the benefit of the outpourings of expert institutions, such as the IMF, and of many individuals well versed in macroeconomic analysis. The lender is confronted by an overwhelming supply of information and analyses. The difficulty, or limitation, is that these analyses are inadequate for the lender's purpose. The lender must judge the likelihood of specific actions, not economic trends alone. Governments can, and do, react very differently to macroeconomic conditions. History is some guide; the action of other governments offers clues; and logical reasoning is possible, even though basic assumptions may be flawed from the beginning. At the end of the analytical process, the lending decision remains to be made, despite the many uncertainties revealed by the analytic process. No line of action can be "proved" to be correct. Only time will tell. At this point, intuition, based on experience, comes to the fore; receptivity to such decisions becomes critically important. Some decision makers rely heavily on statistical concepts of probability that form the basis for actuarial principles, on the knowledge of what others are doing, and on judgments of how others concerned will react to particular decisions.

The awareness of this process is essential to the restoration of creditworthiness. Lenders will not restore creditworthiness because of macroeconomic analyses or the judgment of those making such analyses, even though decisions to renegotiate are greatly influenced by judgments on macroeconomic conditions and policies. The decision to lend is very different from the decision to renegotiate and restructure debt. Restructuring is made necessary by the inability of the borrower to service debt fully and promptly. The lender is confronted by poor choices. To help improve the lender's confidence that the restructured debt will be serviced (in the lender's view, restructured debt is similar to a new loan), the existence of an adjustment program approved by the IMF adds considerably to the comfort level. Moreover, such an agreement may well affect the magnitudes and terms of restructuring—that is, how much of the debt is to be restructured, grace periods, interest rates, and so forth. It might also affect the attitude of regulatory authorities in classifying the loans being restructured. A country whose economic management is being endorsed by the IMF in an agreed adjustment program that is part of a standby arrangement with the Fund is likely to receive a higher (more favorable) classification than a country whose economic management is not so certified. Nevertheless, when all is said and done, a restructured debt results from a nonperforming or potentially nonperforming asset; the bank is satisfied with something far from perfect.

A new loan decision can be made or not made; loan decisions are not automatic. The many factors entering into the decision go far beyond the macroeconomic analysis. The synthesis of these factors, at any time, is the job of management. Banks are eager to make loans with acceptable risks; they are also eager to avoid losses and inconveniences. The result is that new lending requires more favorable factors to be present than restructuring requires. The restoration of creditworthiness is the restoration of normal lending by a lending institution. Decisions to lend that are induced by pressures of an official agency are not indications of the restoration of creditworthiness. In reaching lending decisions that reflect restored creditworthiness, banks cannot be expected to forget their recent experiences in Latin America and Africa. Even if the economic conditions of a developing country in these regions were to meet normal lending criteria applicable to countries that have not lost their creditworthiness, banks may still not be willing to resume normal lending. If they increase lending, the loans are likely to be only for short maturities, for guaranteed transactions, or for very limited borrowers and purposes. This partial restoration may represent progress in the reestablishment of creditworthiness but not actual reestablishment. This is not a matter of semantics or fine shadings. A country or borrower that has established only partial creditworthiness can retrogress quickly as adverse factors arise. For example, it cannot expect to survive a recurrence of arrears in debt servicing or major political disorder. It will not survive otherwise acceptable levels of social and economic instability. In the future, Korea and Taiwan can experience adversities without losing their creditworthiness, even though they may not be any more able to cope with these adversities than Brazil, Mexico, or Argentina. Lenders do not insist that Korea and Taiwan have their economic management endorsed by the Fund, but they have insisted that Brazil, Mexico, and Argentina have such endorsement.

The restoration of creditworthiness must be assumed to take place in an environment of uncertainties and adversities, or it will not take place at all. The world environment—for example, interest rates and commodity prices—will probably not improve enough to make it easy for the borrowing developing countries to have their creditworthiness restored. Domestic conditions and policies in the creditor countries will continue indefinitely to generate uncertainties, and these uncertainties will be major obstacles to renewed voluntary lending by commercial banks and other private entities.

The restoration of creditworthiness requires the rebuilding of the shattered confidence of lenders despite adverse conditions in the borrowing countries and in the world economy. The alternative of waiting for favorable conditions is too likely to be frustrated by adverse changes within the borrowing countries and within the world economy. If the credit restoration could take place more quickly, the ability of developing countries and the world economy, in general, to deal with adversities would be greatly enhanced. Indeed, a number of foreseeable difficulties could probably be avoided.

Thus, the preconditions for restoring creditworthiness cannot be simply stated. They can be made simple only by ignoring realities and uncertainties. Policy advocacy tends to run in fads and fashions. At present, austerity, as a fashionable recipe, is giving way to growth. In earlier years, growth gave way to austerity. Something else might be fashionable in the future. Government regulation and ownership are giving way to deregulation and privatization. In earlier years, market philosophies gave way to planning. In any event, countries that have lost their creditworthiness are not likely to be able to restore their creditworthiness by their own actions and market responses to such policies. Without policies that carry conviction for lenders, restoration is not feasible; in addition, however, other factors will have to be present. The following section outlines measures that could be taken to overcome the lenders' aversion to lending to Latin American countries and some countries in Africa and, thus, to restore creditworthiness.

The Search for Solutions

In economic policy making, as in other areas, it is tempting to prescribe remedies or solutions to problems that reflect the philosophical or ideological views of the authors. Solutions that seem logically right, or that conform to basic theories of societies and economies, are easy to construct. Premises are laid down by the solution designer regarding what is right or wrong; what should happen; and how it can be made to happen. Such premises do not, however, give policy solutions to complicated problems. They often make clear the assumptions on which calculations are made, but these assumptions are frequently beyond the ability of policymakers, commentators, or anyone else to evaluate. Unfortunately, what the expert considers a useful simulation to demonstrate the importance of certain factors and their interrelations often is used as a forecast of what will happen. It is in the world press that public policy alternatives are described, debated, and eventually decided.

To avoid such pitfalls, and to help readers reach their own conclusions on what can be done to avoid the repetition of international financial crises, it would be useful to recapitulate, very briefly, the causes and nature of these crises. In this way, my assumptions will become clear and can be evaluated. My proposals or conclusions for "solutions" rest on these assumptions.

The international debt crisis resulted from a combination of factors that are present in most country cases, though with differing weights. The factor that should be mentioned first was the continuous need of borrowing countries to finance a substantial net inflow of resources. The second factor was the inability of many countries to find sources of financing that matched their usage—largely, financing of long-term, large public sector projects with long gestation periods. Such financing was usually available on terms that were not consistent with the borrowers' low per capita income. The industrial countries enlarged their official assistance, but still in inadequate amounts by this standard. Given the need for external resources and the limited sources of concessional finance, countries turned to commercial sources of finance. Among possible external commercial sources of finance, institutional investors such as insurance companies and pension funds, with few exceptions, regarded developing country borrowers and entities within these countries as not creditworthy for medium-or long-term borrowing on fixed interest terms. Equity investors were also shy, except in particular cases that were attractive to investors and that totaled only relatively small magnitudes. Official export credit insurance agencies facilitated some lending by commercial sources when it was related to export from the credit-extending countries; this lending was significant but, again, small in relation to the total needs of many developing countries. Under these circumstances, commercial banks were sought to finance external deficits of relatively poor countries on a noninsured or nonguaranteed basis. Their financial terms reflected market conditions. The maturities usually available were short in relation to usage or to the longer-run payment prospects of the borrower. Whatever use was made of a borrowed loan, and however the borrower was inclined to service its debts, the overall debt servicing ability of the borrowing country depended on its ability to obtain a net inflow of funds from abroad. This net inflow was likely to be in the form of debt, but the country could expect to be able to borrow more. The supply of commercial funds was adequate, and a borrowing country could retain its creditworthiness by its own management.

The lending banks accepted the so-called transfer risk—that is, the possible occurrences of foreign exchange shortages, whatever the reasons, which would make it difficult, if not virtually impossible, for a borrowing country to provide the foreign exchange needed to service external debt fully and promptly. Collateral was usually not required from governments or their entities—being, in any case, hard to collect, even if available. Central banks, as guarantors of loans by their national entities, were held in high esteem by lenders, but not as eliminating the transfer risk.

Banks took these risks with their eyes wide open. They relied on their country assessments to help evaluate the risks of lending to foreign countries, on their diversification of loans to countries to avoid dangerous concentration of risk assets, and on their management systems to assure implementation of their lending policies. Reserves were increased to meet contingencies. Capital/ asset ratios, however, became more highly leveraged as banks expanded their domestic and international lending more rapidly than they increased capital. Capital was not seen as a decisive influence on the ability of a bank to borrow on acceptable terms from a wide variety of sources, including institutional investors as well as other banks. Banks did not assume that they would be bailed out by their own national monetary institutions, or by any international institutions. Banks had to avoid situations that could bring their own financial standing into question. Private lenders were their lenders of last resort, not the official financial authorities.

The banks misjudged the 1980s; they got into more trouble than they had expected. Many more borrowing countries than expected were simultaneously found to be in serious external financial difficulties—unable to service their external debt to official and private lenders. A major decisive contributing cause was the massive withdrawal of banks from lending to developing countries in trouble, especially in the early 1980s. Banks had expected that borrowing nations would try to keep their creditworthiness and avoid defaults, which they did. Banks had recognized that during business cycle downturns, borrowers often suffered balance-of-payments deterioration. They did not expect, however, that this deterioration would be as widespread, as large, and as persistent as it was. They did not expect that private lenders would simultaneously stop new incremental lending to such countries for a number of years. Short-term withdrawals by individual private banks from lending to developing countries could be managed; wholesale withdrawals, lasting years, created unmanageable conditions.

These events have resulted in very different evaluations of past lending and borrowing. Strong borrowers came to be seen as over-borrowed. Large-scale lending by private banks came to be seen as overlending. Country risk analysis was no longer seen as providing the confidence needed for decision making. Bank superiors became unsure of their own methods. Developing countries came to be regarded prima facie as poor risks, and most as unacceptable risks. Official lenders also began to reflect concerns about their loans. Anticyclical lenders, such as the IMF, could function well but were much too small to substitute for the mass withdrawal of other lenders. Banks did not experience defaults, but they did experience loss of income as parts of their loan portfolio were classified as not performing as required. At the same time, bank earnings were being adversely affected by losses from domestic loans, especially in the oil and farming industries. Losses in the oil industries were seen as understandable—everyone had been wrong in judging the demand for oil and the continuing strength of the OPEC cartel, though many recognized the weaknesses of such cartels. Similarly, poor loan experience in other domestic industries, including agriculture, was regarded as understandable. Deregulation of banking in the United States had further increased the vulnerability of large parts of the banking industry—a worrisome, but understandable development. The remedies in such cases were to work with troubled borrowers, *not* to stop lending to an industry in general or even to troubled firms.

In sharp contrast, difficulties in international banking have been seen as evidence of ignorance, stupidity, or, at best, poor management. The response has been that extreme caution in lending has become equivalent to wise and prudent management. Crisis management became the order of the day for troubled countries, and debt restructuring became a sign of crisis. Adjustment programs with the IMF and negotiations with lenders for restructuring became front-page news in the world press.

Under these conditions, the focus shifted from how to make the borrowing country creditworthy—now deemed a fruitless effort—to how to minimize losses from past lending, reduce reliance on revenues from such lending, switch to bank activities not involving risk to lenders, keep down new lending to troubled countries when some new lending became inevitable as part of an IMF adjustment program, ensure that other banks shared the burden of new lending (lending normally is not a burden to a bank but rather a profit-making opportunity), maximize borrowing from official international institutions such as the IMF and World Bank, and shift responsibility for country risk assessments from the private lender to the international institutions.

"Solutions" to existing balance-of-payments difficulties became "solutions" to the crises—that is, reduce external deficits and, thus, the need to borrow; reduce the amounts of debt servicing obligations; buy time by postponing debt servicing obligations to the more distant future; reduce lending on a voluntary basis; reduce reliance on banks' own risk management systems; be skeptical of initiatives that try to find ways and means for banks to help finance the external deficits of developing countries; and welcome anything that helps borrowers paying interest on their debts.

These "solutions" are not really solutions, because they do not deal with the sources of the external payments difficulties. At best, they buy time. They have helped avoid defaults and more destructive developments, so, in a sense, they have provided breathing time. These are all positive effects, but only at the cost of the withdrawal of the largest and most efficient source of external capital for the developing countries—namely, the commercial banking system.

Thus, my emphasis in trying to find solutions is on how to create conditions in which private banks can again play a major role in providing external finance to developing countries and to indicate that other sources of finance must be available in adequate amounts and on a timely basis to achieve this end. Negativism can be only a temporary answer.

In the solutions given here, I seek, first, mechanisms that will enable developing countries to continue development during periods of unfavorable events abroad that hurt the developing economies. This is done by limiting their adjustments to those required by the unfavorable changes in the external environment but avoiding the further retrenchments made necessary by the withdrawal of external lenders that, with certain feasible changes, can continue to remain lenders during such periods. Thus, the focus is on what can be done to enable such lenders to continue to be lenders when adverse external conditions hit otherwise creditworthy borrowers. With this focus, we will try to stay on the track that the institutions involved can ride, given their fundamental purposes and structures. First of all—what can the borrowing nations do?

What the Borrowing Countries Must Do

Borrowing countries must pursue the policies and practices necessary to obtain external finance. Defining the need for external credit and official assistance and developing policies to instill confidence are ultimately the job of the borrowing country itself. Outsiders can make judgments, but they cannot relieve the country of this key responsibility. Once the need for financial assistance has been defined, the design of supporting policies can follow. However, the domestic policy choices cannot be firmly identified until the external alternatives are known. Borrowing governments must be aware of the likely response of creditors to their domestic policy packages. External sources of credit normally differ in their lending criteria. They may differ, for example, as to what constitutes good economic management. This iterative process goes on today mostly via the IMF, the multilateral development banks, and the collective action of the commercial banks. It has been largely confined, however, to the countries that require renegotiation of their external debts; thus, it is not an adequate guide for judging what is acceptable economic management for obtaining private credit on a voluntary basis.

It cannot be overemphasized, in light of what others are saying and writing, that what is required to solve the immediate debt problem does not necessarily include a large reduction in external debts. Obviously, creditor governments could decide to forgive past loans; this has happened at times. This would reduce the debt and its servicing, and the balance of payments of the borrowing countries would then be easier to manage. In this sense, debt forgiveness can be helpful, but it is not essential. It is a form of foreign assistance, and much depends on whether it becomes a substitute for other forms of assistance. It is not automatically additive. I have long advocated that official loans extended by creditor governments that should have been grants in the first place could well be forgiven, even if that action is not essential for establishing creditworthiness.

Reducing debt servicing by lengthening maturities or postponing interest payments will help temporarily but is also not essential and, by itself, will not restore creditworthiness. Countries with relatively large external debts and high debt servicing obligations may well recapture their external creditworthiness sooner than countries with smaller debts and relatively smaller debt services.

Reductions of outstanding indebtedness are not permanent solutions. The Marshall Plan provided solutions to Europe's reconstruction, not because it provided grants and avoided debt, though that was helpful, but because the countries seized the occasion to improve their productive and trading capacities. Today, Europe would have little difficulty in servicing Marshall Plan aid if it were debt. However, it would not have achieved this capability if the focus had been the grant nature of the financial assistance rather than the economic management of the European countries. The Organization of European Economic Cooperation (OEEC)—the precursor of the OECD—and the European Payments Union, both outgrowths of the Marshall Plan, did more to make European countries creditworthy than the grant aspect of Marshall Plan aid. They did so by their influence on monetary policy, exchange rate stability, and the freeing of intra-European payments and trade, which, in turn, encouraged productive investment and promoted high levels of employment and output.

The domestic policies necessary to restore creditworthiness involve not the fundamental structures of the social, economic, and political systems of a country but, rather, the structure of its management. All kinds of systems can meet the lending criteria of private sources. In this sense, competitive international bank lending has been nonideological. Moreover, the banks have not had to limit their overseas lending to firms that are not competitive with firms in their own countries. In effect, they can and do finance competitors of domestic firms. Now and then, criticisms of such bank activities are voiced, but governments have not interdicted them. Intervention usually takes the form of borrowing countries' limiting foreign banks' activities in order to help their own domestic financial firms.

All countries, even those with the lowest per capita incomes, can become creditworthy for private or commercial bank credit. On a somewhat less fundamental level, experience has shown that countries with relatively large external debts and debt servicing, however measured, and countries that have renegotiated their external debts, even repeatedly (such as Turkey recently and a number of Latin

American countries during the past 30 years), can regain their creditworthiness.

Experience helps us judge the conditions required to restore or maintain creditworthiness. It is tempting to give these conditions an order of weight or importance, but this would be artificial, as their importance varies among countries and over time. Moreover, the significance of any single factor is influenced by the presence of others; one factor alone rarely makes all the difference—not counting as factors actions that, in effect, transfer the risk from the borrowing country to another entity or country, such as an efficient export credit agency in a AAA-rated country or the presence of a major multilateral firm or bank offering similar guarantees.

In the political arena, the important factors for creditworthiness are stability, continuity, and predictability; law and order; efficiency in government; fair and effective judicial systems; the absence of widespread corruption; a record of respect for past and present international commitments; fair treatment of foreigners and foreign entities; and reasonably peaceful and secure international relations. A number of developing countries do not have governments and international relations that meet these criteria, especially those calling for political stability. Countries do not have to meet all of these criteria, and no single criterion can be regarded as the sine qua non— any one of them can be decisive at one time or other.

Different lenders respond differently to these factors, but all will want the sum of pluses and minuses to add to a plus in the judgment of the lender. Sources of information are manifold: governments, international agencies, private firms, academic institutions and not-for-profit institutes, news media, individuals, and officers of the lending institutions. Borrowing countries, as well as lenders, must monitor these sources and must try to know which ones, at any given time, are being used by their principal lenders. It is little comfort for a would-be borrower to point to sources giving views favorable to the country if lenders are relying on information or judgments provided by other, less flattering sources. Since much of the experience and wisdom that is gained is not quantifiable, creditworthiness based on it may be superficially regarded as intuitive and subjective. It is much more, of course, but financing decisions based on analyses that are quantifiable are often considered more objective and more authoritative, even though they often are not.

Political instability may well be unavoidable in some countries.

In those cases, the historical record of how successive governments have met international obligations becomes very important. Italy is an example of a country that has had chronic political instability but is able to retain its creditworthiness because successive governments have honored their obligations. It is a fair reading of experience that failure to meet international obligations in nonfinancial matters will weaken a borrower's standing financially, though the importance given to this factor by individual lenders will vary greatly from one to the other. The borrowing countries must try to have a favorable reputation with lenders. Adverse opinions can be changed, but not if borrowers are ostrich-like, avoiding disagreeable (and often unfair) views. Correcting misunderstandings can be laborious and time-consuming, but the rewards are great. Political leaders—such as heads of state, ministers of finance, and governors of central banks—are usually best positioned to perform this task. Their appearances before banking and related audiences and one-on-one calls on major lenders can be highly worthwhile, giving their audiences an opportunity to judge the quality of the countries' political management and managers. Countries are rarely so highly regarded in financial circles that the quality of their management is taken for granted; thus, such educational efforts are necessary.

As noted elsewhere, Mexico has been highly regarded for its stability, continuity, and predictability, as are other governments of developing countries—for example, Korea, Singapore, Thailand, Indonesia, Tunisia, and Morocco. Brazil, Chile, and Peru are examples of countries that once had reputations for political stability, continuity, and predictability but lost them in the early 1980s, together with their external creditworthiness. To restore creditworthiness lost because of political conditions, it is not necessary to restore previous political conditions. However, until the country is again politically stable and remains so long enough that it seems likely to continue, the road back to creditworthiness can be difficult, if not impossible. On the other hand, countries that have had good economic and political management in the past can restore their good reputations relatively quickly. The world's standards are not very strict; most governments qualify in practice.

Countries such as Bolivia, with its record of very frequent changes in government (measured in months, not years), or countries that seem to be very vulnerable in this regard or vulnerable to international events, such as Iraq and Iran, will find the unfavorable assessments of their countries' political management very hard to change. Turkey, however, has shown that a country with an unfavorable political record in the judgment of lenders can change such assessments after a few years of improved political conditions. The political change in Turkey was significant for international lending not because it was a change from right to left or from left to right, from civilian to military or vice versa, but rather because because the change was from domestic insecurity, disorder,and instability to security, order, and stability.

The criteria for satisfactory economic management are often less subtle and less dramatic than those for social and political stability. They are often equally difficult to achieve, even though in this area, as in the political area, world standards are not severe. Objective economic realities are intermingled with ideologies, expectations of groups and individuals, cultural factors such as national pride and value systems, and institutional policies and practices. Judgments on governments are of major importance in assessing economic performance, because no country leaves economic management entirely to markets. Governments, noneconomic institutions such as churches, and economic institutions such as trade associations and trade unions strongly influence private and public economic decision making. Even "technical" economic issues—such as monetary policies and practices affecting the volume of credit and interest rates, foreign exchange rates, selection of public investments, subsidization, protection, domestic competition, promotion of exports, management of the foreign exchange budget, and the servicing of international debt—are highly politicized in many societies. Even the actions of "technocrats" in top governmental management positions are in fact those of political leaders with economic training making economic policy decisions. Such difficult issues as the population explosion, migrations to cities, massive unemployment, dependency on food imports, and inadequate human development do not remain technical issues because the minister in question has a Ph.D. in economics, a masters degree in business administration, or an engineering degree.

In these complicated mixtures, what do lenders usually look for in economic and financial management? The answer varies and changes, but almost always, particular attention is given to exchange rates, inflation, treatment of the private business sector, efficiency and honesty in public administration, management of public and private enterprises, management of the foreign exchange budget, external financial position, and the economy's vulnerability to adversity in the world economy. Closely related to these are fiscal and credit policies, consumption subsidies, wage policy, the banking system, taxation, and relations between government and productive enterprises. Historical experience weighs heavily in the final judgment.

In judging country risk, many efforts are made to be precise about these factors, but they all fail. The decisions made on creditworthiness do not follow automatically from quantitative analyses, though simple criteria and guidelines are eagerly sought. Judgments provide the crucial links. The ability to make such judgments and self-confidence in the judgments differ and change even within the same lending institution.

Nevertheless, the process of good economic management is not mysterious to judge. Critical factors are usually quite visible. There may be an overvalued exchange rate, excessive budget deficits financed by monetary expansion, all-embracing income indexation, inefficient publicly owned enterprises clobbering the budget, excessive protectionism, inefficient and corrupt government administrators, or inadequate attention to export capability. A government that is seen as willing and able to deal with a number of the causes of its difficulties will get high marks for economic management, even if the policy measures it chooses are not as far-reaching or comprehensive as many would advocate. The government can get high grades even if it does not deal with such structural, fundamental issues as rural rehabilitation, migration, urbanization, population control, education, and health. Decision makers in business cannot be omniscient or perfectionist. Safety in making decisions comes from awareness of limitations and avoidance of wishful thinking. In lenders' judgments of performance, social indicators give way to economic indicators, and short- and medium-term gains are usually more important than long-term gains. Analysts often speak of the structural characteristics and long-term trends in a borrowing nation, and long-term investors may well give weight to such factors, but they are not likely to be of decisive, immediate importance in commercial bank lending or its equivalent.

A country can meet the economic criteria for creditworthiness while continuing to have major economic difficulties. However, current financial practices, such as avoiding repudiation of debt and fulfilling contractual debt servicing obligations, can be of decisive importance. The recapture of lost creditworthiness does not require the elimination of structural maladjustments or weaknesses unless they are causing current difficulties or generating continuous weaknesses. For example, the influence of certain groups in society may create major obstacles to having realistic exchange rates, reducing fiscal deficits, or overcoming rapid inflation. If so, it may prove necessary to deal with these fundamental structures, but if countries find a way to have realistic exchange rates despite these structures, structural change becomes much less important for creditworthiness. The Soviet Union and China have structural problems in agriculture, but they are nevertheless creditworthy because they honor their international financial obligations. Often, in the eagerness to obtain structural changes for other reasons, such changes are regarded as essential for virtually all purposes. The achievement of creditworthiness is not so demanding.

To say this is not to belittle the difficulties in making the policy changes needed to restore creditworthiness. Adopting and keeping realistic exchange rates, reducing public sector deficits, introducing more realistic pricing policies, lowering rates of inflation, restraining increases in real wages that make firms uncompetitive in domestic and foreign markets, renegotiating external debts, welcoming more foreign capital, and privatizing public sector entities are all difficult tasks. Structural features of societies may militate against such changes. Such changes take considerable time, and the benefits are often long delayed. However, governments often, in effect, exist in the short run. The fact that the problems they face are inherited may be of little practical significance for public opinion. Distrust, frustration, anger, and suspicion tend to make governments seek scapegoats and sacrifice them, instead of making fundamental corrections in policies and practices.

Making needed economic adjustments is painful for any nation. Outsiders become impatient with delays that often confirm their already low opinions of the management of a country. It is not a matter of tolerance, or equity, or even knowledge. To know that a country is in difficulties is easy. It is harder to anticipate such difficulties before they become visible, and it is much harder to know how to deal with these difficulties effectively without destabilizing the society and, in the process, losing the consensus needed to govern. Outside institutions such as the IMF can try to help, but to succeed, the IMF has to be seen as an "insider" as well as an "outsider"—a role not easy to achieve in a supercharged, emotional situation that requires difficult economic adjustments. This is particularly true in most developing countries, where the short-run need to diminish balance-of-payments deficits by restraining growth and reducing imports clashes with the need to maintain growth rates essential for social stability and order.

Governments must take remedial steps to restore creditworthiness, but they need not take all steps that can be identified. They must take sufficient steps to gain the confidence of outside lenders that the government and the country are overcoming the conditions that led to the loss of creditworthiness. For this reason, a decisive change in foreign exchange policy, together with more efficient fiscal management and encouragement to the private sector, may restore creditworthiness even though other management problems that have been identified are left unsolved. The aim is the restoration of creditworthiness, not necessarily profound, enduring social or political change. Economic and financial policies that are removed from social issues may offer much more chance of success. A budget that is under better control may still finance subsidization of consumption. Some investments in relatively low-priority, postponable public investments, a considerable amount of administrative waste, and inefficient and inadequate taxation of some groups are not necessarily incompatible with creditworthiness.

The aim is not an optimum-run economy by professional standards but a country sufficiently well run to assume more external debt and to be able to maintain its creditworthiness during the various phases of the business cycle, often with the help of countercyclical lenders such as the IMF. The French expression that the best is the enemy of the good is often applicable in matters of public policy. Perhaps it should also be emphasized that in choosing the combination of public policies needed to restore creditworthiness, governments can choose policies that defend employment and growth. Austerity does not necessarily mean sacrificing growth to balance-of-payments needs. Rather, it means choosing from among the various uses of national output those that combine to improve the balance of payments. This can be done by increasing investment and output in foreign exchange earning activities such as exports and tourism. This includes foreign exchange policies that discourage capital flight and even cause flight capital to return. Measures to induce more private capital inflows are in this category; so are measures to induce more domestic savings. Development can be defended during periods of balance-of-payments adjustment, but it takes strong governments, as well as wise ones, to achieve this aim, because it usually requires changes or reductions in consumption, if nothing else. Food and shelter can become explosive social and political issues, as can jobs and incomes.

The Role of the International Monetary Fund

The major role in reestablishing creditworthiness is necessarily performed by the borrowing countries. The role of the commercial lenders will be examined after some discussion of the roles of the IMF and the multilateral development banks. The focal point here is the reestablishment of creditworthiness with private lenders. Creditworthiness with official lenders is a political decision. It may have economic content—for example, the conditionality of the IMF or the structural adjustment loans of the World Bank—but in the final analysis, lending governments need not be guided by economic criteria, and they often are not.

Debt crisis management in 1981–84 gave a central role to the IMF. As noted earlier, the IMF had long been involved in debt crises involving official creditors and, in the 1970s, had played a similar role in debt crises involving private creditors.

To recapitulate briefly, the IMF is the only major international financial institution whose mandate is to assist, with its own resources, countries suffering from the adverse effects of business cyclical downturns. The IMF maintains a pool of resources through contributions (called quotas) from its members and by borrowing from governments of member countries. The IMF's loans (called purchases or drawings) to its member countries are expected to be short- and medium-term in maturity. Interest rates (called charges) are market-related but somewhat concessional. Outstanding repayment obligations (called repurchases) are not called debt but, in effect, are the equivalent of external debt. Unlike the multilateral development banks, which finance much of their lending by their own borrowings from private markets, the IMF is not a conduit between private capital markets and borrowers. Rather, it is a conduit between or among governments and central banks of countries. It is thus more purely governmental than the multilateral development banks.

The Fund is not guided in its financial operations by the lending criteria of commercial banks or other private lenders. Instead, its lending criteria, or conditionality, reflects the views on economic management of countries acting collectively as members of the International Monetary Fund. Its lending criteria include limits on the magnitudes of drawings related to countries' quotas; the terms of its standby arrangements with countries, which contain the Fund's policy conditions in the form of a letter of intent to the managing director of the IMF, usually from the country's minister of finance; and the financial terms, such as the repurchase period, which is equivalent to the maturity of a loan. These conditions and terms are negotiated by the Fund staff with the country that wishes to have a standby arrangement with the Fund—the equivalent to a line of credit—but they are discussed and finally approved by the executive directors of the Fund, sitting as a board of directors. The managing director of the Fund is also the chairman of the board of executive directors. The board is in continuous session at the Fund headquarters in Washington and usually meets several times per week.

Country conditions are examined and discussed in detail—frequently in connection with a proposed standby arrangement with a member. General policies are framed by the board on recommendations or proposals made by the staff. The Fund considers countries on a country-by-country basis but within the framework of carefully formulated and considered general policies covering such issues as exchange rate surveillance; relations with commercial banks as well as other official institutions; availability of Fund resources for certain purposes, such as offsetting loss of foreign exchange earnings due to declines in export earnings; repayment periods; interest rates; borrowings from member countries; recommendations to member countries on increases in Fund resources; and issues of special drawing rights. The Fund's activities and resulting influence are like an iceberg, as most of its activities are not visible to the public. The Fund must be concerned about protecting the revolving character of its pool of funds, but governments, acting together within the IMF's policies, practices, and mechanisms, decide what is acceptable. The governments have often acted through the IMF's executive board to change the IMF's conditionality, to add to the IMF's resources, or to extend loans to the IMF.

An essential part of the measures needed to restore creditworthiness could be a successful, mutually satisfactory debt renegotiation (as discussed elsewhere in this book) when this is deemed necessary and is agreed among the lending partners concerned. So long as the need remains for the country to renegotiate debt, the IMF is now virtually automatically involved in a key way because of the banks' insistence on prior approval by the IMF of an economic and financial adjustment program, the implementation of which is often supported by the provision of IMF financial and technical assistance, phased over time to enable monitoring by the Fund.

The IMF's role, however, is basically flexible. In recent years, it has broadened beyond activities with borrowing members to include providing information on countries to private lenders, giving opinions on terms of private debt renegotiation, and otherwise counseling lenders and even giving leads on the need for private banks to provide incremental (new) loans to borrowers to help adjustment programs succeed. An interesting and illuminating example of Fund influence was the joint statement by the managing director of the Fund and the president of the World Bank that private banks should support the initiative of the United States—commonly referred to as the Baker proposal—to help ease the debt problems in the member countries of the Fund and the World Bank. United States Treasury Secretary Baker was looking to the Fund and the World Bank to help muster support for a U.S. Government proposal!

The awareness by debtors that the IMF influences their bank creditors, including the availability of new funds, greatly enhances the influence of the IMF. This influence has been enhanced further by the willingness of creditor banks to delay debt renegotiations, interrupt them, or even run the risk of their collapse because of difficulties between the IMF and its borrowing member in reaching agreement on IMF conditions necessary for the IMF to endorse the country's proposed policies and practices or because of countries' failure to implement agreed policies. Recent cases of this sort have included, at times, Argentina, Brazil, Mexico, and Peru.

The IMF has a decisive role in the reestablishment of creditworthiness by helping a country restore a manageable balance of payments. If this is achieved and sustained, it can take the country a long way toward the reestablishment of external creditworthiness. Drastic reductions in imports resulting from monetary, fiscal, and economic policies—often labeled austerity measures—combined with exchange rate changes, can reduce deficits in balance of payments. Similar results can be obtained from government administrative restrictions on trade and payments. Such measures may be eased by the availability of stockpiles of imported goods and, of course, by the availability of external financing. With improvements in the balance of payments, more foreign exchange becomes available for other items in the balance of payments, including debt servicing. However, the achievement of a satisfactory balance-of-payments position goes well beyond reducing external deficits to the level of then-available financing. It involves adopting policies that can be sustained and restoring the growing economy needed to deal with the troubled economic and social conditions in a country, while maintaining political stability. Moreover, this has to be accomplished within the framework of the country's chosen political and economic systems. The achievement of a more manageable balance-of-payments position does not automatically create the preconditions for growth. Developmental growth policies must be integrated with monetary policies—a deep conviction of mine since the 1960s. If they are not, the adjustment program is likely to fail. If this integration is achieved, the IMF-supported program will greatly assist the country in restoring its creditworthiness.

Lenders will wish to be able to conclude that the improvements in country conditions are not temporary in that the policies cannot be sustained, or that the continuation of policies will not seriously damage the longer-run viability of the economy and will provide employment, expand and diversify exports, and reduce inflationary pressures. If these changes do not materialize, the improvements in the balance of payments are likely to prove temporary, as evidenced repeatedly in many countries in the past 30 years.

The IMF has long appreciated that restoring desired balance-of-payments conditions may well take years. It has adapted its own lending policies to this need in its Extended Fund Facility, which provides "extended arrangements" under which a country is given IMF financial assistance for an adjustment effort that is planned to take three years. Under this approach, the member country, the IMF, and others concerned, such as the private banks, have more reason to expect that the IMF's active relationship will last long enough to restore a tolerable balance-of-payments position without policies that result in unsustainable drastic reductions in growth.

A country's use of an annual economic and financial adjustment program runs the risk that the country's adjustment effort could seem unsuccessful because desired improvements in the country's outlook could not be achieved in the time frame of just one year. When additional programs must be agreed upon, questions may again be raised about the ability of the country to restore its creditworthiness, thereby discouraging commercial lenders from voluntary lending. Three-year lending arrangements with the IMF still require semiannual (or more frequent) reviews of the conditions and policies of the borrowing member, but such reviews are not likely to be mistaken for a sign of trouble in the debtor country. These extended arrangements, or longer arrangements, are less likely than shorter-run programs to be causes of political and social disturbances, as they might permit more gradual introduction of required austerity measures.

There could conceivably be a virtual requirement in all debt restructuring exercises that aim at the restoration of creditworthiness for the borrowing country to have an arrangement with the IMF under its Extended Fund Facility or an equivalent arrangement with a longer time horizon. This would not mean that the country could neglect the implementation of IMF conditionality. However it would mean recognition that balance-of-payments adjustments usually take longer than a few years. Indeed, if the causes of problems in a country are not monetary or cyclical, the adjustments may well take much more than three years. Not leaving enough time to succeed is a frequent cause of failure. The appeal of quick success must be tempered by the potential cost of early failure.

Debt rescheduling with consolidation periods of 5 to 10 years and maturities over 10 years could facilitate debt restructuring. It could reduce the need for repeated reschedulings and could give lenders enough comfort to lengthen their leash on debtors. The earlier, short-leash approach has been extended, because the earlier practice of rescheduling payments over a relatively short period created repeated crises, tensions, and ill will. It repeatedly led to the reopening of political decisions that were difficult to agree on and implement, thereby at least postponing the restoration of creditworthiness. Long-term arrangements—supported by IMF lending, if needed—can help restore international confidence in the borrowing country, though it will not restore creditworthiness.

In the case of developing countries that have suffered a loss of creditworthiness, the IMF role has become well defined, but the Fund's role vis-à-vis other developing countries can probably be strengthened. A present shortcoming in the system, from the viewpoint of maintaining the creditworthiness of countries now deemed creditworthy, is that the Fund's views of a country's balance-of-payments position, management, and outlook are not known to the world. Indeed, it can be argued that it should not be known. In addition to greatly handicapping the ability of the Fund to advise and influence governments if its views were publicized, there is the problem that Fund fears and concerns, intended to help avoid difficulties, could precipitate such difficulties by being publicized. Fund endorsement of programs of countries in difficulties is not a prediction that the difficulties will be overcome; rather, it is an indication that the policies the country proposed to follow will, if implemented, have a strong likelihood of meeting agreed targets of improvement. Similar statements could be made about countries that are not in difficulties. The risk comes when the Fund believes that the country is heading for troubles unless external conditions change or domestic policies are significantly altered. Even if the concerns are expressed only implicitly, by what is not said, the effects could be harmful to the country and the Fund.

The answers may be found in the fact, translated into assurance, that the Fund can influence its member countries to follow policies designed to keep their exchange rates realistic and their balance of payments manageable. This assurance does not yet exist. If it continues not to exist, the maintenance of creditworthiness will be much more difficult. An alternative approach is to assure availability of financial resources to "rescue" countries that slide into balance-of-payments difficulties before they lose their creditworthiness. Existing mechanisms are not adequate. Until they are, or until the Fund strengthens its authority, creditworthiness will be vulnerable to drastic and, at times, quick loss. These thoughts form the basis for reforms in the financial system that are recommended in later chapters. The following discussion expands on the role of the Fund in preventing loss of creditworthiness.

To analyze what the IMF can do to keep countries from losing their creditworthiness is, in effect, to analyze everything the IMF does. In a well-run international monetary system, very few countries would lose their creditworthiness. Nevertheless, the question can usefully be asked what the IMF could do to prevent a recurrence of the 1981–86 debt crisis. It is clearly the obligation of the IMF to do everything it can to help members achieve the purposes of the IMF in ways compatible with their international obligations under the IMF's articles of agreement.

The IMF exists to help each member country achieve and maintain domestic prosperity without doing so at the expense of other members. The IMF agreement does not prescribe what countries should do to achieve the desired prosperity or how they should manage their balance of payments, so long as their actions are not contrary to the IMF Agreement. IMF member countries are obligated to avoid both exchange rate practices that are inequitable to other countries and use of restrictions on international trade and payments for current transactions. The IMF cannot be satisfied with the adoption of policies that prolong recessions or constrain international trade. There may well be intense pressure for such practices in some countries, or they may simply seem unavoidable, but their actual use reflects weaknesses in international monetary arrangements. The prolonged world recession of 1980–83 was an example of a malfunctioning monetary system that should have operated to avoid high levels of unemployment and slow growth in the industrial countries and to avoid intense austerity in developing countries. The roots of these conditions, especially the toleration of decades of global inflation, are found in earlier years. The situation was exacerbated by inadequate authority to avoid unrealistic exchange rates and by the lack of adequate financial resources in developing countries.

During the 1981–86 period, the IMF has found itself in a central role in the management of international financial crises. It has worked with available resources and within the policy framework agreed upon by its members. Its actions have tended to reduce the severity of adjustment; to this extent, the Fund's activities have been in line with its purpose of defending world prosperity. It facilitated the process of widespread debt rescheduling. Without such rescheduling and IMF assistance, borrowing countries might have introduced even more deflationary domestic policies and even more restrictive payments practices than they actually did. The weaknesses of the international monetary system were most manifest in the experiences of many of the developing countries. For them, loss of creditworthiness meant external liquidity crises. Their international monetary reserves were not enough to provide external liquidity to offset the consequences of the loss of external creditworthiness. Indeed, this condition hastened the loss of creditworthiness and deepened the liquidity crisis experienced in Latin America and elsewhere.

Illiquidity means lack of cash or near-cash reserves to meet international obligations. Bank loans create liquidity by creating deposits that provide the borrower with needed means of payments; bank loans in foreign currencies create the needed means of payments in foreign exchange. Without such loans, countries have to use their cash or near-cash reserves in foreign exchange to meet obligations. A country with such reserves amounting to a few months' imports is in reasonably good condition. However, when countries are perceived to be entering into balance-of-payments difficulties and loans are not forthcoming, while obligated payments continue to need to be met, reserves fall quickly. Soon—usually very soon—capital flight occurs as people perceive that the country will soon have to devalue its exchange rate, restrict external payments for goods and services, or restrict outflows of funds into foreign countries. What, under normal circumstances, would be a comfortable margin of international reserves, quickly begins to disappear at an ever more rapid rate. Illiquidity is an intolerable state for a country. No country can conduct its international trade on a cash basis when it has no cash! Some countries have come very close to this condition. When they do, there are declarations of temporary moratoriums on external payments or their equivalent, as in Peru in the 1970s and Mexico in 1982. The accumulation of arrears in payments is a forerunner of this condition. Many countries were in payments arrears by 1982 and continued so in the subsequent years.

The events of 1982 did not threaten the major currencies so much. The industrial countries did not experience liquidity crises. They could continue to meet their international payments or had the freedom to convert their currencies into other currencies. The United States could continue to defend the convertibility of the dollar—that is, into other currencies at market rates—by paying internationally in its currency, with no obligation to convert into gold. This was one of the benefits of being an international currency. Other major currencies could be defended, if necessary, with foreign exchange obtainable from official sources such as the IMF, from their international monetary reserves, or from borrowings from private sources if needed. The very existence of these defenses meant that they did not have to be used. The creditworthiness of the industrial countries proved strong, despite widespread questions about international lending. The liquidity of these countries avoided further shrinkage of world trade. Bilateralism in international trade and payments, and other forms of trade and payments discrimination, would likely have become more widespread if the major currencies had not been able to maintain their creditworthiness and had been unable to avoid retreating into inconvertibility of currencies and widespread restrictions on international payments.

The world monetary system escaped this basic threat during the debt crisis years. It was possible for the IMF to focus its attention and resources primarily on developing countries, even though in magnitudes the Fund's resources are mostly there to be used by developed countries. A world of expanding restrictionism and ever-declining trade caused by worldwide illiquidity would have had to be given prime attention. Fewer resources—much fewer resources— would have been available for developing countries. It was the ability of developed countries to avoid use of the IMF resources during these years and instead use other sources of credit, such as the Eurobond market, that enabled the Fund to play a major role in helping the developing countries. During 1980–86, the Fund could concentrate its attention on the developing countries in difficulties, while carrying on its more usual relations with other members.

IMF conditionality is difficult to administer during periods of crisis, though the need for it becomes more obvious. The need is for relatively drastic, quick changes in a country's policies, usually in the form of intense belt-tightening. Political climates in countries contemplating or making such changes become heated and intense. Conditionality can be interpreted as outside interference, and the IMF is then seen as imposing austerity. Such reactions are familiar— almost commonplace.

In the future, the IMF will have to exercise more influence on member countries' policies before critical stages are reached—that is, before creditworthiness is lost. In fact, it has exercised considerable influence for 30 years with varying success, though with ever-increasing sophistication. Countries should be able to assume that adequate IMF financial resources will be available quickly if they are needed for external payments, so long as the country is following, or is prepared to follow, policies the IMF has indicated as its lending criteria. Countries that are unwilling to have such anticipatory relations with the IMF would clearly understand that if they experienced general external payments difficulties, members that already meet IMF criteria would receive priority treatment. Banks and other lenders would be informed as to whether countries were prepared to have such anticipatory relations with the IMF. Banks, in their own country risk assessments, would decide for themselves how much weight to give to greater or lesser certainty of IMF help if needed. The banks could make the provision of availability of IMF assistance a condition of their own lending.

Such an approach would not be a matter of maintaining a "blacklist" of poor policy performers. Instead, it would be an extension of the present practice of having IMF standby arrangements with countries that do not need to reschedule debts or intensify restrictions on payments and show no other signs of major balance-of-payments difficulties. For example, the Fund has had standbys with Korea and Thailand. This approach need not weaken the conditionality role of the Fund. It would extend that role to more countries in practice, but more as a preventive device than as a rescue device. In many respects, this already happens—for example, in exchange rate surveillance—but it needs the sanction of IMF resources and its impact on access to other sources of international credit to make it effective. Such an approach would have been virtually unthinkable in earlier years. The new, intimate relationship established in the past 10 years between commercial bank lending and the IMF make such suggestions acceptable for consideration.

The implementation of appropriate policies in industrial countries, with the advice and encouragement of the IMF, is crucial to the effort to restore creditworthiness to debtor countries. The potential for serious damage to the entire international banking and monetary systems comes more directly from the major industrial countries than from the developing countries, which, even combined, constitute only one-fourth of the world economy. The primary task of the Fund is to avoid a breakdown in the international monetary system, which would be manifested by liquidity crises in the industrial countries, leading to restrictions on payments by industrial countries, the reestablishment of inconvertibility of their currencies, or increased protectionism. So long as this does not happen, the international system can do more to help the weaker countries. That the Fund was too small to meet the needs of the developing countries in the 1980s, even though the developed countries did not need to call on the Fund for financial resources, is a sad commentary on the inadequacy of the Fund. A Fund that, in 1986, must insist on repayments or repurchases by developing countries in fairly short periods, even though they are still in external financial difficulties, is simply underfinanced. The Fund must insist that some way be found to increase its resources, because it will otherwise be too limited in its ability to assist its members in the future. This is a severe restraint on a financial entity that deals with the balance-of-payments difficulties of developing countries during periods of cyclical downturns and weak recoveries. The Fund must be made liquid again, but not by urging members to take further deflationary measures or by creating policies that make poor countries become capital exporters. Bailing out the Fund may well be a desirable thing to do if the cause of the need for the bailout is the inability of its poorer members to create, quickly, the balance-of-payments conditions conducive to repaying the Fund.

If IMF conditionality is to have a much expanded role, it must have the support of the principal actors—the borrowing countries, the creditor governments, and the lending institutions. There has been strong resistance, in some quarters, to the present role of the IMF, especially the conditions on its lending. The changes in present practices suggested later are aimed at achieving the fundamental purposes of IMF conditionality, but so modified in practice and substance as to obtain the needed acceptance by borrowers and other lending institutions.

The Role of the Multilateral Development Banks

The principal multilateral development banks are the World Bank and the regional development banks—the Inter-American Development Bank, the Asian Development Bank, and the African Development Bank. Each is the core of a group of institutions, including a much more concessional arm that is usually modeled on the International Development Agency (IDA), the virtually grant-aid arm of the World Bank. This pattern reflects the judgment that in all regions of the developing world, there are countries whose low level of income and output requires development assistance on much less commercial terms than those provided by these banks. It is to be emphasized that from the borrowers' viewpoints, these development banks also provide concessional terms—that is, terms less costly than those of private commercial sources. The concessional arms of the multilateral banks are even less expensive—in fact, they are virtually interest-free and have very long maturities and grace periods—but this does not diminish the concessionality of most of the banks' loans. In practice, there are some countries in all regions that obtain all of their assistance on the most concessional terms, some that obtain all of their assistance on bank terms, and others that combine or mix the two. In speaking of the role of these institutions in restoring and maintaining creditworthiness, what is meant is the combination of the regular and very concessional development bank lending in each region—for example, World Bank and IDA combined.

The World Bank group includes the World Bank, the International Development Association, and the International Finance Corporation (IFC). The IFC is the "private arm" of the World Bank group. Formed in 1956, its mission is to encourage private sector activities in developing countries. It has its own resources, staff, and international agreements for this purpose. The World Bank is by far the largest of the multilateral development banks, with capital close to $60 billion. Its lending program amounts to about $12 billion per year. The next-largest lending program is that of the Inter-American Development Bank, which, on December 31, 1985, had forty-three member countries, capital of about $35 billion, and a lending program of $4 billion per year. As of the same date, the Asian Development Bank had forty-seven member countries, capital of about $16 billion, and an annual lending program of close to $2 billion. The African Bank has seventy-five member countries, capital of $6 billion, and a lending program of close to $1 billion per year. The capital of the three regional banks combined is less than the capital of the World Bank. Their combined lending programs amount to about $7 billion per year (disbursements are less), or about 60 percent of the World Bank lending. Taken together with the World Bank, these institutions are major providers of external finance to the developing countries, plus the financial activities of their very concessional arms. Their borrowing members, with very few exceptions, have continued to service their obligations to these institutions, despite delays in servicing of other external debt.

These regional banks, following the example set by the World Bank soon after its formation in 1946, have followed the rule, as noted earlier, that obligations to them by borrowing members must be met fully and promptly and cannot be renegotiated and restructured. This rule has applied even when other creditors of these countries were experiencing delays or arrears in debt servicing to them or were restructuring their loans with public and/or private lenders. This preferred creditor position helps these multilateral development banks maintain their very high standings in world financial markets.

These banks have focused mainly on project financing and on technical assistance closely related to project financing. They have helped to induce other lenders and investors to provide many more resources for investment than the banks can provide themselves—recognizing that, at most, they can provide only a small fraction of the development finance requirements of their members. They have also exerted their influence to improve the economic management of countries, mostly in areas closely related to the projects they finance but also, from time to time, on broader macroeconomic issues of development strategy and policies, including exchange rates, industrial policies, and international trade or commercial policies, as well as sectoral issues such as industrial policy and agriculture.

The essence of these multilateral development banks is their ability, through their ability, through their intermediation, to bring private capital to their regions that would otherwise not be available. The loans and resulting financial assistance rendered to borrowing members require the use of budgetary funds only in small part. Their annual disbursements do not add to the budgetary expenditures of the creditor countries within these institutions. However, the credits extended by their very concessional arms or "funds" are budgetary in origin. Thus, for many years, increases in the capital of these banks were much easier to achieve than increases in the contributions to these funds.

The banks are capitalized by member countries, which buy shares with paid-in and callable capital. The paid-in capital is a small fraction of total capital—about 10 percent, or even less in recent capital increases. The bulk of the contribution of members is in the form of callable capital, which is a contingent guarantor obligation against the remote likelihood that the multilateral development bank (MDB) cannot meet its own debt servicing. The MDB borrows in private capital markets. It is able to do so because of the guarantees given by member countries in the form of callable capital. It borrows on very favorable terms, like the U.S. Treasury. Borrowing members get the benefits of the creditworthiness of these development banks. The banks charge their borrowers a margin over their cost of borrowing, but their lending rates are still much lower than those that their borrowers would have to pay in the same markets. These banks are the principal instruments by which developing countries obtain long-term, fixed-interest debt funds.

These development institutions are capable of expansion in their project financing and other financed activities. The World Bank group is already very large, but it is capable of much expanded activities. The World Bank has proved to be a major vehicle for tapping private capital for developing countries, with few actual costs or risks to industrial creditor nations. Given increases in capital resources or changes in existing limitations on lending, it could do more if countries so desired. An important reason why Brazil and Mexico borrowed as much as they did from commercial banks in the late 1970s is that the World Bank encouraged them to "graduate" from reliance on World Bank loans and to seek loans directly from private sources.

The regional development banks are also in position to do much more in transferring private capital for lending to developing countries. Like the World Bank, they do not lend their contributed resources. Instead, they borrow from private markets to fund their own lending. They enjoy high standing in the financial markets of the world and borrow on terms nearly, or virtually, as favorable as those of the World Bank. They, too, pass on the benefits of their creditworthiness to their borrowers, which are not able to borrow at anything close to such financial terms, for longer maturities and at fixed rates. The African Development Bank is a dramatic example of this process. With two-thirds of its members and capital African, it borrows on financial terms very close to those of the World Bank and lends to African nations that are simply unable to get longer-term resources on any terms. Its lending program is nearly $1 billion per year and is expected to go higher in the foreseeable future.

The multilateral development banks are the most important vehicles for obtaining private capital for project financing in the developing countries. Their combined operations are on the order of magnitude of $20 billion per year. Each regional bank is much smaller than the World Bank, but each concentrates on its own areas, whereas the World Bank lends worldwide.

These institutions know their business and enjoy an enviable financial standing, but they are underutilized in dealing with the fundamental needs of developing countries. Aside from their own lending, their role in resource mobilization—for instance, through cofinancing with other lenders and helping to bring other financial institutions into existence—can be a major influence in stabilizing the whole process of international capital flows. Their debt instruments can be an even more important form of international investments, as experience is already indicating. The entire international financial system would benefit from the expanded use of such instruments.

At present, their borrowing and lending are limited, in effect, by a one-to-one ratio with capital, unlike a commercial bank, which is able to lend ten to twenty times its capital. These regional development banks borrow essentially to meet disbursements on loans for a period of time—say, 2 years or more. There is nothing permanent in such policies. The articles of agreement of each bank could be amended, if necessary, to permit the banks to borrow much more. In any case, their funds could be used for much more expanded forms of investments in developing countries, including loans to the private sector and guarantees of loans and equity. These borrowings are from private sources. They are, in effect, using worldwide savings, not government budgets. Such functions performed by the multilateral development banks could transform the entire prospect for the futures of the developing countries. It is only a seeming paradox that the expanded activities of these official institutions can be the mechanisms for shifting the burden of financing development to private sources of finance, rather than budgets.

In addition, another different role needs to be performed by multilateral development banks. At the hub of the problems discussed in this book is the reconciliation of the political and social aims of developing countries and the realities that impose iron constraints. Governments live with emotions and hopes as well as with current economic realities. The task of encouraging reluctant governments to adjust to adversities has been left largely to the IMF. If this continues, there is a risk that the IMF will become the universal scapegoat and will be unable to continue to be an effective intermediary or advisor. The IMF mandate is too narrow for developing countries. Policy advice to them needs the presence of those entities that are given major responsibilities by the international community for promoting development.

Conditionality should become the combined responsibility of the IMF, the World Bank, and the regional development banks. It is often a nasty responsibility, but it is critically important. The close relationships already established among these institutions—for example, in the structural adjustment loans of the World Bank and the corresponding facilities of the IMF—provide the basis for this giant step in collaboration on behalf of their common members. A beginning is being made. It is gratifying that the widely published debt proposal made by U.S. Secretary of the Treasury Baker in 1985 welcomed such changes. The suggestion for such collaboration was made in the 1960s in the World Bank staff proposal on supplementary finance, which was well supported by developing countries and most industrial countries as well as by then-president of the World Bank, George Woods. This proposal, described in some detail in the next chapter, also had the strong support of UNCTAD, then headed by Raul Prebisch. However, it did not have strong support from the United States. The staff of the International Monetary Fund was critical of the role to be performed by the World Bank group. It would have meant that the IMF and the World Bank would have collaborated in dealing with developing countries' problems resulting from unexpected declines in their export earnings. The World Bank would have provided long-term funds to defend development programs from the adversities of cyclical declines, while the IMF would have provided short- and medium-term funds to defend currencies from restrictions on international payments and to help reduce the need for deflationary measures in general. A feasible amendment for Fund-Bank collaboration was put forward by the German government. The support for the proposal was withdrawn by President McNamara of the World Bank, who argued, at that time (1969), that the World Bank's essential financial role was project finance, whereas the supplementary finance proposal would require nonproject lending based on assessments of country performances.

The capital of the regional development banks is still relatively small in relation to the capital flows and needs of their member countries; it is less than 5 percent of such flows. Over the years, the MDBs have gained the experience and management to handle much larger flows. It is suggested, as a first approximation, that the total capital of the three major regional banks—the African, Asian, and Inter-American—be made equal to that of the World Bank, thereby laying the basis for a true partnership between the World Bank and the regional banks.

The regional banks operate with a keen awareness of the conditions of the countries in their areas. They also have a deep, intimate knowledge of, and credibility with, borrowing countries. Despite their closeness to regional members, they have followed the same rules on the servicing of their loans to borrowing members, including implementing preferred creditor practices. Their officials have the respect of countries, as well as their trust. These institutions could play an important role in establishing conditions for international financial support, as is now done by the IMF and to some extent by the World Bank. Programs and policies, including adjustment policies endorsed by the regional bank concerned, would carry more conviction that the conditions of the borrowing countries had been fully recognized and that agreed adjustment measures are needed for future progress in social and economic development. The IMF cannot expect to have this capability; the World Bank comes closer. However, both are global institutions that are closely identified in developing countries with the industrial world in leadership and philosophy.

If they were given a larger financing capability, the regional development institutions could perform a deliberate, strategic, well-planned countercyclical role—helping to protect what they had agreed with members were the top-priority investments and doing so in a fashion acceptable to themselves, to the IMF, to the World Bank, and thus to the international community. To be feasible, such collaboration would have to be on a regular basis, not improvised during crises. This would mean more controversial and more troubled existences for these regional development banks, but it would also mean much larger contributions to the needs of their regional members.

The various development banks have already taken steps to be more helpful in countering cyclical adversities. In the 1980s, they have done more balance-of-payments financing, they have financed higher proportions of local currency needs, and they have accelerated disbursements. What is needed, however, is a recognition that the role of these institutions is to defend development during unfavorable periods as well as to help finance development during favorable periods. Project finance is an inadequate instrument for defending development. It is time-consuming, to say the least, when the need is for quick financial action. Project financing also is handicapped by the budgetary difficulties that borrowing nations experience during global recessions; consequently, investments are cut because of difficulties in providing local currencies for projects. Countries in the various regions of these banks differ, however, and the banks' anticyclical roles must be defined in terms of conditions in their areas and the availability of other external sources of finance. Of critical importance in all of these suggestions is a very large expansion in the capital of these institutions—more than is now being contemplated.

The Role of Commercial Banks

Private commercial lenders can extract a number of essential lessons from recent experiences that would be helpful in creating the preconditions for the return to creditworthiness of debtor countries. First, strong borrowers can unpredictably become unacceptable borrowers. There are many early warning signals, but elements of strength often continue to be present and continue to affect expectations, thus obscuring trends and hampering judgments on risks. Second, the transformation from increasing weakness and erosion of confidence to a critical loss of creditworthiness can be swift; it may take only days or even hours for such a transition through events that indicate that the economic managers, however well respected, have lost control. Certain events are especially damaging. Among such events are delays in correcting overvalued currencies, capital flight, a dramatic loss of reserves, and suspended publication of information on reserves and other significant data. Drastic, unexpected policy changes, such as imposing exchange controls—if interpreted by the financial community as desperate or misguided—can bring on financial crises.

Country monitoring or early-warning systems are likely to be and remain flawed. They cannot be confidently based on published statistics or other published material that is not currently available or on information sources that become silent during critical periods of deterioration. It remains to be seen whether existing institutions, such as the IMF or the new Institute of International Finance, will be able to provide information on deteriorating situations when the final outcomes are still unknown and countries are fearful that unfavorable reports will precipitate a crisis. Banks must be able to make immediate, decisive judgments from their own currently available sources.

A third lesson is that existing mechanisms to assist countries in balance-of-payments difficulties do not automatically go into action when the crisis-inducing event takes place or during the crisis itself. Existing mechanisms take time—days, at best, and often weeks or months. Severe damage can be done before defensive actions are available, even from efficient international institutions such as the IMF and the BIS. International action has helped to limit the damage—as a form of damage control—but it is not preventive or of immediate assistance. Even national agencies, which do not require international acquiescence, move slowly compared to the swiftness of events. The notion of instant counterattack and quick elimination of the problems is not part of the international financial system. The banker, always concerned with liquidity and risk, can never lose sight of this fault in the international financial system. In terms of country risk, it means that entire portfolios of exposure in a country become suddenly at risk, even if the individual credits are sound and have been performing well. To remedy this fault requires major changes in the international financial system.

The fourth important lesson is the need for the solidification of the practice of avoidance of repudiations by borrowing countries that are in balance-of-payments difficulties. Avoidance is now usual, but it is not yet taken for granted. International lending occurs under conditions of perceived benefits to both lender and borrower. The event of balance-of-payments difficulties changes the relationship, at least temporarily. The new stance is one of conflict and potential retaliation, with winners and losers. The lender is in an uncomfortable and vulnerable position. Given the nature of modern banking, the bank is most likely to be highly leveraged, in the sense that its loan portfolio is many times its capital. The exposure at risk in a foreign country will often be a large fraction of total capital—as, for example, in Brazil or Mexico—or even much in excess of total capital. This condition could easily be true of the U.S. bank's exposure in Canada, Germany, or the United Kingdom. In a balance-of-payments crisis, the lending institution is confronted by the possibility of a loss related to its entire country exposure or even its exposure in groups of countries. The lender cannot endure losses of these magnitudes. Small increases in capital, even if achieved, would have made little difference. The lender's risk arises in the nature of commercial banking. The customer's behavior becomes critical for the viability and the very existence of the lender. The lender is aware that the borrower must know this—it is a matter of simple arithmetic, based on published statistics.

The commercial bank's traditional protection has been declarations of default because of failure to service loans as contracted. At best, for such actions, the bank usually has to wait until enough time has elapsed to demonstrate, unequivocally, failure to meet loan servicing obligations. Even if this requirement is satisfied, default is likely to prove a weak remedy. Developing countries in balance-of-payments difficulties are not likely to have assets available to be seized in any significant quantity. Moreover, even if one lender acts before other lenders, it will quickly find others acting likewise. Very little is available for seizure by an individual lender. In addition, action may have to be taken against the borrowing country's government, and Governments are very hard to sue and even harder to obtain judgments against. Defaults are a strong defense in relation to an individual borrowing firm and virtually no defense in relation to a country. This weak bargaining position of the lender helps explain the seeming overreaction to difficulties in foreign countries. At home, even difficulties in a major area, such as petroleum or agriculture, do not immediately involve all domestic loans. However cool and calm a lender may be toward its foreign exposure, it must expect a shock wave, inducing hysteria, to sweep through its institutions at the prospect of a loss of an entire country exposure. When, as in the early 1980s, this fear extends to many countries—and to large and small debtors—it is not surprising that banks withdraw in panic from the field of international lending. A lending institution must be prepared for this contingency if it wishes to profit from international lending and yet avoid the mistakes of overpessimism.

It helps a great deal if the lender can be sure that the borrowing country will not repudiate its debts. Servicing may be delayed—even long delayed—but the obligations, which are the assets of the banks, remain and accrue interest for eventual payment. Therefore, a major improvement from the lender's standpoint would be the certainty that repudiation was out of the question. However, no declaration or assurance by a government can create certainty unless the penalties to the debtor are certain. Collateral in the hands of the lender is, of course, an example of such certainty. Guarantees by unimpeachable entities of the country of the lender, such as an export credit insurance agency, is another example that would eliminate many of the risks inherent in the possibility of repudiation. These remedies have been relatively unusual in international lending to developing countries. Instead, the lender usually relies on the consequences for the borrower as a borrower that are likely to follow from repudiation. The lender is basing its position on the assumed need of borrowers to continue to have a net inflow of funds from foreign sources over an extended period of time and on the assumption that these funds must consist largely of credits from commercial banks. Repudiation of debt for balance-of-payments reasons means loss of creditworthiness with commercial banks in almost all countries for many years. The need for future loans counterbalances the strong bargaining position of the debtor country. This is why lenders are very wary of borrowers that can borrow from countries that do not heed the implications of repudiation. For example, when Egypt could turn to the Soviet Union for credits in the 1950s, it became a much weaker borrower for Western lenders, and when it turned to the West, Soviet lenders presumably were not so comfortable in their positions as lenders.

This reliance on the threat of retaliation by lenders to counterbalance the position of debtors in case of balance-of-payments difficulties can, however, become a blunt and brittle instrument. This weakening occurs when lenders continue to withdraw from lending to a troubled debtor country even though it does not repudiate its debts. If the penalty of not being able to borrow is to be effective in discouraging repudiation, the country must see that refraining from repudiation can have the benefit of facilitating its return to creditworthiness.

Under existing mechanisms, there is no end to this state of uncertainty that further perpetuates the condition of loss of creditworthiness. The fact that a country like Mexico unilaterally declared a temporary moratorium on debt servicing, or that a country like Peru publicly declared that it will drastically reduce its debt servicing, helps keep the fears alive. In addition, the fact that the lenders continue to be reluctant to restore voluntary lending to developing countries that have restructured their external debts keeps alive the advocacy of repudiation by many in developing countries, thereby strengthening the fears that this situation might occur.

This state of unease reflects the inability of the international financial system to give confidence to lender and borrower that it will function in foul weather. In a world of many, repeated surprises and swift changes, an international financial system that functions well only in fair weather is too often not functioning well, which adds painfully to the problems of modern economies. Reform of the international financial system must seek to reduce these weaknesses in the system and make it an efficient instrument in all weather. This has been accomplished in modern domestic finance. It remains to be done internationally.

One solution that is suggested by recent history is the institutionalization of debt renegotiation and restructuring. Countries in difficulties would agree to use the mechanism of debt renegotiation, if needed, and to renounce the use of repudiations. Restructuring of debt would not be seen as implying the likelihood of repudiation. The IMF is likely to be prepared to continue to play an active role in the renegotiation process. For the lender, the IMF's involvement means that the likelihood of recreating conditions for servicing of debt is greatly enhanced, particularly when the borrower is a government or a government-owned entity or the debt is government-guaranteed. There are still many practical complications in debt renegotiations, such as agreeing on acceptable terms with banks and various borrowers, but such difficulties are manageable, as much experience has indicated. The debtor is given a practical alternative to repudiation, since banks presumably would have agreed, in advance, not to declare defaults while the debt restructuring process was going on. The sanctions in the system would be that all sources of international finance from Western private and official lenders would refrain from lending if a borrowing country repudiated its debt during this process, and all such sources would agree to try to be helpful to the borrowing country during the period of restructuring.

Finally, the protection of a commercial bank would be found in measures other than declaring a borrower in default, with its well-known consequences. Default could not be excluded as an ultimate act or sanction if the borrower did not follow agreed procedures. Experience has indicated, however, that protection can be found elsewhere—better country monitoring, a more diversified portfolio, altered terms and conditions of rescheduled debt, more cooperation with other banks in exchanging information and judging risks, support from the IMF and other multilateral organizations, professionalism of staff and others involved in making country risk judgments and lending decisions, and more specific knowledge of foreign countries and country risk management systems.

In view of the number of countries requiring debt restructuring (more than thirty in Latin America and Africa and a few in Asia), the huge magnitude involved (most of the largest debtors in developing countries have been involved), the dire predictions by experts and commentators of collapses of banking systems, and the lending countries' attitudes of bank supervisors and regulators, it is nearly incredible how few national banks or banking systems have experienced unmanageable difficulties. The banks have experienced losses in earnings, a need to increase reserves against possible loan losses, and pressures to improve capital/asset ratios. These adjustments have all been costly but manageable. The causes of difficulties for banks that have experienced serious troubles in recent years have been found more in domestic portfolios than in foreign exposures. Lenders that have country knowledge, sophistication, and carefully designed country risk management systems have done better than others. Banks that followed the lead of others or used less professional methods of country risk assessments and management also did not do badly, as they joined others in the rescheduling exercises, but they are among those that are the most convinced of the dangers of lending to developing countries.

Another major lesson from recent events is the likelihood of the politicization of international banking—that is, the role of creditor governments in decisions regarding international lending by commercial banks in the countries. This role varies from country to country and is hard to document. The United States is unusual among Western industrial countries in the frequently adversarial relationship of government with private business that is curiously intermingled with friendly, helpful relations. Public opinion in the United States plays an important role, especially through the legislative process and in the frequent elections that characterize American local, state, and national political processes.

Banks have large stakes in public policies—taxation, public debt management, monetary policies (especially regarding interest rates, money supply, and exchange rates), banking regulations, and so forth. In the United States, banks have been closely supervised and regulated. These regulations still severely constrain bank activities, though many restraints are being relaxed or removed—for example, constraints on acquisition of nonbanking institutions. Taxation, for example, is a major element in business decisions as international branch banking or activities of affiliates and subsidiaries create opportunities to reduce taxes and increase profits. Banks are close to public utilities in the extent of the importance to them of governmental policies and practices as well as in their importance to the general public. Nevertheless, within these governmental constraints, decisions to lend are essentially business decisions. Convenience, liquidity, credit risk, country risk, profitability, portfolio composition, and opportunity costs have been among the determining factors. Loans have been made to countries that were having political difficulties with the United States or that were in the Soviet bloc. Similarly, governments that continued to enjoy the friendship and, often, the official financial support of the United States could not acquire their ability to borrow from American banks, or it was lost or reduced.

In the 1970s, the exposures of banks in foreign countries were business decisions that were not backed by any governmental lender of last resort. Such loans did not usually have guarantees from creditor agencies or substantial collateral. The banks were at risk, and they knew it. Judgments on risk were made by the banks. They often acted collectively, as in syndicated loans, but the decisions to lend were made individually, and the acceptance of risk was separate, not collective. Political relations with the United States were an important factor in judging country risks, but only a factor to be weighted among others. Major U.S. lenders made visits to the IMF, the World Bank, and other official sources of country information and analysis in the United States, and comparable official entities in Europe were visited by European lenders. However, these governmental sources emphasized their separation from the business decision to lend. They did not feel obliged to provide information, and they felt no responsibility for the usage of information obtained from them or even informal views expressed by their staffs.

Banks were jealous of their independence, and the flip side of independence was full responsibility for their decisions. When bank supervisors and regulators began to classify borrowing countries as risks, in addition to classifying individual loans by credit risk, this step was well discussed with the lending banks and the implications were clearly seen. At times, banks differed in judgments with the official evaluations, but they were bound by these country classifications. There were very few classified countries before the 1980s, however. These classification decisions were governmental and did not imply a bank's agreement with the government's country evaluation; they were regulatory, however, and were obeyed as such. Nevertheless, banks continued to have their own views on country risk and took full responsibility for them. If countries were not classified—the usual situation—it did not imply some kind of responsibility by the regulatory authorities for having judged such countries to be creditworthy. In cases of difficulties, such as Mexico and Brazil, banks could not, and did not, point to the fact that these countries had not been classified earlier as risks by the regulatory authorities.

Recent events have considerably altered practice and perceptions. Governments and central banks now play a vigorous and commanding role in international commercial bank lending. The trigger case was Mexico in 1982. As noted earlier, Mexico's declaration in May 1982 of a moratorium on servicing its external debts came as a shocker. Early warnings were there to see, but optimism about Mexico's ability to avoid a crisis was general. Mexico's declaration of a moratorium came at a time when confidence in the international situation was deteriorating as the waves of the world recession hit one country after another. Mexico, one of the strongest economies in the developing world, was considered by many as the financially strongest in view of its oil production capability. By declaring a moratorium, it galvanized U.S. authorities into crisis action. The chairman of the Federal Reserve, Paul Volcker, reportedly took the lead in mobilizing assistance for Mexico, calling on central bankers in Japan and other leading industrial countries, the BIS, and the IMF. Rescuing Mexico became synonymous with rescuing the international financial system. Calls to central bankers over the weekend and interrupted golf games attested to the sense of urgency the Americans felt and were able to impart to others. Mexico had been borrowing at the rate of billions of dollars per year in the months before the moratorium, as the President of Mexico stubbornly refused to devalue the peso while giving every opportunity to holders of Mexican assets to convert them into U.S. dollar assets. It was financial mismanagement on a colossal scale. The costs—in the billions of dollars—were at the expense of Mexico and all other developing countries.

Which lender could consider any developing country an acceptable risk if Mexico, with a record of nearly half a century of reasonably good economic management and huge oil revenues, could not manage to avoid balance-of-payments crises? Moreover, Mexico accumulated a relatively much larger short-term debt in 1981–82; as Mexico's creditworthiness was weakening, banks were more willing to add short-term Mexican exposure to their holdings than longer-term. Perhaps equally or more costly in the longer run, Mexico ended the convertibility of the Mexican peso into U.S. dollars and other foreign exchange. A critical linchpin had been lost in the Mexican economy. For decades, Mexico had been the proud possessor of a convertible currency. Unlike the currencies of other developing countries, the Mexican peso was convertible during the 1950s, when the European and Japanese currencies were not yet convertible. Keeping the peso convertible provided a built-in mechanism to keep monetary and fiscal policies from becoming excessively inflationary. It was seen that rapid inflation not only made a stable exchange rate impossible to maintain but also threatened the freedom to convert pesos into other currencies. Capital flight always threatens a convertible currency; only cautious monetary and fiscal policies, combined with realistic exchange rates, can prevent such flight. Mexico had been repeatedly threatened with unfavorable conditions, but its governments had usually managed to keep the external difficulties from deteriorating into unmanageable crises resulting in devastating capital flight, and the defense of convertibility had repeatedly been a principal reason for having such appropriate policies.

The handling of Mexico's difficulties became the model. Creditor governments took the lead in international lending. This completed the politicization of international commercial bank lending. Borrowing from the bank had already been politicized in one sense. In the late 1960s, commercial banks lost their aversion to lending to the governments of developing countries for general purposes. In earlier years, banks had adhered to cash-flow lending to private borrowers. Loans had been made only for purposes that resulted in income flows from which credits would be serviced in accord with agreed amortization schedules and interest payments. At some point during the late 1960s, this changed—at different times for different lenders. Governments of developing countries or their agencies and, to some extent, private firms that were able to obtain a government or central bank guarantee could borrow for general purposes not related to cash flow. Country risk and credit risk became one and the same thing for such borrowers. Balance-of-payments analysis became the core of risk analysis. Cash-flow analyses were applied to most credits obtained by private firms, but in magnitudes, they were less important than borrowing by governments or by entities that were able to obtain government guarantees. In the 1970s, government or government-guaranteed borrowing from commercial banks often exceeded private sector borrowing. Debt restructurings, however, are based on balance-of-payments analyses, not cash-flow or credit analyses.

Government borrowings are political acts, whatever the reasons for or ultimate uses of such borrowings. The political aspect may be minor for the lenders, however. On the borrowing side, international banking had become politicized; commercial banks, however, still acted independently of creditor governments, as noted earlier.

Governments monitored this lending but did not interfere beyond existing regulations and supervisory mechanisms. Balance-of-payments difficulties, however, which result in debt restructuring, also transform private lending. Thus, analysis of an individual credit becomes a nearly meaningless act by itself. A country's economic management and its ability and intent to service *all* of its external debt became the critical issue for analysis, judgment, and decision.

In the 1980s, the asymmetry between the politicization of borrowing and the relative nonpoliticization of lending came to an end. The governments of the countries of the lending banks became active participants in the international loan decision-making process involving troubled countries. Regulations and mechanisms came into existence that were focused on international lending to developing countries. Monetary and fiscal authorities, and even legislative bodies, intervened through national or international agencies. Information systems reporting on external debt were greatly improved. The BIS set up a special inter–central bank committee, under the chairmanship of Peter Cooke of the Bank of England, to review and assess what commercial banks were doing and what these supervisory monetary authorities should do. The steps taken were cautious and largely admonitory. The International Monetary Fund became the principal vehicle for creditor governments to influence commercial bank lending to developing countries. The Fund staff and management made these problems their central preoccupation. Private commercial banks, with long traditions of independence, urged these governmental institutions to take the responsibility for judging country risk and for bringing about conditions more acceptable for commercial bank lending. Such judgments guided not only restructuring of past debt but also the extension of new credits. The cases of Brazil and Mexico were outstanding examples of governmental leadership and responsibility for commercial bank lending decisions. The international financial system did not protect the independence of international commercial banking.

In the early 1980s, the international financial system, consisting of a variety of major mechanisms both official and private, could not shift gears without shutdowns and crises. Mexico was not told clearly by private banks that the continuation of their mismanagement of 1981–82 would result in complete loss of creditworthiness and, in the end, of new borrowing—although I can attest, from personal experience, that the Mexicans were repeatedly warned of this possibility. So long as credits were readily available from some private sources, such warnings did not have decisive influence in changing policies. Under existing practices, the IMF could not help induce changes in Mexico's policies until Mexico went into a stage of crisis, lost its creditworthiness, and increased its external debt beyond its ability to service. The Fund could not warn Mexico's private creditors, even if it was very concerned about Mexico's balance-of-payments outlook. Such utterances would have been incompatible with the Fund's international character and Mexico's membership. Individual private banks could not defend themselves beyond stopping lending themselves despite continued lending by others. Banks with good country risk management systems stopped lending before the crisis, but their actions could not prevent the crisis, and the continued lending of others made the magnitude of the problem even larger. Indeed, viewed analytically, the defensive measures of international lenders in constraining new lending—plausible in themselves under existing conditions—aggravated Mexico's balance-of-payments difficulties. They not only reduced the volume of available foreign exchange, but their feared and precautionary measures became known to others and added to the sense of unmanageable difficulties.

These inadequacies in the international financial system are not inevitable. More can be done by commercial banks to make countries aware that they are losing their creditworthiness in the banking community—an exercise in which I participated myself with respect to some countries, such as Brazil and Peru. More can be done by the Fund to intervene in advance of crises. Its policies and practices should permit more active, though discreet, intervention, even if no Fund resources are being requested and the country is not seeking approval for any of its exchange practices. The Fund has come through several major metamorphoses with great differences in its international influence and authority. During recent years, its authority has been closely linked with countries having balance-of-payments difficulties resulting in a loss of creditworthiness with private banks, a need for larger-scale use of the Fund resources, renegotiation and restructuring of external debts, and, in a few cases, the granting of new credits by the banks. The next stage requires a Fund with a different kind of authority—the authority to intervene quietly and discreetly with complete confidentiality, with knowledge limited to the managing director and his staff on a need-to-know basis, in order to prevent crises from occurring; this mode of operation has long been known and practiced by central banks. When crises seem imminent and virtually unavoidable, it is necessary to know in advance how and to what extent the international governmental community can step in swiftly to replace the lost inflows of commercial bank funds or other funds.

This role would require different forms of conditionality than those that now prevail. Conditionality would focus on prevention, rather than on crises. The Fund has taken steps in this direction in the case of Mexico, and the Fund's conditionality has changed greatly over the years. In the 1950s and early 1960s, Fund conditionality for the European member countries and Japan was mainly related to achieving the preconditions for establishing convertibility of currencies by removing restrictions on current international payments and then on to actually achieving convertibility. European countries achieved this status by the end of the 1950s, and Japan did so in 1964. For developing countries, conditionality focused on inflation, reducing budgetary deficits, effective monetary policies, simplifying exchange rate systems, avoiding discrimination through the exchange rate systems, and having realistic exchange rates. In the 1960s, conditionality focused principally on the British pound sterling exchange rate and the defense of exchange rate stability in the industrialized countries. In addition, attention was also given to achieving more open economic systems (fewer restrictions and less protection) in the developing world, while improving their external defenses by such measures as increasing international reserves. SDR creation added to the defense of the international monetary system. Debt restructuring of official debt was experienced by a number of countries but was not a focal point of conditionality. Mobilization and efficient allocation of resources for development were among the concerns emphasized by the authorities of the World Bank in their various forms of consultative groups. These consultative groups aimed to help developing countries obtain more official development assistance and use such assistance in a manner deemed efficient by the World Bank and donor countries.

In the 1970s, Fund conditionality increasingly focused on how to deal with large balance-of-payments crises resulting from the combination of large oil price increases, worldwide inflation, and the recession of 1974–75. With Zaire began the preoccupation with debt restructuring, and commercial banks were the focal point. Other countries—Peru, Turkey, Jamaica, and so on—followed. Unlike the 1950s and 1960s, the emphasis was not on making more progress toward achieving the international financial behavior envisaged in the articles of agreement of the International Monetary Fund but, rather, on defending against the onslaught of worldwide adversities. The Fund did not surrender its principles; it simply changed its line of sight and aimed its activities where the dangers were imminent and great.

The international financial system must again become an efficient, aggressive instrument of progress in growth, monetary stability, and development. To do so, it must help end the era of international financial crises and near-panics. In so doing, it may develop into an efficient system, as we have come to expect of national banking systems. In this system, the commercial banks will again be more their own masters, taking responsibility for their lending decisions, but in a very changed international environment. They may well, again, provide the bulk of finance without guarantees during periods of prosperity and may be more withdrawn from such lending during periods of recession and other general difficulties. Lending will still take place to private firms and governments; during periods of recession, however, official institutions will play a more active role in ensuring an adequate flow of international credit to public and private sectors, either directly or by providing guarantees. This will not be a return to the pre-1980s role nor a continuation of that of the 1980s. It will concentrate on the ability to act quickly enough and in adequate magnitudes to keep difficulties from becoming crises. Effective preventive mechanisms can assure the efficient functioning of the international financial system so that it can safely weather all conditions.

The Role of Bilateral Aid Programs

As discussed earlier, bilateral aid programs have performed an important role in the international financial system since the end of World War II, contributing both financial resources and technical assistance. Fortunately for recipient countries, the various national aid programs have differed in their emphases on uses of funds and on terms. For example, the United States and the United Kingdom have emphasized public sector projects, whereas the Scandinavians have given considerable attention to food production and storage.

In the reconstruction of the international financial system, these bilateral programs are likely to play a changed but still significant role. The bilateral programs are likely to be more coordinated with the multilateral programs. The programs agreed upon with the International Monetary Fund have already had a major influence in the national decisions of countries that grant assistance. As the donor countries achieve general agreement on the need to insist on acceptable economic management as a condition for multilateral assistance, such criteria also become the criteria for bilateral assistance. The exceptions are the clear cases of assistance given for essentially political reasons, such as U.S. aid to Egypt and Israel. In addition, the task of judging and monitoring country performance becomes increasingly the responsibility of the multilateral agencies.

At the same time, the national aid programs can take a leading role in innovations. For example, the U.S. aid program has emphasized certain initiatives in recent years—for example, the Caribbean initiative to give special financial, technical, and trade support to countries in that region. In addition, the U.S. aid program has taken many steps to strengthen the role of the private sector in developing countries. The Private Enterprise Bureau in the U.S. aid program has this as its special responsibility. Its impact has been limited, as it operates within an aid program that, for decades, has been directed principally to the public sector or to government-owned parastatals. These efforts have become increasingly successful, however, as many developing countries in all regions have begun to give a much larger role to the private sector in their development strategies and efforts. There is clearly an interaction between the thrusts of the U.S. aid programs and this increased emphasis by recipient developing countries on the private sector.

Closely related are the efforts to encourage divestiture of publicly owned entities by governments and their sale to private investors, both domestic and foreign. This process of privatization reflects not only the economic philosophy of the U.S. aid program but also the desire by developing countries to encourage inflows of equity capital. It is thus partly a response to the loss of creditworthiness for borrowing from commercial sources.

These approaches culminate in the policies of the multilateral agencies. Because many countries are involved, the views of any one country are merged with the views of others. Nevertheless, the views do merge, and the United States has been, and is likely to remain, the most important single influence. It is not to be expected that U.S. policy in the multilateral agencies will significantly differ from policies followed in its national agencies. Thus, in its bilateral agencies and in the multilateral agencies, the United States is emphasizing policy reforms by developing countries; institution building in developing countries, especially in finance; and facilitation of foreign private investment, especially equity investment. This includes helping to identify opportunities and financing the feasibility studies needed to judge suggested investments and to attract private foreign investors. It means emphasis on achieving viable economies, and it draws attention away from focusing on debt-restructuring and toward creating the preconditions for external creditworthiness.

There is a danger in the tendency toward uniformity among sources of official finance. Good policies are reinforced, but so are mistaken policies. Despite similarities, various bilateral aid institutions serve purposes that differ among nations and that differ from those of multilateral agencies. Like the multilateral agencies, their separate existences reflect a division of labor and functions, reflecting their different purposes. Bilateral programs primarily serve the national needs of donor countries, however beneficial their activities are for recipient countries, and national interests differ. Similarly, multilateral institutions differ in their functions and in the willingness of countries to support them. A strong supporter of one international agency is often a weak supporter of another. Countries have not even been uniform in their support of the Bretton Woods "twins"—the International Monetary Fund and the World Bank—and the differing loyalties changing from time to time.

The national aid programs can be more readily innovative than the multilateral programs. A single country need not wait for other nations to agree on a program. National interests may well indicate support for nations that are not able to meet the criteria of the multilateral agencies, or the needed help may be required sooner than would be feasible for a multilateral agency. The mobilization of support for Mexico by the U.S. authorities in 1982 exemplified the flexibility of national agencies, as did the responses to the African drought in 1983–84.

Thus, it is urged that the judgment of overall country management be primarily the responsibility of the multilateral agencies. National aid agencies can be guided by these country assessments. The multilateral agencies and the bilateral programs can collaborate in individual lending and technical assistance activities, but all institutions should retain their freedom to take separate and independent actions that serve the purposes of their own institutions. As in the case of private lenders, the world economy is best served by institutions that are prepared to cooperate and collaborate closely but do not abdicate their responsibilities or lose their ability to act independently and separately.

Implications for Borrowing Countries

All of the sources of international finance and the mechanisms for capital transfers are involved in the restoration of creditworthiness. In the quest for the restoration of creditworthiness, borrowing countries will naturally wish to avoid a repetition of disrupting balance-of-payments difficulties and external debt crises as much as possible. The most important point, as stressed throughout this book, is that good economic and financial management makes feasible the maintenance of creditworthiness and avoids the need for more drastic deflationary measures resulting from its loss. Good management includes making proper use of available sources of finance. Well-known canons of international borrowing should be followed. Thus, as much as possible of the new borrowing for investments should be at longer maturities. Loans for public sector project financing should be for the longest possible maturities. Short- and medium-term maturities are suited to trade-related needs or working capital. Borrowers should also make every effort to secure resources that will not add to their external debt burden. Every reasonable effort should be made, for example, to attract direct foreign investment and venture capital in available forms and to explore new opportunities for leasing equipment rather than purchasing it. By pursuing these policies, borrowers can contribute greatly to the restoration and maintenance of their creditworthiness with private lenders and investors.

Borrowers must maintain close ties with the international agencies—the IMF, the World Bank, and the regional development banks— and must make efficient use of their financial resources and their very valuable technical assistance. The international institutions do not have sufficient financial resources to meet all the credit needs of developing countries, but close collaboration among the agencies can help countries ensure that adequate resources are available from private and public sources and are used wisely and that current and prospective policy adjustments enhance borrowers' creditworthiness. Innovative financing arrangements involving private and official sources should be explored with open-minded attitude toward novelty as well as expansion of existing practices.

The composition of international lending is likely to change dramatically in coming years, just as it did in the 1970s, when commercial bank financing surpassed official development assistance in overall importance. Borrowing countries will have to become sophisticated in new forms of lending. The relative importance of conventional commercial bank financing, without recourse to acceptable guarantors, may well decline in coming years. However, banks can employ new forms of lending, and umbrellas of guarantees will probably be used increasingly. Cofinancing involving commercial banks and national and international official agencies will probably grow in importance. The IMF, the World Bank, and the regional development institutions will probably significantly increase the use of their resources in such activities. In addition, banks can perform intermediary roles between institutional investors, such as insurance companies, and the ultimate borrowers. Other private financial institutions and instruments will probably become increasingly important.

In the coming period, the main task will be to restore satisfactory growth trends in developing countries. These countries must rehabilitate productive facilities, build inventories, introduce new technology, and encourage their private sectors, as well as carrying on more usual investment activities. Those countries cannot hope to meet such needs from their own resources without creating intolerable social conditions and severe political strains. The debt crises have seriously strained the social and political structures of the countries involved. Very large increases in capital flows to developing countries are necessary. Without such increases, economic management will fail, however resolutely it is tried. Given their rapid population increases and their need for social expenditures and urbanization, developing countries' economies must invest and grow substantially—at least 4 to 6 percent per year in real terms—to keep internal tensions from evolving into destructive disruptions. Rapid job creation requires expanding economies. Emigration from these countries provides only partial and temporary amelioration. Growth is critical.

Austerity must soon be followed by economic growth if rational policies are to be maintained over time. With this recovery of sustained economic growth will come the restoration of creditworthiness, both because of the successful growth itself and because of the pursuit of the policies needed to sustain this growth. Developing countries will continue to be highly vulnerable and sensitive to a decline in, or loss of, creditworthiness due to domestic or international developments or both. For their part, developing countries should make more efforts to make themselves attractive to various private sources of finance in addition to commercial banks. Of primary importance are the key domestic policies, such as maintenance of noninflationary fiscal and monetary policies, realistic exchange rates, pricing policies that encourage savings and direct them into productive investment, and, in general, an environment favorable to innovation and entrepreneurship. Success in the absorption of modern technology is a good indicator, as are lesser but still major policies and practices, such as nondiscriminatory treatment of foreign firms and formation of joint enterprises, with equity provided by domestic private sources and governments as well as foreign firms and the multilateral institutions.

The ad hoc responses to the debt crisis of the early 1980s did not address the fundamental problems facing developing countries and the international financial system. If the world is to be better prepared for future adversities or cyclical downturns in the world economic cycle, recognition must be given to the possibility that these adversities could be severe and could last a relatively long time. The adjustment periods may well be prolonged—perhaps 5 years or more—because world recovery benefits developing countries only partially and with considerable time lags. Balance-of-payments assistance will require relatively long periods to service. The concepts of short, medium, and long term may well have to be redefined for such financing. The short term should perhaps be thought of as covering 1 to 3 years, rather than a period of less than a year, while medium-term loans should be for up to 8 or even 10 years and long-term loans for 10 years or more. Similarly, it should be recognized that long-term structural adjustments may well take a decade, or even a generation, to achieve.

Such redefinitions can be of crucial importance in handling balance-of-payments difficulties as they occur. Future downturns in the world business cycle could hit many borrowing countries long before they reap the benefits of their adjustment policies and the benefits of the recovery of the world economy. Like short-leash approaches to debt rescheduling, balance-of-payments support, which must be repaid in 3 or even 5 years, can be cumbersome, inefficient, and unattractive for borrowers and can cause chronic frustration for lenders. Short-term borrowing is sensible if such financing is a bridge to longer-term available financing. For most developing countries, what starts as short-term balance-of-payments financing will evolve into long-term indebtedness if it is not converted into equity. The individual loan may be repaid or, in the case of the Fund, repurchased in a short period—3 years or less—but other inflows of capital will be needed to make such repayments feasible. Short-term loans may be rolled over—that is, renewed at maturity—or new loans may help refinance the older loans, or equity may make possible the relative reduction of debt. What happens depends on particular conditions in a country. Thus, for example, the World Bank could try to lend more quickly to help a country repay the IMF, thus recreating the country's ability to obtain balance-of-payments support again if, as is likely, it is needed again. In this way, the World Bank could help refinance the IMF in a way that would help the country sustain a satisfactory growth rate. At first glance, this might seem irksome and inappropriate to the longer-term lender, but on reflection, it would clearly serve a legitimate and useful development purpose. An efficient international financial system should constantly use all of its elements to make each element able to function more efficiently. For a country to be the orchestra conductor, it must be familiar with all the instruments, must know the score, and must have rehearsed well before the concert.

Proposals for Strengthening the International Financial System

10

Ways and Means

A NUMBER of ways of coping with the current crisis from the viewpoint of restoration of creditworthiness have been suggested in previous chapters. Others are suggested in this chapter. A useful starting point is the determinants of commercial bank behavior.

Commercial Banks

Lenders wish to reduce their holdings of poorly performing loan assets, loan assets that are likely to become troubled, or loan assets regarded as excessive in light of the bank's capital or portfolio composition. Many ways of doing so are possible, and some are currently being used. Loan assets can be sold directly or indirectly to other lenders who have different views of the risk/reward equations for such assets or have different portfolio needs. Bank loan assets can be refinanced with funds raised by the issue of marketable notes (presumably with floating interest rates). This overcomes the difficulties in making a market for bank loans as such, which are essentially nonmarketable instruments. Banks can write off these undesired loans and take the adverse impact on their income, assisted by tax deductions. They can reduce or lower the value at which they carry such assets—in effect, a partial or entire write-off.

With ingenuity, banks can find other ways of reducing foreign loan assets. This is not the same as withdrawing from the activity of earning income from international banking. Instead of relying on income from loan assets or risk assets, the banks seek less risky sources of earnings, or so-called "off balance sheet" earnings, which result from fees and commissions. Opening letters of credit, cash management, and foreign exchange transactions exemplify these kinds of fee-earning financial services. Simultaneously, the banks can continue to finance short-term trade-related activities, which are risky but usually much less risky than general-purpose lending.

These kinds of devices help deal with a built-in vulnerability in international banking. Loans are made by banks, not by individuals. In case of difficulties, the impact is concentrated in a lending institution that, is a borrower itself and has many depositors or other creditors. In contrast, an individual bond holder in the 1930s who possessed bonds that were not being serviced as contracted could sell them at a discount to other investors and, at times, to the borrower itself. The market thus redistributed the outstanding debt to willing holders, and the total debt was evaluated by the market. Buyers were speculators, attracted by price and yields. Their decisions often proved very profitable, as their longer-range, more optimistic view took advantage of the prevailing pessimism about a country in financial markets.

Banks do not have this flexibility in disposing of their loan assets. They have a variety of interlocking financial considerations, which are made more rigid in significant and highly publicized cases. An effective dispersal mechanism may require the approval and cooperation of the borrower or borrowing government, which may see no advantage or disadvantage in a proposed transaction. For example, a bank may be willing to sell some or all of its exposure in a country at a very large discount because it needs the liquidity and wants to get rid of the inconveniences of holding a poorly performing asset. It may be willing to sell at discounts of, say, 25 percent to 50 percent or even more (as in actual cases in recent years). The borrowing country may be appalled by this publicized "market" evaluation of its creditworthiness. It may be inconceivable that countries that had thought of themselves as A to AAA borrowers only a few years back would now be discounted at 25 percent to 50 percent.

Even assuming that the borrowing government agrees, or that its acquiescence is not necessary, the bank has its own difficulties. If it sells part of a country portfolio at a given discount, will its own comptrollers or official bank regulators insist that the rest of the country portfolio be valued at a similar discount? If one country's loans are so handled, why not do so for other countries in similar circumstances? The bank's nightmare then becomes a reality—loan losses large enough to affect earnings, reserves, and capital seriously and dangerously, even though they represent a small fraction of total loan assets. Memories of the financial panics of earlier decades become vivid, because the bank cannot escape from its institutional existence as a very low risk borrower and a greater risk-taking lender. What is possible when dealing privately with an individual or firm is often not possible when dealing with a country. The magnitudes are almost always relatively large, and the transactions are conducted with the visibility of a goldfish in a bowl. As noted earlier, this vulnerability can also translate into negotiating weakness with the bank's nonperforming debtors. At such times, the management may dream of having capital so large that it can be indifferent to such write-offs, even in major debtor countries. This is conceivable, but it is a pipe dream under existing conditions. Shareholders are intolerant of losses in earnings or capital. The value of their shares is likely to be reduced or dividends may decline or disappear. The equity in which they have a share declines. The market then has a rather dim view of the bank, and it is no time for the management of the bank to go off to market to issue more shares to increase or replace capital. The management has lost most of its options.

Regulators, which must fulfill their responsibilities, are in a quandary. Do they go along with management views and try to minimize actions that require charges against earnings or increases in reserves or charges against capital? What if they choose to take a more optimistic view and adverse conditions continue or get worse—and the future damage is even larger? Are they protecting the public interest, since they have long recognized that the bank is a form of public utility? If they insist on more dramatic defensive measures, will this undermine confidence in the banks or the banking system much more than is warranted? Will it trigger the feared panics? It is not surprising that the regulatory authorities proceed with great caution. Different categories of nonperformance of servicing are created to reflect different levels of concern. Each level of concern is defined in terms of impact on earnings, reserves, and capital. Only a few borrowing countries are declared to be in the more worrisome categories. At the same time, bank supervisors insist on increasing the capital of the banks in relation to total liabilities and assets.

In such sensitive environments, banks hesitate to try to dispose of poorly performing assets for fear of upsetting many apple carts. Many schemes are suggested, and a few experiments are carefully tried, but the system is too vulnerable in difficult periods for major experiments. Thus, nothing has changed drastically in international commercial banking during the 1980s, except that it has become much more cautious. This caution has been evidenced in less reliance on a bank's own country risk evaluations and management systems and more reliance on the assessments of others, particularly the IMF; a drastic reduction in new lending to countries in trouble; more insistence on larger returns on loans made; a move to more traditional forms of international lending; more emphasis on avoiding concentrations in loan portfolios; more building of capital; more emphasis on earnings from nonloan risk activities and so forth. These are not truly new departures. Nevertheless, from the banks' viewpoint, they have helped transform the potentially dangerous international debt crisis into a manageable state of affairs in which panic has been averted. The price paid is a more depressed world economy, increased friction among otherwise friendly countries, a rise in protectionism, accelerated inflation in many countries, and prolonged deflation in others. For U.S. banking, the withdrawal from international lending has meant a weakening financial ties that had taken a hundred years to build in Latin America. For the future, the obvious need is to strengthen the international financial system so that these high prices for defending the banking system need not be paid.

Leaving aside for the moment the possible roles of the IMF, the World Bank, and regional development banks in reinforcing the system, what more can I suggest that the banks do, other than agreed measures to cope with the existing stock of past debts? The following suggestions, like the others in this book, are based on my personal experiences in international banking and in the U.S. Treasury, the International Monetary Fund, and the World Bank.

A New Finance Institution

The commercial banks could establish a new institution along the following lines, sketched here to exemplify the kinds of measures that can be taken and to inspire further thought. Many variants and improvements are conceivable. The banks can establish a new entity that would be prepared to engage in the business of purchasing unwanted bank loans at an appropriate discount from their face value. The new entity could be a sort of Bank for International Settlements, but it would be owned by the private banks and, possibly, other investors. The face value of the notes acquired from the banks in this manner would be collected by the new entity over time, with the originally discounted portion of that face value taken in as income.

Many banks may be willing to sell significant amounts of their claims in one or more countries. In so doing, they would be motivated by a clear preference to liquify a portion of their claims (that is, the face value of the notes net of the discount), rather than continuing to hold them to maturity. The selling banks would consider the discount as the equivalent of a loan write-off chargeable to current income. Apart from liquifying certain loan claims in this manner to realize liquidity, banks might be able to make other desirable adjustments to their international loan portfolios, thereby avoiding continuing criticism by regulators or shareholders.

The commercial viability of the new entity, including its level of profitability, depends primarily on whether the purchased loans are fully repaid and, of course, on the sizes of the discounts that were negotiated between the new entity and the selling bank.

The new entity would not be a commercial bank; rather, it would be a special finance company that would not accept or create deposits. In an imperfect way, it would provide the banks with a privately owned source of liquidity. The entity would then have the option of either holding the paper until maturity or redeeming it in local currency and using the proceeds for sources of equity for promising export-oriented projects. An institution of this sort could significantly strengthen the international financial system. The commercial banks would have an alternative to holding unwanted assets that interfere with acceptance of new cross-border exposures.

The shareholders would elect a board of about twenty directors, which would meet periodically. It would become, at a minimum, a meeting place where bankers could privately exchange their views and concerns on the international financial situation in addition to directing the new entity.

The debtor nations would remain in debt but would now be more able to borrow again from the commercial banks. The incentives to pursue economic management policies that would make them creditworthy with commercial lenders would be greatly strengthened by this new possibility of borrowing. The IMF and other resources would still be available, but with enhanced ability to be successful in implementing programs agreed with them because more international resources would be available.

A Safety Net

To help overcome fears about the viability of the international banking system it is suggested that consideration again be given to some additional form of safety net, constructed by the private banks themselves. In the latter part of the 1970s, I proposed the formation of a form of "international safety net." The proposal was based on the conviction that the keystone in the international banking system is the international correspondent bank relations of the major national banks. If a relatively small number of banks in a few key countries—say, thirty or forty banks in five or ten countries—were to agree that they would keep their correspondent bank lines with each other intact during periods of concern, any difficulty, such as the recession of 1982–83, would not raise fears of or actually cause a "domino" effect. The major banks would demonstrate their confidence in the creditworthiness of the others by not withdrawing their lines or deposits and would expect to be treated likewise. A relatively small number of U.S., British, French, German, Japanese, and Swiss banks would be the core of the system. Other banks, such as the Belgium, Canadian, and Swedish, would be important but not key. Disturbances in any country, or in a few countries simultaneously, could be handled if they did not spread. The proposal was discussed with key leaders in international banking and was well received. It was not critically needed and did not come into existence; therefore, it was not available to help in the 1980–84 events. It should be reconsidered in light of recent events and carefully studied by those who are eager to preserve private banking by emphasizing mutual self-help to meet unexpected banking difficulties.

An International Banking Council: An Improved Country Risk Management System

At the same time, a proposal was made to establish an international banking council for commercial banking, the equivalent of the BIS for central banking. In the 1970s, it was evident that the banks had no mechanism for quiet consultation and exchange of views with each other on emerging trends and events. A conference was much too large for such purposes. Informal, unstructured luncheon chats, or occasional office calls, were too haphazard and likely to be too late to help avoid emergencies. Experience in the IMF and World Bank executive boards and in the monthly meetings of the governors of the BIS had shown the advantages of small, deliberative groups that meet confidentially in a process of continuing fact-finding and exchanging of ideas. Again, the suggestion of a council was canvassed and well received, though the process of selection of membership would clearly be difficult. In the meantime, it was decided to form an institute of international finance in Washington, which could perform some of these functions. The Institute of International Finance now exists. It operates on the assumption that external debt servicing difficulties can be anticipated and avoided. A major element in the success of such an institution is being fully informed. The mechanism for exchanging critical information must be flexible and quick-acting—this is more important than precise accuracy. Decision makers need to know what is important and must judge current events accordingly, because what is important is constantly changing. There is a need to build on formal knowledge and analysis, and judgments, when needed, must be made by those who are qualified by experience to make such judgments. An international banking council could help significantly in this process. The new Institute of International Finance could service such a council.

Given the types of changes foreseen or suggested in this book, particularly in this chapter, country risk evaluations and management systems of commercial banks would be considerably altered. The environment for voluntary lending would be greatly improved, and lending would be made more reliable for the borrower. The attraction of commercial banks to borrowers, despite market financial terms, remains their ability to act quickly, compared with official sources of financing, and their ability to lend without rigid ceilings on their total lending to any one country. Such considerations as credit and country risks and portfolio composition place practical limits on lending, but not to creditworthy borrowers with creditworthy projects in a creditworthy country. The lending private bank either can finance an entire project itself or can put together a syndicate for this purpose.

Banks have not been reliable sources for new lending when conditions in borrowing countries have become adverse, even when the adverse changes resulted from events beyond the control of borrowers. With the proposals made herein, lending institutions can assume that borrowing countries will not be overwhelmed by difficulties.

This should prevent overreactions by banks during periods of wide-spread balance-of-payments difficulties.

To prevent the danger of encouraging excessively lax lending criteria, banks should have strict internal country assessment and management systems and internal comptrollers and regulators of such systems should be closely scrutinized. The banks would have the benefit of outside views, such as those of the IMF, the World Bank, and BIS, and the regional development banks, as well as information provided by the new institute. International lending would continue to have risks besides those characteristic of domestic lending. However, the framework within which individual loans are made—namely, the country risks seen in these loans and the magnitudes and terms deemed appropriate—would become more flexible and would be influenced by external institutional factors that reduce such country risks. Banks would still not be fully reliable sources of finance, but they would be much more so than they are now.

The future of voluntary international lending to developing countries will also reflect the changes in the banking or financial services industry. In the United States, banks are merging and are being deregulated. The number of banks is therefore being reduced, and the remaining banks are becoming larger and are offering a wider spectrum of financial services. Automation, computerization, and other modern technology, as well as new debt instruments, are being introduced everywhere. Consumer and corporate banking techniques are being revolutionized. Multinational production, trading, and finance are overcoming the strangeness of things foreign. Finance is more readily internationalized than production and even distribution. The environment of international lending is changing dramatically, which will affect future notions of country risks and of acceptable magnitudes, terms, and purposes of international lending.

Handling Debts

These suggested changes can strengthen the international banking system and can help in the restoration of true creditworthiness with private lenders in banks or capital markets. Nevertheless, there remains the problem of past debt—a problem that simply will not, and cannot, go away until creditworthiness is restored. This is a vicious cycle that must be broken somehow.

Accumulated debts to governmental lenders are being handled by the Paris Club. They can be rescheduled in any way that is acceptable to creditors and debtors. Governments are free to act without the constraints that exist on commercial, privately owned banks. Forgiveness of debt does mean loss of revenue to national treasuries, but the governments can agree to forgo, or reduce, such revenues. Governments have voters and taxpayers, but they do not have shareholders. Official debts have often been forgiven by creditor governments, though usually only after endless discussion and efforts to avoid this solution. War debts and reparations for the 20 years between World War I and World War II illustrate this situation. Debts to developing countries have been forgiven by some creditors, such as the United Kingdom, as a form of foreign aid. This can be done quickly and drastically, or slowly and gradually. For example, it is possible to convert most or all outstanding development loans from governments into IDA-type credits—with 20-year grace periods, 50-year maturities, and very low interest rates. Loans guaranteed or granted by official export credit agencies could be restructured more drastically with interest payments capitalized—that is, total principal increased and maturities extended. The multilateral financial institutions could continue to enjoy a preferred creditor position, but with expanded new lending to their borrowers and in forms permitting much more rapid disbursements. Having done this, the creditor governments could (and do) continue to lend and provide grants if that seems to be in their national interests. The key issue is the political desire and will of creditors to assist debtor countries despite their own budgetary constraints. National interest—not profit and loss statements—should determine the decisions.

Debts to private commercial banks are very different. They are dominated by financial impacts on profits, capital, reserves, and so on. Private banks are sensitive to shareholders and regulators. Of the two, regulators are the more decisively important. Banks may disagree with the judgments made by regulators, but they are bound by judgments that become regulations. Banks do not lend to "classified" countries. They do not lend to countries the regulators regard as nonperforming. Banks can capitalize interest payments or even reduce interest rates below the costs of funds to the lending bank—that is, they can take losses from such actions—but if they do, such loans are "under water." New lending thus becomes very constrained. If the bank has other means of earning revenues in a country—such as a branch banking system or fees earned from such financial services as trading in foreign exchange—it may be able to absorb losses from its loan portfolio with little pain, but this situation is unusual. For most banks, losses from poor loans are difficult to offset. Even if bank regulators are not very concerned because of the bank's overall strength, shareholders might be worried and might be critical of bank managers and sell their shares, thereby depressing their values.

Banks need to get rid of unwanted loans, and various ways to do so have been suggested earlier. Unless this is done, the restoration of creditworthiness becomes much more difficult.

One alternative not yet mentioned is to distinguish clearly between new and old loans or debts. One way to do so is to reinforce creditworthiness for new loans with guarantees by national or multinational agencies in such a manner as to destroy the negative implications of past debt and debt servicing records for new loans. In effect, the banks could resume new lending because of the guarantors for new loans. Borrowing nations would be creditworthy for such new loans. This would not be restoration of creditworthiness because of the continual need for guarantees. It would be more comparable to the ability to borrow from the IMF or the World Bank when the country is not able to borrow from the commercial banks.

If private banks can otherwise get rid of unwanted holdings, they will be more prepared to make new loans on a truly voluntary basis, with fewer defenses against country risk. Debtors can help by pledging resources to serve past debt; for example, in 1986, Peru pledged to use 10 percent of its foreign exchange earnings for this purpose. Suggestions that propose interest rates lower than costs of funds to banks, thus resulting in losses, may be accepted as the lesser of evils but, by themselves, may mean the cessation of lending or a great delay in the restoration of voluntary lending.

New Forms of Lending

It may be that the event that will unlock creditworthiness will prove to be growth, especially in an environment of lower interest rates, drastically reduced oil prices, and a more realistic value of the U.S. dollar. Brazil and Mexico could lead the way back to creditworthiness. A borrowing economy that is being managed well, that is growing in productive capacity and export capability, and that is being partly financed by multilateral institutions that endorse a country's economic policies and management may become so well regarded by banks as a source of revenues that existing overhangs of past debts would be treated as much less important in deciding country exposure limits. This road is conceivable, but it is likely to be most cautiously regarded and to be slowly taken, if at all. A quicker, more certain, and more rapid restoration of creditworthiness requires not only deliberate changes in domestic policies and practices but also changes in the policies and practices of the international institutions.

Lending to developing countries in the future is likely to involve expanded use of newer forms of lending as well as expanded (and contracted) forms of well-established mechanisms. Among these relatively newer forms is the application of domestic investment techniques to international business undertakings. Developing countries need capital goods, which can be bought, borrowed, or leased. They can be owned by nationals, by foreigners, or jointly. The needed funds can come from nonbank institutions. For example, the three major automobile companies in the United States—Chrysler, Ford, and General Motors—are major lenders for a wide variety of purposes. Such firms can be major sources of international credit, as they are already thoroughly acclimated to international business.

The ingenuity and inventiveness of domestic financing is not yet typical in international development finance. It is only necessary to speculate on the current trends of nonbanking giant firms, using their financial, industrial, and commercial resources to provide banking services, to see their potential application internationally. The provision of financial services is highly competitive. Margins of profits are small for lenders, but the volume of business can be very large, and total income can be very satisfactory. The borrowing developing countries are the higher-growth countries that have rapidly modernizing sectors that require modern financial services. As portfolios grow, or as lending to such countries becomes part of the highly diversified activities of a business entity, the criteria of acceptable risk, or creditworthiness, again changes. It is for such reasons that I see private international lending, in one form or another, expanding greatly in the foreseeable future, with innovation and invention gladly or reluctantly undertaken.

Multilateral Institutions

We now focus on suggestions for coping with external payments difficulties of developing countries that involve changes in multilateral official institutions, especially the IMF, the World Bank, and the regional development banks. The issues raised have preoccupied me for many years—going back to the 1950s and increasing steadily in the 1960s and 1970s. Herein are given, in very brief form, suggestions for improvements from earlier decades as well as new ones resulting from more recent experience. Old proposals are restated herein only to the extent that they have not been adopted and implemented and are regarded as still relevant for existing conditions and prospects. They are offered as a set of proposals that reinforce each other. The aim is to help create an efficient, reliable international financial system that would be capable of sustaining growth and development in all phases of the business cycle, including during adverse conditions in the world economy, and that would be helpful to countries in any stage of capitalization and modernization.

The International Monetary Fund

Before dealing with possible reforms, let us briefly review the international monetary system that provides the framework for the international financial system. Before suggesting reforms, it may be useful to recapitulate—very, very briefly—some key characteristics of the international monetary system and the role of the International Monetary Fund. The Fund is, in effect, a major credit-creating institution, but it is not a commercial bank concerned primarily with risk and profitability. More than 150 member countries have joined together to achieve an international monetary environment and system deemed desirable by its members. This international monetary system is intended to promote economic growth and international specialization by promoting nondiscriminatory, competitive international trade and flows of productive capital. These purposes were originally to be accomplished by having a system of relatively stable exchange rates, agreed upon by the international community, and by avoiding the use of governmental restrictions on international payments for goods and services. International trade was expected to benefit from a high degree of certainty in exchange rates.

This system no longer exists. An entrepreneur engaging in commerce or industry is faced with foreign earnings whose value, in the currency of the trader or producer, is subject to a wide range of uncertainty. Trade and investments, which are profitable at existing exchange rates, become unprofitable if exchange rates change.

The international monetary system does serve the objectives of high employment and greater productivity in the world economy by its rules and actions in avoiding or reducing restrictions on payments for goods and services. Foreign exchange shortages in the 1970s and 1980s, however, caused countries to use such restrictions, as they rationed their foreign exchange income in accordance with foreign exchange budgets established by governments. Whatever the attractiveness of these techniques in economizing on the use of foreign exchange, they do not serve the purpose of promoting international trade on a competitive basis, leading to greater, more efficient specialization in the world economy and increases in global output.

The events of the 1980s caused major setbacks in the international monetary system. The 1970s had already ended the system of stable exchange rates that were agreed upon internationally. Instead, the world system became based on fluctuating exchange rates, which proved disappointingly volatile and unable to assure realistic exchange rates in the 1970s and 1980s. In the 1980s, the developing countries had to resort to intensified use of restrictions on current payments. Fortunately, the developed countries were able to avoid this backsliding.

By using its financial resources, the Fund was supposed to help countries avoid such restrictions on payments, but it did not have sufficient resources. Moreover, its mode of operations proved unsuitable for many developing countries. The Fund usually operates on the assumption that within a fairly short period of 1 to 3 years, most borrowing countries can adopt policies that can reduce their external deficits and enable the borrowers to repay credits obtained from the Fund. This is a reasonable expectation in the case of industrial countries or the unusual developing countries, such as Saudi Arabia or Venezuela, that have manageable balance-of-payments positions, because of oil. In the case of most developing countries, the fulfillment of these expectations depends largely on world economic conditions. During the 1950s and 1960s, when the world economy was on a strong upward trend and when downswings in the business cycle were mild and short-lived, developing countries could bring excessive deficits under control rather quickly. Import demand and other needs for foreign exchange, including debt servicing, tended to exceed available foreign exchange from earnings, but remaining needs for foreign exchange could be financed from available capital inflows. When foreign exchange difficulties arose, feasible changes in monetary, fiscal, and wage policies, combined with exchange rate adjustments, often brought quick results.

At times in the 1950s and 1960s, these remedies proved short-lived, but they could be repeated. There were continued instability and setbacks, but the growth trends in the developing countries were upward and mostly exceeded the rapid population growth trends. Living standards rose. Under these conditions, developing countries could meet their financial repayment obligations to the Fund and could agree to the conditions countries had to meet to obtain financial assistance from the Fund.

Conditionality on the use of Fund resources has been practiced consistently by the Fund since the early 1950s. Conditionality in the Fund, however, was greatly influenced during these earlier years by the central role of the Fund in relation to developed countries. The British pound sterling exchange rate and the sterling area payments restrictions were the principal matters of concern. The United Kingdom repeatedly needed to use the Fund's financial resources. Much of Fund conditionality evolved from relations with the United Kingdom. The United Kingdom could, and did, meet Fund conditions for use of its resources by adopting remedial policies that worked successfully long enough to enable it to repay the Fund—often ahead of schedule. The United Kingdom had originally been a strong advocate of unconditional, or automatic, access to the Fund's financial resources, but by the end of the 1950s, it came to see that it could meet Fund conditions and repay any financial assistance. The United Kingdom's and other European nations' resistance to conditionality ended by the 1960s, and these countries became strong advocates of conditionality. The United States always supported conditionality in principal, but with great flexibility in application to individual country situations.

Member countries of the Fund were chronically uneasy in the 1960s and 1970s about their ability to adopt adjustment measures that would enable them to repay financial assistance from the Fund in a few years. These countries lobbied the United States and other donors. The outcome was a variety of Fund policies and facilities in the 1960s and 1970s that provided for both limited amounts of Fund assistance without domestic policy adjustments and additional amounts with conditions, usually called "higher-credit tranche drawings." Time limits for repayment were usually 3 years or less, for amounts much like those countries could obtain from the Fund.

As the years went on and the hardships of the 1970s were experienced, new Fund facilities were devised that increased the amount of assistance developing countries could obtain. Poorer countries were helped to meet interest costs by providing for interest subsidization. In some cases, the contractual period for repayment was lengthened. At the same time, conditionality continued for larger amounts of Fund assistance. Developing countries tried to avoid access under the tougher conditions, but the events of the 1980s compelled their usage, and the Fund found itself playing a much more influential and even an authoritative role in the affairs of developing countries. The insistence of commercial banks—and then other sources of financing, such as the World Bank and the export credit agencies of industrial countries—that borrowing countries meet IMF conditionality transformed the Fund. It became the central agency in managing the flows of funds to developing countries.

Fund conditionality is not the same for developing countries as for developed countries. International rules are not uniform in practice. Similarly, IMF conditionality is not uniform with respect to repayment nor, in effect, interest costs. Countries are increasingly being given a larger number of years—say, 3 years or more (not a uniform period)—to improve conditions along lines agreed upon between the country and the IMF. It is recognized that until a developing country has resumed satisfactory growth, it remains in a situation of emergency difficulties. This has not meant, however, that the time period for a program or the repayment period is stretched to cover the entire recovery period or to extend into the period after the recovery, when a country becomes able to repay the Fund and accumulate international reserves. IMF conditionality must be even more open to long-term time horizons—beyond 3 or 4 years—if IMF-supported adjustment programs are to be considered sufficiently long to restore satisfactory growth. Conditionality cannot provide merely for improvements in the balance of payments or in fiscal and monetary conditions.

Conditionality that recognizes the special circumstances and needs of the developing countries must encompass development needs, practices, and policies. This will involve more frequent collaborative relations among the IMF, the World Bank, and the regional development banks. Supporting funds can come from all of these institutions, and there can be a consensus on which adjustment policies would be appropriate. Just as the BIS is a natural close collaborator with the IMF in dealing with the OECD-type countries, the multilateral development banks are the natural intimate collaborators with the IMF in dealing with developing countries.

Relations among Multilateral Institutions

A recent initiative taken by the United States—the so-called Baker proposal—envisages closer collaboration among the IMF and the World Bank, the Inter-American Development Bank, and probably also the Asian and African Development Banks. The idea of involving the multilateral development banks in assessing domestic adjustment programs of developing countries in collaboration with the IMF, and of conditioning assistance to countries on the implementation of such agreed programs, is not new. Much collaboration has been going on for years, but the multilateral development banks have not played a major, responsible role in the international effort to achieve acceptable adjustment policies. Now they are again being urged to do so. For me, it is a return to the 1960s, when these matters were intensely discussed among nations and international agreements to this end were almost reached. Recalling the experiences of that period may help those responsible now to achieve more success. A brief glimpse at history may be useful to the reader. It is recommended that those responsible for policymaking in these matters delve much more deeply into these past experiences.

In the 1960s, the United Nations Conference on Trade and Development (UNCTAD) adopted a resolution asking the World Bank to consider the problem of the disruption of development programs caused by unexpected declines in export earnings. The resolution was introduced by the United Kingdom and received unanimous approval of member countries. It was generally assumed that if any finance was necessary, it could be part of the financial operations of the World Bank and the International Development Association. This resolution was offered essentially as an alternative to international commodity agreements in dealing with the problems caused for many developing countries that were primary product exporters by the volatility of these commodity prices and the long-term downward trend in their so-called terms of trade—that is, the relationship of export prices to import prices. Prices of imported manufactures have tended to rise for decades, while commodity prices—exports—had tended to decline. Primary products were mostly agricultural and mineral, aside from oil and precious and rare metals. These conditions for primary commodities repeatedly created severe balance-of-payments difficulties. Not only did those poorer countries normally need a net inflow of foreign resources to supplement their own resources and savings, but declining export prices, often coupled with rising import prices, meant large increases in balance-of-payments deficits that were not caused by larger imports in real terms of goods and services.

The use of international commodity agreements to stabilize world commodity prices had been advocated since the early years of the twentieth century. Some commodities—for example, tin, rubber, sugar, and coffee—had been the subject of international agreements. A cocoa agreement had been discussed for decades. As always, the difficulty in reaching such agreements was caused by differing views of consuming and producing nations. Consuming nations wanted to have prices as low as possible; producing nations preferred the reverse. Few international agreements had been signed, and even fewer worked. The coffee agreement was among the more successful. The "terms of trade" issue remained throughout these decades and still is an issue among economists and governments.

In any case, many developing countries relied heavily on foreign exchange earnings from these commodity exports, and these earnings were unreliable and unpredictable. The International Monetary Fund had established a facility in 1963 to help countries facing such difficulties, but the magnitudes of assistance were limited by policy, by the limitations on the Fund's financial resources, and by the need of the Fund to limit such assistance to relatively short maturities of only a few years.

The World Bank: A Supplementary Finance Scheme

The World Bank staff studied the matter in the 1960s, as requested by UNCTAD. It responded to another salient feature common to most developing countries—that developing countries are trying to accelerate the process of social and political change by governmental policies and practices. Even where private institutions, mechanisms, and markets exist, these official policies are strong determinants of activities and events. Often, the government is also the owner and manager of enterprises producing goods and services. Government determines what is profitable or unprofitable. It greatly influences consumption, savings, investments, prices, availability and cost of credit, wages, and other production costs, even physical availability of goods and services. Given this prevailing broad view of the role of government, most developing countries developed a planning or programming approach to the management of their economies. Expertise in this field became highly developed, encouraged by the use of econometric techniques and aided by electronic computation. Forward planning is almost universal, as it is in most business organizations and international organizations.

Planning, often combined with close government regulation and even ownership, was a response to the nature of mixed economies. The tasks of ordering economic life were not left to markets alone. Governments needed to budget ahead, even years ahead. In developing countries, a critical need was to know what foreign goods and services would be needed for accelerated development and what foreign exchange was likely to be available to pay for them. The needed foreign exchange would come mostly form earnings from exports. Even when foreign and/or private credits are important, the bulk of foreign exchange comes from export earnings. Countries' planning started with a few key income assumptions, such as income/savings ratios. Another critical assumption—expected foreign exchange earnings—was the linchpin of the entire planning effort. Out of this need and process came the projection of foreign exchange earnings or total foreign exchange receipts from all sources.

The World Bank's staff's proposal addressed the question of what happened to the development efforts of well-managed countries when export earnings fell significantly below the expectations of foreign exchange availability that had been built into the entire development effort. Analysis and experience indicated that under such conditions, development was seriously disrupted by reductions in investments. Governments found that their own expenditures were largely politically and socially motivated, and popular consumption was hard to constrain. Faced with the need to tighten belts because foreign exchange was less than originally assumed in their plans, development—that is, investments in the public and private sectors—bore the brunt of retrenchment.

The IMF did not have the responsibility to defend development. The World Bank did. However, the lending programs of the World Bank and the IDA were mostly tied to large-scale new investment projects, almost all in the public sector. The existing practices did not operate to defend development against the significant shortfalls between expectations of foreign exchange and actual availability. This was a recurrent and major problem, even during the 1950s and 1960s, when the world economy was in a long-term prosperous phase. It was feared that if the world experienced a serious recession, developing countries would be severely hurt—as did happen later in the 1970s and 1980s.

The problem I have described was explored over many months by the World Bank, resulting in a staff proposal for supplementary financial measures in December 1965. The proposal provided for the World Bank group to be prepared to expand its financing of a country's development program when such was required by unexpected declines in the country's export earnings. The proposal was vigorously championed by Raul Prebisch, the head of UNCTAD, by various developed and developing countries, and by the staff of the World Bank. Unlike similar measures in the IMF, it was specifically targeted to defend development, and the terms of financial aid were those of multilateral development finance—that is, those of the World Bank, the IDA, or a mixture of the two. Assistance was conditional on prior agreement with the World Bank (later modified by a German proposal to include the Fund in a joint evaluation procedure) that the country was pursuing sound development objectives, policies, and practices. If this proposal had been brought into existence, the 1980s need not have seen the drastic setbacks to development. Such defense mechanisms still do not exist.

The mechanism proposed by the World Bank staff would have provided developing countries with the foreign exchange needed to carry on internationally agreed development programs if foreign exchange earnings fell below the magnitudes that had been projected in their development planning. Unlike the IMF's compensatory financing facility, the proposed World Bank mechanism did not relate its assistance to declines in export earnings. Rather, it was related to the difference between expected earnings and actual earnings. Problems can arise even when export earnings are rising. Actual experiences illustrate the difference. When the price of oil is rising, experts and countries can agree on what they expect oil prices and international sales to be. For example, the international community may well agree that it is reasonable for a country to project a 20 percent per annum rise in earnings from oil sales for a 5-year period and may plan an investment program assuming the availability of this foreign exchange. However, conditions may change. Oil prices may not rise as much, and world demand may be less. Earnings may rise, but only 5 percent per annum. Investments have already begun on the basis of a rise of 20 percent, and capital has been sunk into the projects. The international community has scrutinized these investments and has found them worthy of international support. The country is unable to find other investable funds from domestic or foreign sources. Consumption cannot be significantly compressed further to provide increased private savings, and the budgetary conditions cannot generate more governmental savings.

The remaining adjustment step is to cut back on investments. Short-term external borrowing could temporarily delay such a need, but the need is for financing for long-term investments, and the unfavorable conditions may not be reversed, even after the initial cause of the change has disappeared. Short-term funds provide temporary net inflows of funds, but repayment meant outflows. If the repayment obligations come sooner than enduring improvements in the external position of the country, the short-term borrowing does not solve the immediate balance-of-payments problem of the borrowing country. It increases the amount of debt servicing obligation without resulting in a corresponding simultaneous increase in ability to service debt. If the short-term borrowing reflects the ability of a borrowing country to obtain external funds even when its export earnings are not as strong as expected, such a borrowing country could carry on its investment program and not need outside assistance from the international community to do so. This, however, would be an unusual case.

The authors of the World Bank scheme were well aware that other "unexpected" developments could have adverse effects similar to those of shortfalls in expected export earnings, especially increased costs of capital goods and food and rises in interest rates. However, export earnings were a large proportion of total receipts. The prices of capital goods were an important though usually only small proportion of external payments. Interest rates were still largely fixed; in any case, they were relatively low in the 1960s. For many countries, food imports were much more substantial. A very large rise in the costs of food could also be devastating. The World

Bank's supplementary finance scheme did not cover these contingencies, and this was recognized as a shortcoming of the scheme. The World Bank staff focused on shortfalls in export because this was requested by the countries represented in UNCTAD. The international community was responding to the alternative suggestions for commodity agreements.

If the scheme were evolved under the conditions of the 1980s, more attention would have to be paid to possible movements in import prices and interest rates and to possible adverse changes in the availability of foreign capital. It is a logical evolution of the purpose and mechanism of supplementary finance to assist countries experiencing sharp *unexpected* increases in import prices and interest rates—for example, oil as in the 1970s—or sharp reductions in net capital inflows. In such cases, adjustments to these adversities could otherwise require substantial reductions (and losses in sunken capital) in investments. Thus, if the supplementary finance scheme had gone into effect in the 1960s, the developing countries would have been better able to cope with the negative developments of the 1970s and 1980s and more able to expand its approach to other important areas in the 1970s and 1980s. Not only would more external resources have been available in the 1970s to cushion the impact of unexpected external adversities, but the assistance would have been a long-term basis, with much less reliance on short- and medium-term bank borrowing. In this environment, commercial banks would have been used less and, to the extent used, would have had much less reason to be nervous about their international exposures in developing countries. Their response of drastic withdrawal in the 1980s would have been less likely to occur.

Such speculation on history is "iffy" at best, however. I am convinced that many of the difficulties of the 1970s and 1980s could have been averted if the international community had accepted the principle of defending development as decisively as it had accepted the principle, in earlier decades, of defending convertibility of currencies. Failure to have done so is water over the dam, however. Speculations about what might have been are interesting, but their usefulness is more in what they teach us about the inadequacies of the international financial system. The international financial system is still not designed to defend development, nor does it function satisfactorily without design. Therefore, ways and means to remedy this deficiency are major components of suggestions to reform the international financial system to make it suitable for the world economy. Because of the critical role that could be played by some similar schemes to defend development, somewhat more is said here about the international reaction to the World Bank's supplementary finance scheme.

The supplementary finance proposal had the strong support of a large number of governments of industrial and developing countries. Among the warmly supporting industrial countries were Canada, Germany, Switzerland, and Sweden. Germany supported it with the provision that there should be close World Bank–IMF cooperation in administering the scheme. The United States was a lukewarm supporter, being fearful of the budgetary requirements—that is, that it would require a larger IDA than otherwise would be necessary. Some members of the World Bank staff were fearful that such activities would take place at the expense of project financing. Balance-of-payments financing for development was not in fashion with much of the World Bank staff, and these views were shared by the new president of the World Bank, who came to this position in 1968. In addition, some members of the Fund staff feared a diminution of the influence of the Fund and lobbied strongly against international support for the scheme. The Fund staff involved in these matters argued that the Fund was able to handle these conditions without World Bank involvement. The proposal was shelved toward the end of the 1960s.

One positive consequence of the World Bank proposal was to facilitate an increase in the IMF's compensatory financing facility. It helped set the stage for the creation of new IMF facilities in the 1970s, in response to the difficulties created by the large oil price increases. However, the need for this major improvement in development finance remained. Developing countries continue to base their investment activities on estimates of future foreign exchange availability and other factors, such as costs of imports and finance. However well done, such forecasts can go wrong—and a developing country has little margin for handling adverse changes, even with the help of the IMF facilities, which provide assistance in the short or medium term, not for the well over 10 years needed, or shorter maturities that must be continuously renewed or rolled over.

Experience is replete with examples of how unexpected adverse changes in the world environment can disrupt sound development programs. When such changes occur, there are pressures within a developing country to maintain noninvestment public expenditures, including subsidization of consumption. Too often, topflight investment projects are sacrificed to more immediate political and social needs and purposes. Either local currency financing is cut back to reduce public investment expenditures or scarce foreign exchange is otherwise used. There is a need for a mechanism to defend top-priority investments. Part of the mechanism already exists—international endorsement of investment programs for projects that meet international standards. The international community can do more to have countries follow policies designed to encourage larger flows of private capital, particularly equity capital. Another part of the mechanism involves ensuring that the international development institutions can provide, directly or indirectly (via guarantees), additional financing to offset, in whole or in part, the unexpected shortfalls in foreign exchange earnings. Such financing would enable countries to continue their development programs, thus helping to maintain growth and employment and reducing social and political instability. If the world environment is seriously impaired, domestic adjustments in real income in developing countries would inevitably be required, but their impact would be less severe and less costly to long-term growth and development if financing to defend development was available. The experience of Southeast Asian and Far Eastern countries in recent years indicates, in part, the beneficial effects of the important presence, during generally adverse conditions, of multilateral development banks that do not cut bank lending during such periods. Such countries have the additional benefit of finding it easier to defend their creditworthiness with private banks, to attract foreign equity capital, and thus to have continued access to private sources of external finance for their development programs.

As noted earlier, the experience of the 1970s and 1980s indicates that the concept of preventing disruptions resulting from unexpected export shortfalls must be expanded to cover other unexpected difficulties that are caused by factors outside the control of borrowing countries, including unexpected increases in certain import prices, such as oil and food prices; unexpected higher interest rates; and unexpected obstacles in access to private financial markets.

The Baker Proposal

The 1985 proposal of U.S. Treasury Secretary Baker to deal with the international debt problem and the gloomy prospects facing many developing countries, especially those in Latin America and

Africa, opens up the possibilities of again considering the equivalent of the World Bank's supplementary finance scheme, with major roles to be played by the World Bank and the regional multilateral development banks in Africa, Asia and Latin America, in close collaboration with the International Monetary Fund. The blueprint exists in the supplementary finance scheme. The essential ingredients of the Baker plan are a clear recognition of the need for more lending by commercial banks to developing countries, an expanded role of the World Bank and the regional development banks in close cooperation and collaboration with each other and with the International Monetary Fund, and the acceptance by borrowers that external financing is conditional on the international acceptability of their economic management of their countries. The original countries suggested by Secretary Baker for such assistance may not necessarily be those that would need or qualify for such a scheme, but the choice of countries has not been an essential feature of his proposal.

The Baker proposal has serious shortcomings, however. The amounts to be provided by the commercial banks and the multilateral development banks are much too small to deal with the realities of the problems facing giant developing countries such as Mexico or Brazil, or Korea in the future. The significance of the Baker scheme, however, is its recognition that the external debt problem is not being handled successfully by current methods and that it cannot be treated in isolation from newly expanded international lending by private and official entities. Such lending is inevitably related to meeting the lending criteria of the private and public sources of finance, categorized as economic management. These lending criteria have to recognize the special needs and conditions of developing countries, and the scope of such conditions must include developmental as well as monetary criteria. Therefore, the interests of the international community are better reflected in a combination of the World Bank, the regional development banks, and the IMF than in any one of these institutions alone. The multilateral development banks had already begun to move in this direction—with, for example, the structural adjustments loans of the World Bank and the project financing of the African Development Bank. These moves have to reinforce each other, and doing so will require much closer cooperation and collaboration. The Baker proposal left many issues unanswered, but it pointed to a way to deal with a major weakness in the international financial system.

The Baker plan is a major effort to jump over the high obstacle of the lost creditworthiness of the borrowing countries. It attaches great importance to expanded lending by private banks to countries regarded as not meeting their lending criteria for new money. The Baker plan does not, however, provide a mechanism for the restoration of creditworthiness—an essential ingredient.

Another major weakness is the absence of needed large commitments by the United States and other industrial countries to provide external funds bilaterally, by loans or guarantees, or multilaterally, by greatly expanding the multilateral development banks and the IMF.

However, the lid is off the box. The international community can again think more realistically and more boldly. Experience can be heeded. The supplementary finance scheme of the 1960s came from a background of euphoric optimism and international recognition of the need to be helpful to the poorer nations. The 1960s was the "first development decade," but there was no worldwide emergency or crisis. The need to change required feats of the imagination and a commitment to creativity and novelty—not a favorable environment for major international financial innovation. The 1970s was a decade of crises. In the early 1980s, deep and prolonged recessions, an overvalued U.S. dollar, food shortages, continuing global inflation, high interest rates, and unrealistic and volatile exchange rates kept the world economy reeling and lurching. Falling oil prices and interest rates helped many oil-importing developed and developing countries, such as Germany and Brazil, but hurt oil exporters, such as Mexico, Egypt, and Venezuela. The 1980s became a decade of crises and concerns, resulting in worldwide caution akin to endemic pessimism. The opening made by the Baker plan has a fighting chance to result in a major improvement in the management of the world economy, because it is a response to an urgent need that is felt around the world. The outcome is likely to be very different (and this book is offered in the hope that it will help in the process of finding lasting solutions), but the impetus given by the Baker plan can make it more possible for the world to look at the problems squarely, face the need for major reforms, and move to make these reforms.

From a longer-run perspective, perhaps the most significant aspect of the Baker plan is its recognition that the self-adjusting mechanisms that exist in national economics and in international economic

relations cannot by themselves be relied upon to give acceptable results. Instead, solutions are sought that are compatible with the conditions of modern societies. Such concepts as self-reliance, growth,
and income distribution are abstractions until they are translated into
political realities. The world is not self-adjusting. Society-inspired
expectations remain strong forces, and governments respond using
combinations of national and international institutions, both private
and official, to cope in such a way that they can have reason to hope
for acceptability and success. Incentives and disincentives of a material kind—profits, wages, money supply, interest rates, exchange
rates, subsidies, taxes, credits—remain the strong levers of action,
but the movements and positions of these levers are not left to autonomous forces. Governments choose and, in so doing, take responsibility for economic behavior. Developing countries will continue
to give a major role to government, but they must give it a changed
context that is more likely to succeed in achieving societal aims. With
this philosophy, the world becomes freer to choose but also becomes
responsible for choosing wisely. The multilateral financial institutions—the IMF, the World Bank, and the regional development
banks—become much more important, because they are instruments
of governments, more reflective of global interdependency, and more
likely to succeed than any single national entity or policy can hope
or expect to be.

Primary Product Issues

Closely related to the issues involved in supplementary finance is the
problem of the volatility of primary product prices and their secular
downward trend. As noted earlier, these conditions have long been
recognized as a major source of difficulties for borrowing developing
countries. The literature on this subject is very large. Countries have
tried to agree on international commodity agreements, and assistance
has been given by multilateral institutions to the functioning of these
agreements. Only a few successes have been experienced, however.
Even relative success stories, such as the tin agreement, have had
disastrous difficulties. The problems of volatility in commodity
prices and declining trends do not go away. Copper prices in recent
years illustrate the problem for Chile, Peru, Zaire, and Zambia. Oil
prices are the dramatic example of the 1980s. Other commodities
will probably be problems in the future, reflecting cyclical down-

turns, technological changes, and structural changes in world consumption. The techniques tried thus far in agreements governing coffee, tin, and a few other commodities have included establishing floor and ceiling prices and using buffer stocks held by the authority managing the agreement to keep prices within agreed ranges. These agreements have also included ceilings on production and export quotas. Existing international arrangements can conceivably be strengthened; for example, there could be more financing to hold buffer stocks. Also, however, new and different approaches may be found. Various U.N. agencies are well qualified to explore, in detail, ways and means of dealing with the problems caused by volatility and declining trends in commodity prices. It is obvious that these conditions result in grave balance-of-payments difficulties, a serious weakening creditworthiness with private lenders, and setbacks to needed growth and development.

My own preference is for approaches closer to the supplementary financing measures described here, because the fundamental remedy is to overcome the dependency of developing country primary producers on foreign exchange earnings from exports of primary products. Even strong primary products, such as oil and tin, are unreliable earners of foreign exchange. Feast follows famine, and chaos rules. Such dependency can be overcome only by diversifying export products and markets, and development achieves this diversification.

Cooperation between Multilateral Institutions and Private Institutions

Another way to strengthen the international financial system is by much greater use of international mechanisms that rely successfully on private sources of finance. Developing countries need larger and more flexible access to private sources of finance. Expanding the role of existing multilateral institutions to increase the flow of private capital is a tried and feasible way to help accomplish this objective. This can be done in various ways—expanding the ability of these banks to borrow from private markets to fund loans to developing countries, increasing cofinancing with other institutions, greater use of their guarantee authority, and encouraging formation of private international financing institutions.

The multilateral banks are all engaged in important schemes that include outside sources of financing, often involving a substantial multiple of the banks' financial input. This cofinancing is an established part of international finance, but it has not flourished as much as it could. The multilateral bank is often in the position of advocate of the borrower, seeking best terms for the borrower. The private bank is a commercial lender; it is not in the foreign assistance business. It does not welcome outside pressures to reduce earnings, and this has limited its enthusiasm for cofinancing with official institutions.

Cofinancing takes place more readily among similar lenders. A regional development bank finds a ready and willing partner in the World Bank, and vice versa. A commercial bank finds a ready and willing partner in another commercial bank or, often, in a large number of them in a so-called syndicate or club. The combination of private and official lenders is harder to make work—but it does work from time to time in significant magnitudes. If the private lender is uneasy about the country risk in lending to a particular country, the simultaneous presence of a multilateral lender may reduce the perception of risk to an acceptable level. One mode is for the commercial bank to participate in the earlier or shorter maturities, which are less risky for it, while the multilateral bank takes the longer maturities, thus adapting to the particular risk preferences of lenders.

Experience creates new opportunities and modes, but the inherent differences continue. The commercial bank wants to make loans, its principal source of income. Commercial banks are risk avoiders, however. The multilateral banks want to promote development and are risk accepters. The ideal for a commercial bank is satisfactory profits and virtually no risk to the bank—an ideal rarely achieved in practice. Risk aversion and earning revenues from lending must be reconciled. Cofinancing helps in this reconciliation, but the presence of the multilateral bank does not go all the way toward eliminating risk. Cross-default clauses, even if the lenders involved can agree to them, are largely empty gestures. The multilateral development banks is not so concerned about repayments. It has the benefit of being a preferred creditor; its loans have not been renegotiated, and servicing is regarded as a firm, nonnegotiable commitment by the borrower. Moreover, it has no regulatory authorities to classify its loans and insist on write-offs, write-downs, or increases in reserves. The obligations of the multilateral development banks for funds raised in capital markets are ultimately guaranteed by the callable capital of its shareholders of sovereign countries such as the United

States, the United Kingdom, Germany, Japan, France, and so on, as well as developing countries. The multilateral bank does worry about how its borrowers service their loans. During the current external payments crises of many member countries, these banks have experienced arrears in payments to them. They cannot contemplate declarations of defaults, but they have the leverage that comes from their ability to continue lending (or disbursing) on past and new loan commitments. They do not withdraw from new lending because their borrowing member is in balance-of-payments difficulties. If anything, quite the contrary is the case. Thus, their view of a lender is profoundly different from that of a private lender. They often make willing but uneasy partners. More can be done if the private banks are encouraged to initiate lending in which they involve the official institutions, rather than the reverse. Cofinancing is helpful, but it cannot be regarded as a major remedy for the present inadequacies of the international financial system.

Other measures are needed to tap private savings in the industrial world for use in lending to developing countries. Among the most obvious have been the greatly expanded official aid programs that use budgetary funds that tap domestic savings. However, these programs need the political support of governments. Though increases in such support have occurred in the 1970s and 1980s, it has been clear since the 1960s that they have been made most reluctantly—increasingly so in the United States and some other industrial countries. This condition is not expected to change. The proposals made in this book stress the use of private sources of finance, even when multilateral official institutions are the intermediaries.

Private New International Development Finance Institutions

Inspired by the combination of developing countries' need for more external capital and creditor countries' budgetary difficulties, I proposed to various multilateral development banks during the 1980s that they use their resources to bring into existence institutions that would be able to mobilize additional private funds for developing countries without going to national budgets. The essentials of this proposal are as follows:

1. Each multilateral development bank would help to capitalize,

from its accumulated reserves, a new international lending institution, which could be a commercial bank or an investment bank, or both. The new entity would be essentially private, not governmental.

2. The bulk of capital would be provided by private investors around the world.

3. The regional multilateral development bank would be an investor—not a manager—and a minority shareholder. It could sit on the board of directors, but the board would *not* represent governments. The board would be composed of private individuals representing all shareholders and voting as such.

4. The management would be chosen by the board and would come from private financial backgrounds.

5. The new bank would be profit-oriented, but its portfolio would be limited to developing countries (or to a particular region if capitalized in part by one regional development bank).

6. The bank could be chartered as a bank and could leverage its capital. It could be an investment or merchant bank, raising funds for individual projects or having pools of funds for a collection of projects.

7. The total capitalization could start with about $1 billion, with the multilateral development bank holding 20 percent of the shares.

8. The new bank would borrow from private capital markets, as do other commercial banks, and all care would be taken to safeguard the essentially private character of the new institution.

9. The multilateral development banks would be prepared to make available to private investors the results of their project investigations, particularly in industrial and other activities of potential interest to private investors or lenders.

I explored this proposal widely to test its feasibility. It was well received by potential private investors and bank regulators, and it was seen as adding substantially to the resources available to developing countries. It was originally designed in terms of the Inter-American Development Bank but, with that bank's permission, was brought to the attention of the Asian Development Bank and the

World Bank. The proposal was closely studied and discussed within the Inter-American Development Bank and is reported to have helped in the formation of a new international investment entity—an affiliate of the Inter-American Development Bank that serves the similar purpose of encouraging private investment in Latin America but is essentially an official—not private—institution.

A new private institution of this kind could provide additional financial resources; relatively reduce reliance on official sources of funds; and involve the private sectors more deeply in the development process. The new institutions could better assume country risks because of the presence of the multilateral development banks as project evaluators, members of the board, and investors, while enjoying freedom from severe constraints, such as the so-called gearing ratios of these inter-governmental multilateral development banks. These banks limit lending to capital on a one-to-one basis and consider guaranteeing of loans as equivalent to loans. If a commercial bank is not deemed appropriate, the new bank could be structured as an investment bank or an investment pool. The total commitment of all governments combined would be only one-fifth of the total capital, and that would be contributed through the ownership of shares by the multilateral development banks. No new funds would be needed from governments. The new bank could pass the requirements of regulatory authorities and meet the high standards of rating agencies.

A major issue is the commercial, private character of the proposed bank. Would an intergovernmental entity—a multilateral development bank—help bring into existence a commercial bank directed and managed by others coming from the private sector and responsible to a board of which a majority come from the private sector? This would obviously be a major innovation. It can be done without having a budgetary impact on creditor countries and without weakening the influence and scope of the official institutions. These official institutions would not have to give up existing useful practices, such as project evaluation in the industrial field, because of their own existing financial limitations as lenders. Because of these limitations, these institutions must husband their lending authority for other high-priority needs, such as rural development, education, and health. The proposed institution could operate actively during adverse periods in the world economy. Its existence and activities would strengthen the creditworthiness of the borrowing countries

with commercial bank lenders while the multilateral agencies continued to carry on their essential functions.

This proposal points to a more general need. The multilateral
development banks (MDBs) need to expand the scope of magnitude
of their activities greatly. They have outlived their prime emphasis
on financing relatively large-scale public sector investments, such as
roads, power, irrigation, and education. They need to become part
of the day-to-day economic life of a country, sharing the burden of
managing economies to achieve the goals of economic and social development. Thus, the multilateral development banks must be able
to do much more financially. For example, these banks must perceive
of themselves as having a much more important countercyclical role.
This can be done through their traditional lending activities—particularly project financing, various forms of balance-of-payments financing, expanded cofinancing, closer collaboration with the IMF in
the formulation and monitoring of conditionality—or through new
forms such as the supplementary financing proposals described here
or more flexible use of their guarantee authority. There is much more
for the MDBs to do. The case for a larger role for them—including
arguments for more concessional assistance through entities like the
IDA, and the African Development Fund in the African Development Bank—has been made strongly and effectively. The point to
be emphasized herein is that the larger the multilateral agencies, the
more creditworthy borrowing countries will be for private sources
of financing. Given the expanded need for development finance, the
fear that more done by one lender will be at the expense of others
seems groundless. It is more likely that there will continue to be
shortages of all finances combined. If this proves wrong, ground
rules can then be more clearly defined for the areas best served by
different lenders.

The proposed role of the multilateral development banks can be
summed up in the phrase *defense of development*. Like any credit-
creating mechanism, the MDBs will have to be concerned that their
lending operations, whatever they are, meet high standards of evaluation and continuous monitoring. As a financial institution, an
MDB intends to have profits—that is, net income after costs of funds
to it plus administrative costs. If it were a private commercial bank,
it would also have to take into account taxation and would have to
be prepared to pay dividends to shareholders. It may wish to incur
costs similar to taxes, such as contributions to local communities or,

more important, to their concessional arms—for example, the IDA. Having done this, these banks can still be handsomely profitable, because they borrow at interest rates and maturities that are available to the strongest borrowers and lend at interest rates above the costs of funds. They earn profits even though they will not charge their borrowers as much as commercial sources would. In this way, their borrowers get much of the benefit of the creditworthiness of the development bank. Nevertheless, borrowers will still pay enough to earn profits for the multilateral development bank, thus, among other effects, helping the development bank continue to access financial markets as favorable rates.

Another way to strengthen the international financial system is to expand the guarantee activities of the multilateral development banks. Guarantees can be used to overcome the weak country risk standing of the developing countries. The mechanisms are largely in place and can be adapted to new conditions and needs. The multilateral development banks have the authority. Because their ability to lend, guarantee, and borrow is tightly limited to capital, increased guarantees require more capital. The multilateral development banks do not have to use budgetary funds to expand their capital base. With an expanded capital base, they can expand their lending and guarantee functions with funds from private sources. Their borrowings from private sources are already much larger than was deemed feasible in the past. The essential feature of this capacity to borrow is the willingness of their member country shareholders to guarantee, collectively, the borrowings of the multilateral or regional development bank. In 40 years, this guarantee has never been invoked, and it is most unlikely that it ever will be invoked. It would take a continuing combination of global catastrophes to create the need to invoke such guarantees. Yet the existence of these guarantees is what creates the creditworthiness of these institutions. These institutions have a combined capital of considerably over $100 billion; it can be expanded much more—to $300 billion—without drains on budgets.

A drawback is that many regard these development institutions as official aid. Much of the explanation for this attitude is, of course, the aforementioned guarantees given by member countries. In addition, borrowing governments must guarantee loans made to entities in their countries, whether private or public. Perhaps more important is that MDB loans have been mostly for public sector projects. These conditions can be readily changed, however. Instead, governments can agree to give guarantees automatically to all private sector loans granted by a multilateral development bank. The provision could become merely a formality. The private sector could become a major source of loan demand. This would be a drastic change in the orientation of these development banks, but it would be quite feasible.

Within these frameworks, the development banks can make much more use of existing private financial institutions by using their guarantor authority instead of direct loans. That practice would deepen the role of such private institutions in the development process and make them more willing to play such a role without the presence of the multilateral institutions.

If the financial capabilities of the MDBs are sufficiently expanded, these multilateral development banks could become both the major defenders of development and, together with the IMF, the principal instruments for creating the preconditions for continued lending by private financial institutions during downswings of the business cycle and other adverse developments. The development process would gain something that it is now missing—namely, a built-in defender. As the defenders, the MDBs would have great influence on national development planning, programming, policies, and practices, including the relative roles of the private and public sectors. By so doing, the MDBs would help greatly in creating the preconditions for the restoration and maintenance of the creditworthiness of developing countries with commercial banks and other private lenders.

The order of magnitude of the capital of the development banks must be a multiple of existing sizes. This assumes that these institutions would play a full-fledged developmental role—directly or indirectly, via guarantees—including, where necessary, financing international exchange of goods and services, rehabilitating decapitalized economies, increasing private and public investments, transferring and adapting technology and management, and offsetting unexpected shortfalls in export earnings or unexpected increases in costs of imports. To do these tasks, the development banks must be increased by factors of three or four, with the increased capital allocated among the World Bank and the regional development banks or given to a new entity if, for some decisive reason, increasing the capital of existing institutions had to be ruled out as impossible. As a rough rule of thumb, it is suggested that the capital of the three major regional banks in Africa, Asia, and Latin America should equal the World Bank's capital. This would enable these banks, combined, to make commitments in the tens of billions of dollars per year—$25 billion to $30 billion per year would be a feasible level for the foreseeable future. Compared with the orders of magnitude of international trade, world savings and investments, international capital flows, debt servicing of past debts, and so forth, these magnitudes would still not be large. The availability of these resources could provide the catalyst for other sources of funds, but in any case, the great bulk of the resources would come from private sources via the multilateral development banks. Government budgets would provide only a very minor portion of such funds. The restoration of a viable international financial system need not await improvements in the budgeting conditions of the United States and other industrial countries.

It is appreciated that this implies that much larger debts would be owed by developing countries. As noted several times in this book, it is not the size of debts or debt servicing burdens that is of crucial importance for a developing country; rather, it is the need for new capital inflows to finance its balance-of-payments deficits, which include amortization and interest payments on external debts. The debt crises exist because international private lenders will not— it may be said, cannot—lend sufficiently when they perceive country risks to be excessive. They must withdraw. As suggested herein, ways and means can be found to prevent this loss of country creditworthiness. Such measures can help banks continue lending during adverse world and domestic conditions, and they are also likely to encourage more equity inflows. In such ways, debts can be serviced and restoration of creditworthiness can be achieved, even when the world economy is experiencing cyclical or other difficulties.

The consequences, however, will be a virtually continuously rising level of external debt, even if foreign equity investment also rises. The rising debt is the financial counterpart to the building of physical assets in the developing countries. It is external debt, rather than entirely domestic debt, because domestic savings are not enough to finance the physical investments required. As with domestic debt, it is desirable to increase the share of equity, but debt remains a principal instrument for transforming savings into physical capital. External debt accumulation will go on as long as a developing country is growing, until its own domestic savings are able to sustain a satisfactory growth rate. To regard the accumulation of external debt as erroneous or sinful is simplistic and misleading. What is an error or a sin is using borrowed funds unproductively and losing creditworthiness, which converts the benefits of capital inflows into the burden of servicing such inflows without the resources to do so. Theoretically, increased savings and higher productivity combined with reduced living standards can cope with the need to service external debt without a net inflow of new resources, but in the real world, this can translate into widespread misery, social disorder, and political upheaval—witness the global catastrophes unleashed by the Great Depression of the 1930s. It may seem paradoxical, but the road back to the restoration of creditworthiness requires more debt accumulations and a willingness to have conditions that enable external debts to rise even further.

Attention has been given thus far to how the commercial banking system and the multilateral development banks can be strengthened and, thus, can strengthen the international financial system. The suggested measures are aside from those needed to deal specifically with the current external debt crises. Of course, these suggestions are not an exhaustive list of possible improvements; it is hoped, however, that they will open doors. In addition, there are ways and means of strengthening the International Monetary Fund, which is the central manager of the international monetary system whose transcendent importance has repeatedly been emphasized herein. The International Monetary Fund needs to be strengthened, not only financially but also through more flexibility in its practices and procedures. The IMF must serve its agreed purposes—a growing, prosperous world made possible by expanding international trade in goods and services and flows of capital needed for productive investments.

The International Monetary Fund has a number of distinct functions that are all important for an effective international financial system and for the restoration of the creditworthiness of developing countries. First and foremost are its responsibilities as manager of the international code of monetary behavior embodied in its articles of agreement, policies, and practices. This code determines the policy priorities of the IMF. The Fund is not a freewheeling entity that decides its priorities as it sees fit. As discussed elsewhere, it must be guided by its own purposes; its modes of operations are circumscribed by its articles of agreement and by policies derived from these articles. Thus, it focuses on short- and medium-term balance-of-payments behavior and management, especially exchange rates and rules for international payments for current transactions (trade and services, including interest on debts). From these responsibilities comes its involvement in other aspects of domestic policy, especially domestic monetary, fiscal, and income policies. Savings and investments are important determinants of balance-of-payments behavior, so the IMF includes them in its agenda of adjustment policies or conditionality; development programs—their content and their financing—are closely related to these broader concerns, and so forth. The starting point, however, is the balance of payments, not the pace or content of social and economic development. Given its global responsibilities, the IMF's most important responsibility is the behavior of the major industrial countries whose monetary systems, and their interrelationships, constitute the international monetary system. The U.S. dollar exchange rate with the other major currencies—the pound sterling, the Japanese yen, German deutsche mark, the French franc, and others—are of key importance for the entire world economy. The exchange rates with the Brazilian, Mexican, or Korean currencies are not of the same global importance, but they are still significant. The importance of currencies reflects the magnitudes of economies and their roles in international trade and capital flows. These magnitudes and usages change gradually, but major shifts result over time—for example the relative economic rise of Japan and decline of the United Kingdom and the increasing use of the Japanese yen in international payments. Policies that further the international usage of a currency and encourage international capital flows or the evolution of a national currency into an international currency exemplify the central preoccupations of the international monetary system.

This central importance of the Fund's role vis-à-vis the industrial countries can be obscured by the relative attention given to other activities, such as the external debt problems of the developing countries, debt restructuring, and the adjustment programs agreed by them with the IMF. These are obviously important activities, but they are not central to the international monetary system.

Even from the viewpoint of the developing countries, the critical role of the Fund is the management of the international monetary system and its major constituent parts—that is, the monetary behavior of its economically largest and globally most important member countries. It is the function of the Fund to provide an environment that promotes the expansion of international trade, encourages capital flows for productive usage, and makes possible the achievement and maintenance of high levels of employment and growth in national economies. In brief, the Fund has a key role in achieving a favorable global economic environment. The global environment is principally determined by the major industrial countries. Instability of their exchange rates, unrealistic patterns of exchange rates, restrictions on international payments (directly via exchange controls or indirectly via trade restrictions), deflationary domestic policies, and persistent inflation are examples of what the Fund is supposed to help avoid. If the world economy, consisting mainly of the industrial countries, achieves a high level of employment and output—and the Fund is supposed to have a major part in achieving this—the developing countries can have more hope of coping with their own sets of problems.

If the Fund is to make a decisively larger contribution in assisting developing countries, more emphasis must be given to its role in achieving global prosperity. The world has failed to have satisfactory growth rates and levels of employment or to have stable or realistic exchange rates, orderly exchange markets, and avoidance of discriminatory trade practices by industrial countries. These are failures of the international monetary system. The other parts of the international financial system cannot overcome these failures; however, it can—it must—accommodate to them to try to limit their harmful effects.

To play a more decisive role in improving the international monetary system, the Fund needs strong support from its member countries, especially the United States and other large industrial countries. This means recognition of the need for further subordination of national policies to common monetary objectives—a view frequently expressed in declarations of summit or similar meetings but not sufficiently implemented in practice. Perhaps the reason for inadequate action lies in the fact that aside from the exchange rate for the U.S. dollar, the weaknesses of the international monetary system have not been of overwhelming or critical importance in the crises of the 1980s. The continued convertibility of the major currencies, the universal acceptability—thus far—of the U.S. dollar, and the ample liquidity available to the developed countries, in combination, have meant that the current financial crisis has not encompassed the developed countries. The danger is to regard this combination of favorable factors as durable, which is not necessarily so. It is understandable, even laudable, that the Fund has given much of its efforts to countries in trouble, but its central preoccupation remains the developed countries.

In dealing directly with the external payments difficulties of the developing countries, the Fund's role has been paramount. Mainly, the Fund has provided much needed external funds in the form of the equivalent of loans, not grants. The Fund owns its assets; thus, they are, in a sense, the collective property of its members. The Fund's assets are protected against loss or depreciation. Many of these funds have been provided to needy members on a virtually automatic basis. As automatic facilities have been depleted, more financial resources have been available on a conditional basis, embodied in a "Fund program" setting forth the economic policies to be pursued by governments to which Fund financial resources are made available. These activities have been spelled out in earlier chapters. At this point, in considering how the international financial system can be strengthened and how creditworthiness can be restored, attention is drawn to the need of the Fund for much larger resources, which would enable it to be of much greater assistance and influence over longer periods of time.

The greatest need is to decide how to increase the Fund's resources—larger quotas, more borrowings from official sources, borrowings from private sources, or more reliance on SDR creation. Most of these methods have been used repeatedly, except borrowing from private sources. It is desirable to consider using large-scale borrowings from private sources of finance, though always continuing to be mindful of how this would affect future access to official funds obtained by increases in members' quotas, borrowings from official sources, and expanded use of SDRs. Such borrowings could be loans or credits, or they could be standby lines with commercial banks, to be drawn if needed.

The starting point is that the IMF is the world's prime countercyclical institution. Fortunately, through its regular consultative procedures with its member countries, it can help anticipate difficulties and consult quietly with countries on different ways of coping with possible difficulties. The experience of the past few years may well make countries more receptive to this anticipatory advice. Publicity hampers this crucial role. The Fund has received much publicity in connection with its role in the external debt problem. This has made the Fund much better known and respected but has probably constrained it in its ability to be the trusted advisor and mediator. The IMF's role is to protect the international monetary system and, thus, protect the world economy's essential framework. Public awareness of the Fund is gratifying, but the measure of its success is how the world economy is functioning, not how widespread is public recognition of the Fund's name.

The IMF must prepare its member countries to deal with future cyclical downswings. Emergency measures taken during the downswings are welcome, but the name of the game is anticipation and prevention. If they are not anticipated, the next and future cyclical downturns will again have to be met—and they will be met in some way—by improvised emergency adaptations of existing institutions and practices, reinforcing the serious anxieties inherited from recent years. Among other things, this could lead to even more cautious pulling back by private lenders and could cause more developing countries to plunge into external financial crises even more serious than those since 1982. The international financial system will need to cope with strong cyclical changes in the future. The central role will be played by the IMF.

For many years, I have advocated a Fund with total financial resources of $300 billion or more, to enable it to perform its countercyclical role and to avoid the kinds of crises the world has experienced since 1982. The Fund's role is not to finance deficits still remaining after severe austerity programs, but rather to reduce the need for severity and to help countries resume noninflationary growth (with reduced unemployment and more income and output) as quickly as possible. The aim is to defend and promote prosperity. This responsibility may prove much more onerous in future business cycles if large industrial countries also need financial help. The current difficulties have been exceptional in that no important industrial country has needed major help from the IMF.

A Fund of $300 billion in quotas or other forms of financial resources would be large, but the effective use of those resources is likely to be much smaller. It is assumed that most quota payments of the IMF will be in national currencies, which are not used by other countries to meet international payments. Thus, much of the increased size of the Fund has to be discounted at the outset if it is in the form of increased quotas. Moreover, the IMF, as a revolving fund, has to safeguard its liquidity by keeping a substantial margin of usable funds unused. Large-scale need for IMF funds might well last for 3, 4, or more years cumulatively; repayments or repurchase can be slow, lasting well over 5 or even 10 years. Thus, in practice, even a $300 billion IMF is not sufficient, by itself, to substitute for the constrained lending by a fearful commercial banking system and consequent hoarding-dominated attitudes toward international monetary reserves by individual country holders. A $300 billion Fund would give confidence to private lenders that would otherwise disappear.

If quota increases of these magnitudes are not feasible because they require budgetary expenditures, other nonbudgetary sources of funds are available. As in the past, it may be possible to achieve these huge resources by a combination of relatively small quota increases, which require budgetary expenditures, and larger borrowings from governments and from private sources. If they are done in very large magnitudes, such borrowings from private sources may require, in time, guarantees by governments, but much borrowing could probably be done before this condition is reached. IMF borrowings could expect to be rated as high as the multilateral development banks— that is, AA or AAA ratings. It might be possible to fulfill the Fund role with an addition of $50 billion of increased quotas of industrial countries and $100 billion of borrowings, because the borrowings would provide needed and generally usable currencies that are not diluted in effectiveness by contributions in inconvertible or unusable currencies or currencies of countries that are themselves in balance-of-payments difficulties.

It may be queried why such large magnitudes are necessary. Of primary importance is that a very effective IMF would encourage private lenders not to withdraw during difficult periods. Among the other reasons are the large swings in external balances in recent years; the fact that a number of countries can be in deficit simultaneously; the possibility that the difficulties can persist for years; the fact that no country, however big (including the United States), is immune; and the fact that the first line of defense of the monetary system obviously has to be large enough to make academic the question of its capability to defend the system. In practice, this means not only defending the system per se—that is, the agreed regime of exchange rates and freedom from exchange restrictions—but also avoiding deflationary measures domestically, which are made necessary by foreign exchange shortages. In order of magnitude, actual usage of Fund resources for decades, may not exceed $20 billion to $30 billion per annum cumulatively for, say 3 or 4 year, but the needs are unpredictable and the supply of funds must be available to meet simultaneous demands virtually instantaneously. A central bank does this for the domestic banking system. It can finance any budgetary deficit, and it can assure full and prompt payment of government debt. There is no world central bank, and there will not be until there is a world government. Short of this utopia, however, there is a need for a lender of first resort to avoid global, deep, and prolonged recession and collapses of social and political order. The IMF has the mandate, the experience, and the institutional structure to meet this most important responsibility.

The suggestions made herein, as well as those made earlier, are designed to achieve the restoration of creditworthiness. As always, the critical input is the management of countries—but efficient, feasible institutional arrangements are still needed. It is hoped that the suggestions given herein, and those made in earlier chapters, will be treated together as a package, not separately.

The following chapter brings these threads together and summarizes the suggestions made in this book for a combined program of action.

11

Summary of Proposals

V ARIOUS suggestions have been made throughout this book on how to improve the international financial system and restore the creditworthiness of borrowing countries with commercial banks and other sources of private finance. These suggestions are intended to reinforce each other, though some can usefully be taken separately. When a suggestion has already been discussed in some detail, I will merely refer to it here; if a suggestion has not been discussed earlier in any detail, I will elaborate somewhat.

The suggestions cover three main areas: the international monetary system, international banking, and the multilateral development banks, including the World Bank and the African, Asian, and Inter-American Development Bank.

It is appreciated that the global environment is a critical factor in any evaluation of proposals. For the past decade, the industrial countries have pursued disinflationary policies of varying degrees of severity. Monetary policy—especially control of the money supply, interest rates, and exchange rates—has been the principal instrument. Most recently, more strenuous efforts have been made to restrain government expenditures and to reduce budgetary deficits. This combination has resulted in lower rates of inflation and changed expectations of inflation—from expectations of accelerating inflation to expectations of stable or falling rates of inflation. The price paid for these results has been high unemployment by postwar standards, slow growth, and faltering of international trade. Nevertheless, persistent inflation, still exists. Until inflation and expectations of persistent inflation are ended, it cannot be assumed that industrial countries will choose to shift gears into high-growth, low-unemployment policies. The international financial system has to be able to function efficiently whether the industrial countries stay on their present course of policies or shift in other directions.

The developing countries will have to adapt to prevailing world conditions. They must choose their priorities clearly. They alone can make social and economic development the top priority in practice. It is assumed, herein, that they will so choose.

The policies pursued by financial institutions will be different depending on these choices, but the institutions involved must be able to function in a manner suited to existing conditions. National banking systems function in all phases of the business cycle and during periods of drastic structural changes. Thus, the proposals made herein do not assume favorable or unfavorable world economic conditions. Their usefulness and feasibility are not predicated on such assumptions. The system has to function well in foul weather and in fair.

Another major characteristic of the international financial system is that they consist of public and private institutions with changing but considerable degrees of government supervision and regulation. These "mixed" institutions perform simultaneously and have different but interrelated functions. They must mesh smoothly, each changing speeds and directions separately, but together providing the financial services needed by society. The international financial system is also mixed, with different international institutions servicing different though, at times, overlapping functions. They, too must mesh smoothly and efficiently. Each institution, while performing its own function, must be able to assume that the others are performing their functions reasonably well. If not, the system falters and can enter into states of crises, as seen in the 1980s. To assure that each institution performs as needed, it is essential that they can be understood well and that they be prepared for continuing adaptation to unpredictable changes. A world of sustained recession or weak growth, inflation, and rising protectionism is evidence of a failing international financial system.

The starting point for strengthening the international financial system is a strengthening of the international monetary system. The present weaknesses are in the formation of exchange rates, the role of capital markets, and the provision of liquidity to members that are short of liquidity. Exchange rates must be more stabilized, and the international community should set up procedures for correcting unrealistic exchange rates. This effort need not involve a return to the par value system established at Bretton Woods, with its links to gold, although that system permitted much more flexibility in exchange rate changes than is now commonly understood. It can be based on the assumption of managed paper (fiat) currencies. Some volatility in exchange rates can be tolerated. The strengthening effort should recognize that foreign exchange and other markets are much more sophisticated than they were in earlier decades in providing hedges against exchange rate changes, thereby reducing the uncertainties and risks. It can start with maintaining free exchange markets and convertibility of currencies. It should provide for international cooperation and initiatives and concurrence on exchange rates and their changes. It can provide for intervention by central banks and the BIS, or it can give the key intervening role to the International Monetary Fund. There is no shortage of practical suggestions. Basically, the choice depends on the extent to which countries are prepared to dilute their sovereign powers in changing exchange rates for their currencies and in intervening in exchange markets, as the Western European countries do in the European Monetary System. In any case, countries would retain the ultimate authority to pursue domestic policies that, in time, will determine the values of their currency domestically and internationally. Inflation leads to currency devaluations, and inflation is primarily caused by national policies. Moreover, countries are, in any case, limited in their ability to determine foreign exchange rates, because other nations are involved and can take countermeasures. Witness the intense international negotiations in 1985 and 1986 to achieve better exchange rates for the U.S. dollar. Under the present system, the U.S. dollar rate cannot be decreed or determined by the United States. This determination requires cooperation from at least Germany and Japan and also France and the United Kingdom.

The world must end the uncertainties created by the present system of floating exchange rates. The acceptance of exchange rate stability as a goal does not mean rigidity. Changes in exchange rates can and will occur. It does mean, however, that continuing accelerating inflation must be eliminated by the major industrial countries. Inflation rates are too likely to vary, and varying inflation rates mean eventual changes in exchange rates, which hit with unpredictable timing and magnitudes. So long as accelerating inflation was typical of almost all industrial countries, exchange rate stability was not achievable under any system. With low and declining inflation rates, stabilization becomes a more attainable goal. Exchange rates could well be a subject of a new Bretton Woods conference, if the desire was for a new look from the viewpoint of the more distant future.

Another major area for reform is international capital flows. The Great Depression of the 1930s and World War II wrecked the earlier systems of international capital flows. Such flows became relatively unimportant in the 1930s. Governments proved unwilling to give up national controls over movements of funds into and out of their countries. The Bretton Woods agreements did not give the IMF or the World Bank jurisdiction over capital movements. The only major rule was that the Fund was not to be used to finance such capital movements. The absence of any agreed code of behavior has meant that governments act purely nationalistically in this area, though they have recognized that international cooperation and agreements are essential in the international exchange of goods and services and in international payments for them. Capital movements from one country to another have come to dominate foreign exchange markets. Instead of exchange rates being determined by relative prices or, more broadly, by relative economic conditions in countries and their foreign trade, exchange markets and exchange rates reflect capital movements. These movements result from the desires of individuals to move funds from one nation to another for a great variety of reasons, such as expectations of exchange rate changes, differentials in interest rates, the behavior of national stock markets, relative investment opportunities, and political safety. These capital movements bring about unrealistic exchange rates—such as the U.S. dollar exchange rates during the past 10 to 20 years—which are harmful to or even destructive of national prosperity, expansion of international trade, and global well-being. They have been major disturbing elements—what economists call *disequilibrating*.

The Fund does not have experience in the field of capital movements comparable to its experience in areas in which it has international jurisdiction. Nor has the World Bank this experience, though its area of responsibility is capital movements for developmental purposes. It is recommended that the international community give a joint mandate to the Fund and the World Bank to consider the need for a code of international conduct for capital movements and to make specific proposals for the consideration of member nations. The aim should be to facilitate the international flows of savings that encourage international divisions of labor and increased world output and efficiency. Capital flows that disrupt the world economy must be discouraged and supervised. This might well be a major item on a new Bretton Woods–type conference, however it is organized.

A third area of international monetary reform is the need for increased liquidity for countries whose ability to grow is seriously handicapped by a shortage of international liquidity. The provision of foreign exchange to countries in balance-of-payments difficulties is a prime function of the Fund. It makes possible domestic policies of growth and high employment. Most important for the world economy are the policies of the largest countries economically. The United States is the very largest. Now that the world has entered into a stage of low inflation and weakened inflationary expectations, the role of the Fund becomes clearer—to avoid deep and prolonged recessions in the industrialized countries, which are caused by inadequate international liquidity. For the 1980s, this shortage of liquidity has been primarily a problem for the developing countries.

SDRs have been created to meet any liquidity needs of the industrial countries. Measures should be considered for ensuring their acceptability and expanded use, if needed, in the future. This is not critically urgent, because the disinflation of recent years has not been due to liquidity shortages in the industrial countries. The resolution of these issues, however, takes time. It is essential that the SDR mechanism be reevaluated in light of the crisis of the 1980s and the prospects for the future. It is likely that the Fund is already doing this, but the danger is that discussions may be overly influenced by current conditions, especially concerns that SDR creation will become a vehicle for dealing with the current liquidity problems of the developing countries.

The developing countries are repeatedly in need of liquidity. They need to be able to turn to the Fund as the principal counter-cyclical institution in the world economy, thus avoiding otherwise undesirable social and economic policies. The available liquidity should be ample to avoid otherwise unnecessary and undesirable austerity. To keep members' policies from resulting in inflationary policies or failures to adjust to changing world conditions, the Fund would have to continue its conditionality on the use of its resources. However, the content of conditionality would now be influenced by the ability of the Fund to provide many more resources and, if needed, for longer periods. It has been suggested in an earlier chapter that the Fund's holdings of generally usable currencies be increased by $100 billion to $150 billion. These increases can be achieved by borrowing generally usable currencies from governments and private markets and by some relatively small increases of the Fund quotas for the industrial countries, whose currencies are generally usable. If necessary, some guarantee mechanism could be used to facilitate borrowing in private capital markets, as is done by the multilateral development banks, though this may not be necessary. The Fund has a strong reputation in financial markets. Its members have honored their repayment obligations, with minor exceptions, and it owns very extensive holdings of gold.

Whatever its size, if the Fund is to be able to act in a timely fashion, it needs informal understandings with all member countries in advance of difficulties, so that the members know whether, and to what extent, they can count on immediate help if needed. Prevention of crises would be the test of success. Fund understandings of this kind would be kept confidential.

Given this improvement in the international monetary system, the international banking system and other sources of private finance could be expected to have a very different attitude toward lending to developing countries. This would be reinforced by what is suggested for the multilateral development banks. Restoration of creditworthiness would be much easier to accomplish. As suggested earlier, the commercial banks would nevertheless have to strengthen their systems of international risk assessments and portfolio management. The banks could also create an "international safety net," as suggested earlier, and the equivalent of the BIS for private banks, also suggested earlier. They could benefit from available sources of information and continue efforts to strengthen their capital base.

These efforts to reestablish the role of commercial banks would be greatly facilitated by measures to end the debt crisis. Specific suggestions have been made in earlier chapters. Banks must be prepared to extend the present debt restructuring—to, say, 10 years or more. They must move away from being unwilling holders of risk assets. They have to recreate the environment in which new loan opportunities are considered separately by each lender in light of its own conditions and aspirations and the conditions in the country, apart from past debts. Concerted lending must give way to voluntary individual lending. The debt restructuring mechanism can be used for new and remaining cases, but not for new lending on a voluntary basis. Banks must consider—generally, and on a country-by-country basis—what their institutional requirements are for resumption of normal lending and what their longer-run plans are for earnings from international activities. Such strategic rethinking will position banks to react to changes in the world environment that greatly influence their judgments, including institutional changes in the roles of the International Monetary Fund, the World Bank, the regional development banks, and bilateral aid programs.

Simultaneously, borrowers should be seeking to learn what the preconditions are for the resumption of voluntary lending to them by private banks. In addition, they should be exploring further the new instruments for borrowing from the private capital markets. They should seek the widest spectrum of sources of finance, with the understanding that for all sources, they will, in the end, be compelled to accept market judgments on their economic management and creditworthiness. They will need to know what other borrowers are doing as well as what various lenders will do. They should give more attention to using their collective strength to achieve conditions for the existing international institutions that would enable those institutions to be more helpful to developing countries, guided more by policies designed to be helpful. The debtor countries should act together to bring the debt crisis to an end in such fashion as to facilitate the restoration of their creditworthiness and the resumption of access to the largest sources of funds in the global economy—the capital markets and the banking systems. Such steps include a renunciation of repudiation and a welcoming of foreign equity inflows.

Clarification is needed of the role of the Fund in relation to private lending institutions. The Fund must be able to deal with its own responsibilities to its members. Its influence inevitably extends beyond its formal jurisdiction, but that results from the quality of its performance in meeting its formal responsibilities. A major consideration for the Fund is its continuing relationship with its member countries, separately and collectively. This relationship is fundamentally not one of confrontation or bargaining or even negotiation of parties with conflicting or competing interests. The members of the Fund with which the Fund "negotiates" *are* the Fund. The staff and management of the Fund are employees of an institution made up of member countries; thus, they are employees of the members. Fund programs of adjustment are programs of their members. If the staff and management cannot accept a prepared program as the basis for financial assistance from the Fund or for any other Fund purpose, they cannot endorse the program and recommend its support by the Fund's executive directors. In such a disagreement, they are not in conflict with the involved member. There is no question of leave it or take it; there are no victories or defeats; there are simply failures to agree. Such failures do not lead to discontinuity in membership or relations. Because of its continuing responsibilities, the Fund may agree to programs because, on balance, it regards the policies being taken as progress—as steps forward—even if they still leave much more to be done. Such judgments are not made by standard, uniform criteria; nor do they necessarily meet the needs of other institutions, especially private lenders. They are judgments felt to be justified by the existing conditions and outlook. The judgments are largely technical in content, but the presumption is one of agreement in a friendly relationship. No offense is meant by disagreement, and it is hoped that no offense is taken.

Too often, in the heat and tension of policy formulation, differences and disagreements, the process is transformed into a conflict in which there are perceptions of victories and defeats. The Fund cannot fulfill its given responsibilities in this manner. It has the financial ability to help countries follow policies deemed appropriate by the international community. In this sense, it has financial inducements. It also has limited sanctions to withhold approval. At any given time, this combination of inducements and sanctions may be reinforced by the policies of other institutions that make Fund approval the precondition for their approvals. The debt restructuring exercises and the provision of new money for IMF-agreed adjustment programs are cases in point, but a Fund program is to be guided by its own responsibilities. Another case is the insistence, by a development finance institution, that the member abide by its agreements with the Fund. At any time, this combination of factors can give great weight and power to the Fund, making it seem like a conflict between David and Goliath. Yet the Fund cannot endure in this role.

The member countries are in a voluntary association with the Fund. They must trust its intentions to be helpful to all members, and they must trust its technical integrity and competency. They must see the staff and management as eager to be useful to them and as maintaining an unending, uninterrupted relationship with them for the foreseeable future and beyond. Coerced agreements or policies are paper victories, or even Pyrrhic victories. Because of the special character of the Fund and its relations with members, it needs the trust and goodwill of its member nations. Countries cannot be expected to accept having their conditions critically examined and made bases for international action if they fear hostile or public use of information and exchange of views.

The Fund must have insights into economic situations and policies, which requires confidential information of the most sensitive kind. Without such information, the Fund flies blind. It will not have such information if the countries providing the information fear disclosure or hostile use. It is a task of truly professional diplomacy and international management to carry on discussions of sensitive policy issues with members in difficulties, to disagree on some, and yet not destroy the process. To safeguard this process, the Fund is limited in its service to non-Fund institutions. It can be of greater service to institutions of similar official character and membership— for example, the World Bank and the regional development banks.

The multilateral development banks can make the crucial difference in strengthening the international financial system and in restoring creditworthiness. To achieve these aims, their purpose must shift from being mainly a project finance institution to defending development and the developing countries. All forms of development assistance—project financing, balance-of-payments support, local currency financing, direct lending to the private sector, guarantees of loans from private sources, trade financing, and so forth— are acceptable. These banks cannot have a uniform definition of their activities for all countries, just as they do not have a uniform definition of their projects for countries nor a uniform content for their structural adjustment loans. The critical difference is the acceptance of an active, broad developmental role. They should strive to enable countries to continue productive investments in the private and public sectors during unfavorable periods. To this end, they can play an active role with borrowing members in choosing suitable development policies. These banks can collaborate with the Fund and with the regional development banks in agreeing with countries on the conditions required for immediate assistance from the Fund, the World Bank, and the relevant regional bank. These supportive mechanisms could, if needed, quickly substitute for private institutions that withdraw because they must be more concerned with immediate risks. At the same time, these private sources would become much less likely to withdraw, because they would be less likely to regard conditions as too risky. Banks do operate during unfavorable periods of the business cycle or other adverse conditions. Indeed, during such periods, they may be eagerly seeking foreign loan assets to offset declines in loan demand in their own economies. International borrowing from private sources flourished during the 1980s for borrowers other than the troubled developing countries. Thus, the strengthening of the multilateral institutions may result in relatively much greater use of the private sector institutions, as the strengthened multilateral institutions stand by in case of need. The BIS is an outstanding example of a successful financial institution embodying this principle.

In any case, the multilateral banks are already a major vehicle for transferring private resources to the developing countries. They can do much more in performing this function. They can become a much more important source of development finance without the use of budgetary funds. This fits with budgetary constraints in the United States and elsewhere. Their callable capital would have to be greatly enlarged, however, because this capital acts as the ultimate guarantee of the borrowings of these institutions from the private markets. This callable capital is not a drain on budgets. The multilateral development banks would have to see themselves as serving all the needs of development—private as well as public—not as official aid agencies promoting the public sector and, more particularly, public sector projects. The multilateral development banks can take the initiative in creating new international private financial entities, as suggested herein. It is suggested that the capital of the World Bank be increased to $200 billion and that the regional development banks be given a combined capital equal to that of the World Bank. This $400 billion would be nearly all in callable form, not requiring budgetary forms, thus providing the ability to tap private sources of world savings in these orders of magnitudes.

In combination, the measures set forth here and in other chapters would give us an international financial system that would be able to encourage and finance noninflationary growth and development in developed and developing countries with minimum reliance on budgets. It would merge the progress made in the 1960s and 1970s with the innovations of the 1980s into a system capable of functioning well in the future. These suggested proposals conform to four overriding conditions that are likely to prevail for years: eagerness to keep down budgetary expenditures in developed countries, eagerness to resume higher growth rates in the developing countries, eagerness to operate through mechanisms that respect national sovereignty despite the interdependence of the countries that make up the world economy, and eagerness to use private and official institutions in so doing.

Epilogue

12

A New Bretton Woods?

D URING recent years, many have called for a new Bretton
Woods Conference, presumably modeled on the conference in
1944 that agreed to the formation of the International Monetary
Fund and the World Bank. Most recently, the inspiration has come
principally from the external debt crisis, but the need is for a tho-
roughgoing reexamination of the entire international financial system
and a redefinition of the functions of its major institutions.

The equivalent of a new Bretton Woods Conference is inevitable,
but not to deal with the external debt crisis. It may not be a conference; in many respects, the process is already going on within the
framework of the wide variety of institutions and mechanisms that
already exist, ranging from the entire United Nations system to the
IMF, the OECD, the BIS, the European Community GATT, the
annual five- and seven-country economic summits, and bilateral discussions such as those between Japan and the United States. Nevertheless, there are many fundamental issues in international economic
and financial relations that cannot be resolved by temporary pallia-
tives, that avoid considering what the world must do about the world
economy or, more precisely, avoid examining the international rules
by which countries wish to conduct their international financial and
commercial relations. Some misgivings have been expressed with the
international exchange rate system and growing protectionism, but
they were not the genesis of a call for a new Bretton Woods.

During the early 1980s, there were many calls for a new Bretton
Woods, as the debt crisis spread throughout Latin America and
much of Africa, and countries in these regions suffered serious setbacks. However, such calls often added to the hysteria and overreaction to the international payments crises of Latin America and Af-

rica. It is recalled that the rapid buildup of international debt, followed by the widespread need to renegotiate and restructure debt, were seen as precursors of the collapse of the international lending system.

There was an abundance of schemes for dealing with the external debt difficulties, but unfortunately, they were often presented as alternatives to imminent repudiation, default, collapses of banks, and so forth. These suggestions ranged from forgiveness of debt to restructuring of principal of debt while servicing interest and postponing interest payments by so-called capitalizing interest—that is, transferring part or all of interest due into principal outstanding, to be paid at the end of the maturity period for past debts. Other suggestions were to sell unwanted external assets to investors needing funds to invest in developing borrowing countries. Banks could sell some of their assets in a country, which could not be serviced in foreign exchange but were available in local currency to foreign investors who required local currencies for their activities and would reimburse the bank in foreign exchange. This required the permission of the debtor countries. Suggestions have also been made to transform the fixed debt of commercial banks into marketable debt by the buying and selling of such debt, as is done in huge quantities on international financial markets with a great variety of debt instruments. There has thus been no shortage of suggestions of how to deal with the great debt crisis of the 1980s. Unfortunately, these suggestions did not deal with the basic causes of the loss of creditworthiness or its restoration. Furthermore, many suggestions were simply not institutionally feasible.

The world believed, and gave serious attention to, the views of professionals and nonprofessionals on solutions to solving the debt crises. The fashion was to sound alarmist and mostly pessimistic. A new Bretton Woods has been strongly urged in this context. Thus, the focal point of calls for a conference was the external debt problem, rather than the appropriateness of the international financial system for the entire world economy, including both developed and developing countries. Yet it was the malfunctioning of the world economic system, as well as the conditions of the borrowing developing countries, that had caused the external debt problem.

The international financial system has not been adequate by global standards. It is this system that should be the focal point of a thorough review. The external debt problem is the current manifestation of deeper weaknesses. Between World War I and World War II, similar errors were made in concentrating world attention and efforts on the problems of reparations (a form of external debt) and war debts of World War I. While these futile discussions went on, the world economy collapsed. Naziism and fascism repudiated the concepts and practices of a liberal international trade and payments system. The Soviet Union had already done so, but it was much less important in the international economic system. Autarky flourished, and international trade became a form of economic warfare, while nations met repeatedly to consider now-forgotten ways and means to deal with war debts and reparations.

This is what is threatening to happen again, in a modern context, of course. An efficiently functioning world economy and international financial system can readily handle the debt problems of the developing countries. It is the failures of the world economic system that need solutions. In this, the international financial system is of prime importance.

Thus, the world economy and the international system are not merely the background of the international debt crisis; they are the soil in which the weed of debt crisis flourishes. Therefore, although this book has dealt considerably with the evolution of the international debt crisis and how it has been managed, the "solutions" offered have dealt with the management of the world economy and the international financial system, as well as with the external debt crisis.

It is now possible to consider, less emotionally, the need for the equivalent of a new Bretton Woods Conference. The experience of the most recent years has begun to drive home lessons that were already there to be learned for years—that there are fundamental weaknesses in the international financial system, that there is a worldwide community of interest in trying to find better ways to deal with these problems, and that current manifestations of these difficulties may be solved temporarily, only to be followed by other major difficulties caused by the basic weaknesses. A new Bretton Woods could deal with these fundamentals.

A new Bretton Woods does not necessarily mean a conference of nations designed to set up new institutions or a conference held outside the auspices of existing institutions. It may be organized by existing international organizations and may even be one of a series of meetings of such organizations for such purpose, analogous to the meetings of governors of the International Monetary Fund and their deputies that have been taking place for years. The purposes and content of a new Bretton Woods, however, would not be to review these institutions or to make new decisions for them, though this might well be much of the outcome. The meeting would discuss the fundamental prerequisites for world growth and prosperity and would try to find a road back to the economic and financial conditions that are needed for world peace. The purposes would be grand and ambitious, but it would be a meeting of governments to consider, realistically, what could be done and what long-term commitments countries were prepared to make. As in the case of the original Bretton Woods, this might require years of prior preparation, international discussions, and negotiation. The meeting would not try to map a plan for the future. Rather, it would aim at agreeing on the rules for the conduct of international economic relations. It would not be a detailed negotiation on details, like the Multilateral Trade Negotiation or the annual separate consultations of the IMF with its members. It could review the purposes of existing international rules, mechanisms, aid, adequacy of resources, and so forth. It could model itself on the historic Bretton Woods Conference, which proved markedly successful. Its spirit would be collaborative and cooperative, not confrontational. Ideas and solutions could compete, and some solutions would "win" over others, but countries would not "win" or "lose." Conflicting ideologies would be present and important, but the resulting agreements would be empirical and pragmatic, leaving much for the future in the way of adaptation and implementation.

The Analogy to Bretton Woods

The Bretton Woods Conference was held during World War II, in 1944. It had been preceded by more than two years of intensive discussions between the United States and other friendly governments, especially the United Kingdom and Canada. Within governments, especially in the United States and the United Kingdom, the lead roles were taken by the treasuries or ministries of finance, but the central bank, the Federal Reserve in the United States, foreign offices (for example, the U. S. State Department), and other agencies were vigorous participants. The national and international discussions that laid the groundwork for final agreement at Bretton Woods for the formation of the World Bank and International Monetary Fund did *not* deal with the current problems of those years, even though most of the individuals involved were simultaneously dealing with current problems in their other activities. Many were university professors, but in these deliberations they were acting as government officials or advisors.

During those war years, the current international financial problems arose out of the conduct of global war. Provision of military and other critical supplies to Allied nations, purchase of such supplies for the war effort in various countries, rules for contracts for military supplies, preclusive purchasing abroad of goods to deny their use to enemy nations, treatment of enemy properties, allocation of available international shipping, treatment of enemy gold holdings, shipment of gold and silver to friendly nations, management of foreign-held banking accounts, conduct of military governments installed in victorious areas, issuance of special military currencies for use of Allied troops, and so forth, were the current problems of international finance during the war. Most of the principals who engaged in the discussions on postwar international financial relations were engaged much more with the problems of war finance.

Thus, unlike the usual calls for a new Bretton Woods today, the first Bretton Woods was not called to deal with current problems. It was not center stage for most of the principals, compared with their current concerns and responsibilities. Bretton Woods grew out of the war in the sense that it was motivated by a desire to eliminate major causes of the breakdown of the international political system that had led to the war. It began with a vision of the future and how to achieve it. It was based on historic experience combined with imagination of the future, deduced from analysis and intuition. One of the ingredients of the success of Bretton Woods was that it did not get involved in the controversies raging around the existing war issues. Rivalries of institutions, individuals, and ideas could be largely transcended because the future was the framework; yet all agreed on the need to ensure that the future was not a repetition of the past. Compromise was made easier because the compromises would not have meaning for years ahead. At the same time, the principals were men of affairs—some technically well grounded, others not. They did not seek optimal solutions; they sought working compromises to which nations could commit themselves in practice. While these compromises for the future were being found, the day-to-day problems of war finance were being resolved through the established mechanisms.

The guiding vision was that world prosperity was a precondition for world peace. Countries with deep economic disequilibria could not be expected to fulfill international commitments for orderly international relations. World prosperity was indivisible, like world peace. Depression anywhere threatened the entire world economy. World prosperity could be achieved, but not without cyclical fluctuations, which could occur simultaneously in a number of countries. Cyclical fluctuations could be tolerable and not threatening to world order if countries were helped to avoid policies that deepened and widened prolonged depressions. Adversities caused by business cycles could be made temporary and need not disrupt the strategy and course of national growth. Unexpected events, such as droughts, could upset sensible economic national policies and management, but their adverse effects could be ameliorated by temporary financial assistance to countries experiencing the adversities.

Countries with differing social and economic systems, even the Soviet Union, could join in an international code of behavior designed to achieve these objectives. It was feasible for differing systems to adapt their own policies and developments to the environment created by this agreed international code of behavior. Laissez-faire or "liberal" international economics were compatible with planned and even socialistic domestic systems. Countries could agree and pledge that desired exceptions to the code of international monetary behavior would require international approval. Countries could rely on the goodwill and understanding of other countries to give their approval to such exceptions.

Countries could seek the use of international financial resources, if needed, to avoid policies that deepened or lengthened depressions, if the need for such deflationary policies might result from shortages of foreign exchange. Countries could be entrusted to repay or return such borrowed resources to the international organization to which they were entrusted—namely, the International Monetary Fund. The authority to police the international system could be effectively exercised by this international organization that was formed by governments. Its authority could thus be respected by governments throughout the world. The international flow of capital for development could be encouraged by guarantees given by the world community, or could be helped by new loans given by a new international institution—the International Bank for Reconstruction and Development. This institution could borrow in private capital markets because of guarantees to its creditors given by the collective membership of the World Bank. Other international capital movements could be left to the workings of the capital markets and the actions of national governments.

Thus, the Bretton Woods vision embodied a view of the world—its need to prosper and how it was to prosper. Its philosophy was largely the philosophy of the United States, combined with the various ideologies of other governments and countries, especially the United Kingdom. It had agreed purposes and mechanisms to implement those purposes. Countries agreed to allow the new institutions the flexibility to deal with different and changing situations, but within a general framework of agreed principles.

These principles were disputed, and the mechanisms were disputed. The Soviet Union was a participant at Bretton Woods but never joined the Fund or the World Bank. The more planned, autarkic, and socialist-minded governments, such as New Zealand, had deep qualms and joined with strongly expressed caveats. No one "won" at Bretton Woods. The United States dominated, as it was dominating in all world affairs at that time. If Bretton Woods can be deemed a "victory" of the United States, it was a by-product of Allied victories in Europe and the Pacific. Countries could see themselves helped in recovering their own independence in domestic policies and philosophies by participating in a global system based on liberal economic principles. The fact that Nazi Germany and fascist Italy had by and large repudiated these principles in practice gave cognition and sentimental support to philosophies contrary to the philosophies of those countries.

The Need for a New Bretton Woods

A new Bretton Woods must start with the quest for agreement on a vision of the future, not with a multilateral negotiation for dealing with current problems. There are already many international bodies dealing with current problems: the IMF with its many mechanisms; the World Bank group—the African, Asian, and Inter-American Development Banks; the Development Committee of the Fund and the World Bank; he ad hoc groups of governments, such as the Group of Five, Seven, 22, 77, and so forth; UNCTAD; the regional economic commissions in Africa, Asia, and Latin America; the European Community in its many forms; the OECD; the United Nations and its countless specialized agencies; the Bank for International Settlements (BIS); and others. All provide international mechanisms for dealing with current affairs; elaborate policies and practices and large staffs guide them.

Then why do we need a new Bretton Woods? A new Bretton Woods is needed because our vision of the future has become too blurred and uncertain; countries are not agreed on general purposes and principles to which they are prepared to subordinate national policies; there are no generally accepted guidelines by which to conduct and judge current policies; and friction in international economic relations is eroding peaceful and constructive international political relations. Priorities for the future are not known. The existing institutions are unclear about their purposes and functioning in many critical areas, even though they are very active and useful in many areas. It is not to be expected that fundamental changes will be proposed by existing institutions, and conclusions that endorse their usefulness and continuation would be suspect as self-serving.

A conference to agree on solutions to the differences in the great variety of current international issues would be a Tower of Babel, ending in frustration, anger, and lasting ill will. It could destroy what does exist in the way of internationally agreed behavior in economic and financial matters. Government ministers, meeting in a broad attempt to deal with current problems, could not hope to agree on the solutions to the many differences that still remain, despite numerous and serious past international endeavors to deal with them.

A new Bretton Woods would seek a new vision of the world focused on the future—say, the world after 1990 or 2000. It would aim to agree on the vision, the priorities, and the mechanisms for achieving them. The danger is in repetition of worn-out slogans and cliches, empty phrases, and meaningless compromises. This was also the danger at the original Bretton Woods Conference. The danger was avoided then by making the purposes and mode of achievement the center of discussion and by not meeting until there was sufficient agreement on purposes, priorities, and modes to enable the formal conference to be the final agreement on codes of conduct and the mechanisms to enforce them.

This can be done again, but the subject matter must be considered apart from current issues and must be discussed intensively and extensively among governments; discussion must be carried on until agreement is reached for more formal international action and must be freed from the disruption of decision making on current issues. The participants must be government officials, getting help from wherever they want. Their mandate would be to discuss and find common ground—not to negotiate a final agreement until asked to do so. They could ask the existing international organizations to help. They could have bilateral, regional, and subregional discussions, but the global mandate would be given by governments to a worldwide group of their representatives. Confrontational politics would be taboo. An existing institution, such as the IMF, or a group of institutions could be given the responsibility for organization and coordination but must not dominate the discussions intellectually.

The Agenda for a New Bretton Woods

The international understanding and rules by which countries will seek to find more satisfactory rates of growth, reduce unemployment, and end inflation need the kind of attention that would be made possible by a new Bretton Woods.

The following are some suggestions for the agenda of a new Bretton Woods. A new Bretton Woods would be difficult to organize and carry out. It could be done successfully only if the needs are felt keenly by governments around the world. The needs must be clearly delineated and generally agreed upon. Major achievements cannot take place without such consensus. Full descriptions and analyses of the urgent needs would take volumes, but it would be useful to summarize some main elements of these needs, as follows:

1. There is a need for an international financial system to provide the framework for world prosperity, sustained growth, and structural change. The present system is unable to defend developing countries from serious injuries. High unemployment, low growth rates, and inadequate savings in developed as well as developing countries also reflect the failures of our present system.
2. There is a need for an international monetary system, resulting in a pattern of exchange rates that can be generally regarded as realistic, equitable, and usually stable. For many years, the U.S. dollar exchange rate with other major currencies has been out of line

by all criteria—undervalued in the 1970s and overvalued in the 1980s. Overvaluation of the U.S. dollar has given a substantial competitive edge to U.S. foreign competitors' world markets. It has created large trade deficits for the United States, has brought protests from injured U.S. industries, has caused increased pressures for protectionism, and has created serious ill will between the United States and otherwise friendly nations, such as Japan, Korea and Brazil. No international monetary system can be regarded as adequate with these major faults. A new method of creating international exchange rates must be found. It should not be approached as a variation on the present system but should be looked at afresh with the benefit of experience but without commitment to the present or to the past.

3. International capital movements need reexamination. Disequilibrating capital movements have repeatedly disturbed national economies and international business. At the original Bretton Woods Conference, this issue was neglected. Capital movements had become minor during the Great Depression. They are decisive factors in our modern world, however, and they should be reconsidered at a new Bretton Woods. Is a code of international behavior feasible and desirable? If so, what agencies should administer this code?

4. The world needs to end persistent inflation. How can this be achieved? Rapid inflation is still chronic in many countries. The industrial countries have not learned how to end persistent inflation and avoid the recurrence of accelerating inflation without serious deflation, which, if sustained, could threaten social and political stability. Is a growth attack on inflation—instead of the disinflationary approach—feasible without causing accelerating inflation? The answer is not to be found in pursuing the same policies as have been followed in the past decade. A new Bretton Woods should probe and clarify national priorities in private and public consumption. It should encompass the entire economy, not concentrate on public budgets alone. It should aim to reexamine public expectations of material well-being; help choose among the many options; see better how the market mechanisms can function to register, reflect, and ratify these choices; and discuss and find ways to create the savings needed for production and structural changes in the industrial countries and in developing countries. Such discussions will not yield quick results and should not be based on easy assumptions about ending expectations of persistent inflation. They should explore the possible use of changes in exchange rates as the principal adjustment

mechanisms, rather than changes in growth and employment. In so doing, should the central role, internationally, be performed by the institution that manages the international monetary system— namely, the International Monetary Fund? As nations clarify their own understanding of what is feasible and what kinds of mechanisms they prefer to achieve these preferences, the stage will be set for a successful effort to end persistent global inflation.

5. Do the existing governmental rules and practices serve world business, which has become interdependent and integrated to a degree that represents a quantum change from the past? Modern technology, especially in communications and transportation within and among economies, has involved the bulk of humanity in this interdependence and integration. All nations have their own islands of modernity that link with others. These islands now dominate economic change, even when people in various countries are still largely engaged in traditional economic activities, such as food production in India, Pakistan, or Nigeria. The changes may be beneficial, such as increased land productivity, or they can be harmful or even disastrous, bringing intolerable urban congestion, depopulation of the countryside, expansion of desert in Africa, famine, disease, and epidemics.

Interdependence and global integration have created a world in which nations and their businesses have lost their freedom of action, however reluctantly and angrily. The varying impacts of the oil price increases on national economics gave many illustrations of the limits on the freedom of action of nations and their governments. Individual firms are now part of a worldwide productive and marketing process. Trade unions may well find themselves more eager to raise wages in other countries than in their own in basic defense of their jobs. Business firms seek intermediate parts, technology, partners, finance, skills, and so forth, anywhere and everywhere in the world. World markets supply what they need and buy their products. In practice, the position of firms and the impact of policies on industries have been neglected as international cooperation has focused on nations and their governments. In the interdependent and integrated world, close attention must be paid to the global links of firms and industries. National policies, which are seen as justifiable in light of national conditions, may be unacceptable because of their disruption of international market linkages and efficiencies. Nations have to agree on whether they will be bound by rules that maximize and protect the linkages of world markets. This means new definitions of what is national, what is meant by national interest, and what is meant by unfair national competitive practices.

6. Is the international financial system suited to a world that has become very different because of the miracles of modern technology? Technology transfer and adaptation increasingly dominate international economic relations. We need to know where the world wants to go and by what principles it proposes to get there.

The world cannot avoid addressing these issues in one form or another. Through its existing institutions, the world is addressing current problems in a rather orderly and thoughtful manner. The future is inevitably neglected, however, as the agenda of current problems is lengthy and crowded. The future needs separate attention. Intellectual leadership is needed, and the prime candidates to provide this leadership are those who are already providing leadership in dealing with our current serious problems.

Bibliographical Note

T HE sources of information used in the preparation of this volume are all primary. The book distills the author's experience of over forty years in international economics and finance. Senior positions in the U.S. Treasury, International Monetary Fund, the World Bank, Citibank, and the First Boston Corporation, followed by advisory positions with the African, Asian, and Inter-American Development Banks gave the author extensive opportunities for analyzing economic conditions in most countries and for exchanging views with officials and private experts. In addition, he participated in the activities of other institutions like the Bank for International Settlements, the OECD, and the GATT.

The institutions mentioned above, including the commercial banks, originate much of the statistical and nonstatistical information used in international economics and finance. These institutions publish monthly bulletins; annual reports; world economic surveys; regional and country analyses; special subject technical brochures; less-technical journals; training and educational materials; press releases; speeches by governors (usually Ministers of Finance) from over 150 countries; addresses of senior management; official histories and so on. These primary sources of information were used by the author to prepare this book, but analyses and interpretations are, however, the responsibility of the author.

The principal sources of the statistics used in this volume are:

International Monetary Fund: annual reports; *International Financial Statistics* (monthly); *International Financial Statistics Yearbooks*; *Balance of Payments Statistics* (monthly issues and yearbooks); *IMF Survey* (bimonthly); *World Economic Outlook* (semiannual); *World Economic Outlook, April 1985* (from 1980 to 1984, the World Economic Outlook was published as part of the Occasional Paper series); occasional papers—for example, no. 1, *International Capital Markets* and no. 3, *External Indebtedness of Developing Counties.*

International Monetary Fund and World Bank: *Finance and Development* (monthly).

World Bank: annual reports; world debt tables; *External Debts of Developing Countries* (annual); *World Development Reports* (annual).

Organization for Economic Cooperation and Development (OECD): annual reviews by the Development Assistance Committee; *Twenty-Five Years of Development Cooperation: Efforts and Policies of the Members of the Development Assistance Committee; Economic Outlook* (semiannual); *Main Economic Indicators* (monthly); *Financial Markets Trends* (three times a year); *Financial Statistics Monthly; External Debt of Developing Countries—1983 Survey* (April, 1984); *Geographic Distribution of Financial Glows to Developing Countries 1981–84* (January 1986); *Internatinal Banks and Financial Markets in Developing Countries* (November 1984).

Bank for International Settlements (BIS): annual reports; *International Banking Statistics* (annual); *Maturity Distribution of International Bank Lending* (annual).

BIS/OECD: *Statistics on External Indebtedness* (semiannual).

African Development Bank: annual reports; *African Development Bank 1964–1984.*

Asian Development Bank: annual reports.

Inter-American Development Bank: annual reports.

United Nations World Economic Survey 1986 (annual).

Appendix:
Glossary of Selected Terms

THE definitions provided here are based on current usage of the International Monetary Fund, the World Bank, and commercial international banking.

Capital Flows

COMPONENTS OF CAPITAL FLOWS   International movements of capital may come from either official or private sources. Official sources are (1) governments and governmental agencies (also called bilateral lenders) and (2) international organizations (called multilateral lenders). Private sources comprise (1) commercial suppliers and manufacturers, which provide export credits for the purchase of their goods; (2) commercial banks, which provide export credits or cash loans; (3) other private investors, who invest in foreign enterprises in which they seek a lasting interest (direct investment) or purchase stocks or bonds issued by foreign companies or governments (portfolio investment); and (4) charitable organizations, which provide financial aid, goods, and services as grants.

CONCESSIONAL FLOWS   International lending on terms more favorable to the borrower than those obtainable through normal market transactions. Concessional flows are usually defined as those having a grant element of 25 percent or more.

DIRECT FOREIGN INVESTMENT   Investment made to acquire a lasting interest in an enterprise operating in an economy other than that of the investor. The investor's purpose is to have an effective voice in the management of the enterprise.

EQUITY FINANCING   Investment that confers whole or partial ownership in an enterprise and entitles the investor to share in the profits from its operation. International equity financing flows may be included in either foreign direct or portfolio investment.

EXPORT CREDITS   Finance provided by lenders in a given country for exports of specific goods or services. Conventionally, one distinguishes between private and official export credits. *Private export credits* consist of (1) supplier credits, which are extended by the exporting company to the foreign buyer, and (2) buyer credits, which are extended by commercial banks in the exporting country on behalf of the exporters. *Official export credits* are extended by an agency of the exporting country's government.

GRANT   A current transfer of capital, goods, or services to a foreign country that results in no current or future obligation to make a like transfer from the recipient country to the donor.

GRANT ELEMENT   The extent to which a loan can be considered a grant is determined by its grant element—the difference between the original face value of the loan and the discounted present value of debt service, as a percentage of the original face value. Thus, a true grant has a grant element of 100 percent. A discount rate of 10 percent is conventionally used in the calculation. The grant element is used to compare the concessionality of assistance provided under differing terms and conditions.

NET FLOWS OF LENDING   Loan disbursements less amortization of principal.

NONCESSIONAL FLOWS   Lending on or near terms prevailing in private financial markets.

OFFICIAL DEVELOPMENT ASSISTANCE   Loans and grants made on concessional financial terms from official sources, with the objective of promoting economic development and welfare. It includes the value of technical cooperation and assistance.

PRIVATE NONGUARANTEED DEBT   External obligations of private debtors that are not guaranteed for repayment by a public entity of the debtor country.

PUBLIC AND PUBLICLY GUARANTEED DEBT   *Public loans* are external obligations of public debtors, including national governments, their agencies, and autonomous public bodies. *Publicly guaranteed loans* are external obligations of private debtors that are guaranteed for repayment by a public entity of the debtor country.

Trade and Finance

BALANCE OF PAYMENTS   A systematic record of the economic transactions between a nation's residents and nonresidents during a given period, usually one calendar or fiscal year. It covers the flows of real resources (including factor services, such as the services of labor and capital) across the boundaries of the domestic economy, changes in foreign assets and liabilities resulting from economic transactions, and transfer payments to and from the rest of the world. Balance-of-payments accounts comprise two broad categories: the current account, which measures merchandise trade, factor and nonfactor service income, and transfer receipts and payments; and he capital account, which measures changes in domestic and foreign capital assets and liabilities.

CURRENT ACCOUNT BALANCE   A representation of the transactions that add to or subtract from an economy's stock of financial items. It is given as the sum of net exports of goods and nonfactor services, net factor income, and net transfers. Official capital grants are excluded.

DEBT REORGANIZATION   Any change in the payment arrangements associated with an existing stock of debt mutually agreed upon by the borrower an the lender. In *debt refinancing*, new loans are negotiated to meet debt service obligations on existing debt. In *debt rescheduling*, arrangements are agreed upon for postponing payments of principal or interest or otherwise changing the terms of repayment or of interest charges.

DEBT SERVICE   The sum of interest payments and repayments of principal on external debt. The debt service ration is usually total debt service divided by exports of goods and services.

EXTERNAL DEBT   Debt that is owed to nonresidents. Different reporting systems vary in coverage. For precise usage, each data source must be understood. For example, World Bank data, unless otherwise specified, cover external debt that has an original or extended maturity of one year or more and that is repayable in foreign currency, goods, or services. Transactions with the International Monetary Fund are excluded (with the exception of trust fund loans). A distinction in medium- and long-term debt is made between private nonguaranteed debt and public and publicly guaranteed debt.

INTEREST RATES   The nominal rate on a given loan is the percentage stipulated in the loan contract and may be expressed as a *fixed rate*—that is, an interest rate that is constant over the duration of the loan—or as a *variable, or floating, rate*—an interest rate that is recalculated at fixed intervals (such as every 6-months). Variable interest rates consist of a base rate (such as the 6-month London interbank offered rate) plus a margin, or spread. *Market, or world, rates* reflect the terms of borrowing at any given time in private capital markets; market rates are usually differentiated as *long-term rates*—the current rates payable on financial instruments, such as bonds, having maturities of more than one year—and *short-term rates*—rates on such instruments maturing in one year or less. The *real interest rate* is the nominal rate adjusted to account for changes in the price level.

INTERMEDIATION The process whereby a private or official financial agency accepts funds from investors and onlends them to borrowers.

MATURITY For a loan, the date at which the final repayment of principal is to be made. *Short-term loans* are those with original maturity of a year or less; *medium- and long-term loans* are those with original or extended maturity of more than one year.

RESERVES A country's international reserves comprise its holdings of monetary gold and special drawing rights; its reserve position in the International Monetary Fund; its holdings of foreign exchange under the control of monetary authorities; its use of IMF credit; and its existing claims on nonresidents that are available to the central authorities. Reserves are also expressed in terms of the number of months of imports of goods and services they could pay for.

RESOURCE BALANCE The difference between exports of goods and nonfactor services and imports of goods and nonfactor services.

SPREAD The difference between a reference rate used to price loans and the rate at which funds are lent to final borrowers. A widely used reference rate is the London interbank offered rate, LIBOR—the rate at which banks participating in the London market are prepared to lend funds to the most creditworthy banks; another is the U.S. prime rate.

TERMS OF TRADE A measure of the relative level of export prices compared with import prices. Calculated as the ratio of a country's index of export unit value to the import unit value, this indicator shows changes over a base year in the level of export prices as a percentage of import prices.

TRADE BALANCE The difference between merchandise exports f.o.b. and merchandise imports f.o.b.

National Accounts

GROSS DOMESTIC PRODUCT (GDP) The total final output of goods and services produced by an economy—that is, by residents and nonresidents—regardless of the allocation to domestic and foreign claims. It is calculated without making deductions for depreciation.

GROSS NATIONAL PRODUCT (GNP) The toal domestic and foreign output claimed by residents. It comprises gross domestic product adjusted by net factor income from abroad. Factor income comprises receipts that residents receive from abroad for factor services (labor, investment, and interest) less similar payments made to nonresidents abroad. It is calculated without making deductions for depreciation.

INVESTMENT The sum of gross domestic fixed investment and the change in stocks (or inventories). Gross domestic investment covers all outlays of the private and public sectors for additions to the fixed assets of the economy, plus the value of change in stocks (or inventories).

SAVINGS   Gross domestic savings is defined as the difference between GDP and total consumption; gross national savings are obtained by adding net factor income from abroad and net current transfers from abroad to gross domestic savings.

Definitions of External Debt

EXTERNAL DEBT   Debt that has an original or extended maturity of over one year (long-term debt) and that is owed to nonresidents and repayable in foreign currency, goods, or services. A distinction is made between *public debt*, which is an external obligation of a public debtor, including the national government, a political subdivision (or an agency of either), and autonomous public bodies; and *publicly guaranteed debt*, which is an external obligation of a private debtor that is guaranteed for repayment by a public entity.

PRIVATE NONGUARANTEED EXTERNAL DEBT   An external obligation of a private debtor that is not guaranteed for repayment by a public entity.

Categories of Creditors

OFFICIAL CREDITORS   Debt from official creditors comprises (1) loans from international organizations (multilateral loans), including loans and credits from the World Bank, regional development banks, and other multilateral and intergovernmental agencies (excluded are loans from funds administered by an international organization on behalf of a single donor government, which are classified as loans from governments); and (2) loans from governments (bilateral loans), including loans from governments and their agencies (including central bank) and loans from autonomous public bodies.

PRIVATE CREDITORS   Debt from private creditors comprises (1) loans from suppliers, including credits from manufacturers, exporters, or other suppliers of goods; (2) loans from financial markets, including loans from private banks and other private financial institutions and publicly issued and privately placed bonds; and (3) loans from other sources, including liabilities on account of nationalized properties and unclassified debts to private creditors. For private nonguaranteed debt, contractual obligations of a direct-investment enterprise to a foreign parent company or its affiliate are shown separately when these data are reported.

Country Groupings

DEVELOPING COUNTRIES   (1) Low-income economies, with 1983 GNP
per person of less than $400; and middle-income economies, with 1983
GNP per person of $400 or more. Middle-income countries are also
divided into oil exporters and oil importers, as identified herein.

EAST ASIA   All-low- and middle-income countries of East and Southeast
Asia and the Pacific, east of, and including, Burma, China, and
Mongolia.

EAST EUROPEAN NONMARKET ECONOMIES   Albania, Bulgaria, Czech-
oslovakia, German Democratic Republic, Hungary, Poland, Romania,
and USSR. This group is sometimes referred to as *nonmarket economies*.

HIGH-INCOME OIL EXPORTERS (NOT INCLUDED IN DEVELOPING COUN-
TRIES)   Bahrain, Brunei, Kuwait, Libya, Oman, Qatar, Saudi Arabia,
and United Arab Emirates.

INDUSTRIAL MARKET ECONOMIES   Members of the Organization of Economic Co-operation and Development, apart from Greece, Portugal,
and Turkey, which are frequently included among the middle-income
developing economies. This group is commonly referred to in the text
as *industrial economies* or *industrial countries*.

LATIN AMERICA AND THE CARIBBEAN   All American and Caribbean
countries south of the United States.

MAJOR BORROWERS   Countries with disbursed and outstanding debt estimated at more than $15 billion at the end of 1983, including Argen-
tina, Brazil, Chile, Egypt, India, Indonesia, Israel, Republic of Korea,
Mexico, Turkey, Venezuela, and Yugoslavia.

MIDDLE EAST AND NORTH AFRICA   Afghanistan, Algeria, Arab Republic of Egypt, Iran, Iraq, Israel, Jordan, Kuwait, Lebanon, Libya, Morocco, Oman, Saudi Arabia, Syrian Arab Republic, Tunisia, Turkey,
Yemen Arab Republic, People's Democratic Republic of Yemen, and
United Arab Emirates.

MIDDLE-INCOME OIL EXPORTERS   Algeria, Angola, Cameroon, People's
Republic of the Congo, Ecuador, Arab Republic of Egypt, Gabon,,
Indonesia, Islamic Republic of Iran, Iraq, Malaysia, Mexico, Nigeria,
Peru, Syrian Arab Republic, Trinidad and Tobago, Tunisia, and
Venezuela.

MIDDLE-INCOME OIL IMPORTERS   All middle-income developing countries not classified as oil exporters. A subset, *major exporters of manufactures*, comprises Argentina, Brazil, Greece, Hong Kong, Israel, Republic of Korea, Philippines, Portugal, Singapore, South Africa, Thailand,
and Yugoslavia.

SOUTH ASIA   Bangladesh, Bhutan, India, Nepal, Pakistan, and Sri
Lanka.

SUB-SAHARAN AFRICA   All thirty-nine developing African countries
south of the Sahara, excluding South Africa.

Multilateral Bank Debt Restructuring

BANK ADVISORY COMMITTEES   Also called *coordinating committees*; a limited number of banks designated by the authorities of a country to act
on behalf of and as a liaison group with all bank creditors. Once an
agreement is reached with the advisory committee, it is then submitted
for approval to all participating banks. Typically, membership of advisory committees is determined on the basis of the banks' exposure
and to secure a regional balance. The bank with the largest exposure
usually heads the committee, and member banks often act as regional
coordinators.

COFINANCING   Loans to developing countries made by commercial banks
or other lending institutions in association with the World Bank and
other multilateral development banks.

CONCERTED BANK LENDING   Equiproportional increases in exposure to
a restructuring country, coordinated by a bank advisory committee.
There has generally been a close linkage between disbursements of concerted bank lending to a country and performance under a Fund-supported adjustment program.

CONSOLIDATED PERIOD   The period in which amortization payments to
be rescheduled or refinanced under the terms of a restructuring agreement have fallen due or will fall due.

CRITICAL MASS   Minimum amount of bank commitments to a new money
package, giving reasonable assurance to Fund management that the financing assumptions of an adjustment program are realistic and that
the program can be submitted to the Fund executive board for
approval.

DEBT REFINANCING   Either a rollover of maturing debt obligations or the
conversion of existing or future debt service payments into a new medium-term loan.

DEBT RESCHEDULING   Formal deferment of debt service payments, with
new maturities applying to the deferred amounts.

DEBT RESTRUCTURING   Rescheduling or refinancing of debt service payments in arrears and/or of future debt service payments, undertaken in
response to external payments difficulties.

ECONOMIC SUBCOMMITTEE   A subcommittee of a bank advisory committee appointed to evaluate economic prospects of a restructuring
country.

EVENTS OF DEFAULT   Any event that allows creditor banks to declare the outstanding principal, as well as all accrued interest, due and payable on demand.

FLOATING RATE NOTES   Unsecured notes that pay interest at rates varying with the yield on a reference interest rate such as the LIBOR.

MORATORIUM   An official declaration or decree by a government, postponing all or certain types of maturing debt for a given period.

MULTIYEAR RESTRUCTURING AGREEMENT (MYRA)   Restructuring agreement in which the consolidation period covers more than 2 years beyond the date of the signing of the agreement. These arrangements aim principally at eliminating a hump in scheduled amortization, which may prevent a return to normal market access. In the context of MYRAs, banks have sought special monitoring procedures to ensure that adequate financial policies would be followed once the restructuring country no longer is using Fund resources. As part of these special monitoring procedures, some restructuring countries have requested that the Fund enhance its Article IV consultations.

TRADE DEPOSIT FACILITY   Facility under which participating creditor banks make foreign exchange deposits at the central bank of the restructuring country. These deposits may then be withdrawn by these banks to finance specified foreign trade transactions.

ONLENDING   Redesignation of credits originally granted to a government of central bank for general balance-of-payments purposes as loans to parastatals or private sector borrowers.

REDENOMINATION CLAUSE   A clause that, in the context of a debt restructuring agreement, allows banks to redenominate their loans in their home currency. The agreement normally specifies the amount, timing, and currency eligibility of such redenomination as well as the applicable reference interest rates.

STANDSTILL   An agreement between bank creditors and a government on a temporary deferment of amortization payments on long-term debt and on a freezing or rollover of short-term debt. Its principal objectives are to prevent a deterioration of the payments situation during the restructuring negotiation period and to preclude an uneven reduction in debt to some banks.

Multilateral Official Debt Restructuring

AGREED MINUTE   A document embodying the terms agreed upon in a multilateral rescheduling meeting. The Minute provides guidelines for the debt relief that subsequently is arranged on a bilateral basis between the debtor and each creditor country. The Minute normally specifies the coverage of debt consolidated, the cutoff date, the consolidation period, the proportion of payments to be rescheduled, the provisions regarding the downpayment, and the repayment schedule for both the rescheduled debt and any deferred debt.

ARREARS Unpaid amounts that fell due before the beginning of the consolidation period.

BILATERAL AGREEMENTS Agreements reached bilaterally between the debtor country and agencies in each of the participating creditor countries, establishing the legal basis of the debt rescheduling as set forth in the Agreed Minute. Information on the terms of bilateral agreements is regarded as confidential. Bilateral agreements normally specify financial terms, such as the interest rate on amounts rescheduled (moratorium interest), which is agreed bilaterally between the debtor and each creditor. Although the Agreed Minute now always refers to the interest rate being set on the basis of the market interest rate, in the past some Minutes had stipulated that each creditor country should make the maximum effort to keep the rate of interest as low as market conditions and legal considerations permit. The latter stipulation has not been made in more recent agreements, as creditors have indicated their desire that the question of the interest rate be determined solely on a bilateral basis.

BILATERAL DEADLINE The date by which bilateral agreements must be concluded. The period for concluding bilateral agreements is now generally eight to nine months from the date of the Agreed Minute.

CONDITIONAL FURTHER RESCHEDULING The provision in some Agreed Minutes setting forth the terms of rescheduling for payments that fall due in a specified subsequent future period and the conditions for such a rescheduling to become effective without a further Paris Club meeting.

CONSOLIDATION PERIOD The period in which debt service payments to be consolidated or rescheduled under the terms applicable to current maturities have fallen due or will fall due. The beginning of the consolidation period may precede or coincide with the date of the Agreed Minute.

CURRENT MATURITIES Principal and interest payments falling due within the consolidation period.

CUTOFF DATE The date before which loans must have been contracted in order for their debt service to be eligible for consolidation.

DE MINIMIS CLAUSE The provision whereby creditor countries whose claims eligible for rescheduling total to less than a specified amount are excluded from the rescheduling agreement. In the past, the de minimis amount was set at around SDR 1 million, but two-thirds of the agreements in 1983 and 1984 provided for limits of SDR 500,000 or SDR 250,000. The debtor is expected to pay all claims excluded from the rescheduling by this clause as soon as possible and, in any case, by a specified date.

DOWN PAYMENT   Payments falling due within the consolidation period.

EFFECTIVE RESCHEDULING PROPORTION   The proportion of total payments eligible for consolidation that are rescheduled or otherwise deferred until after the end of the consolidation period.

GOODWILL CLAUSE   The creditors' willingness, as expressed in the Agreed Minute, to consider further debt relief in the future, subject to fulfillment by the debtor country of certain specified conditions.

GRACE AND MATURITY PERIODS   The more recent practice of the Paris Club, to measure grace periods and maturities from a date six months after the midpoint of the consolidation period.

INITIATIVE CLAUSE   The standard undertaking in the Agreed Minute that the debtor country will seek renegotiation of debts owed to other creditors on terms comparable to those outlined in the Agreed Minute. The clause appears as one of the general recommendations and reads as follows:

In order to secure comparable treatment of public and private external creditors on their debts, the Delegation of [debtor country] stated that their Government will seek to secure from external creditors, including banks and suppliers, rescheduling or refinancing arrangements on terms comparable to those set forth in this Agreed Minute for credits of comparable maturity, making sure to avoid inequity between different categories of creditors.

LATE INTEREST CHARGES   Additional interest charges that may be levied as a result of obligations being overdue beyond a specified period. In some recent agreements, late interest charges have been listed specifically among debt service to be excluded from consolidation.

MATURITY PERIOD   The grace period plus the repayment period.

MORATORIUM INTEREST   Interest on amounts deferred or rescheduled under the Agreed Minute.

MOST-FAVORED-NATION CLAUSE   The standard undertaking in the Agreed Minute that the debtor country will accord to each of the participating creditor countries a treatment not less favorable than that which it may accord to any other creditor country for the consolidation of debts of a comparable term.

PREVIOUSLY RESCHEDULED DEBT   Debt service obligations arising from previous debt reschedulings.

SPECIAL ACCOUNT   An account established under some Agreed Minutes by the debtor country with the central bank of one of the participating creditor countries into which monthly deposits in an agreed amount are made. The total amount to be deposited usually approximates the amounts estimated to be payable to all participating creditors during the year; the debtor country would draw on the account as bilateral implementing agreements were signed and specific payments under these agreements became due.

Acronyms and Initials

ADB   Asian Development Bank or African Development Bank; sometimes written AsDB and AfDB.

BIS   Bank for International Settlements.

DAC   Development Assistance Committee of the Organization for Economic Co-operation and Development, composed of Australia, Austria, Belgium, Canada, Denmark, Finland, France, Federal Republic of Germany, Italy, Japan, Netherlands, New Zealand, Norway, Sweden, Switzerland, United Kingdom, United States, and the Commission of the European Communities.

EC   European Communities, comprising Belgium, Denmark, France, Federal Republic of Germany, Greece, Ireland, Italy, Luxembourg, Netherlands, and United Kingdom.

GATT   General Agreement on Tariffs and Trade.

GDI   Gross domestic investment.

GDP   Gross domestic product.

GDS   Gross domestic savings.

GNP   Gross national product.

GNS   Gross national savings.

IBRD   International Bank for Reconstruction and Development.

IDA   International Development Association.

IDB   Inter-American Development Bank.

IFC   International Finance Corporation.

ILO   International Labour Office.

IMF   International Monetary Fund.

MDB   Multilateral development bank.

ODA   Official development assistance.

OECD   Organization for Economic Co-operation and Development; members are Australia, Austria, Belgium, Canada, Denmark, Finland, France, Federal Republic of Germany, Greece, Iceland, Ireland, Italy, Japan, Luxembourg, Netherlands, New Zealand, Norway, Portugal, Spain, Sweden, Switzerland, Turkey, United Kingdom, and United States.

OPEC   Organization of Petroleum Exporting Countries, comprising Algeria, Ecuador, Gabon, Indonesia, Islamic Republic of Iran, Iraq, Kuwait, Libya, Nigeria, Qatar, Saudi Arabia, United Arab Emirates, and Venezuela.

SDR   Special drawing right.

UN   United Nations.

UNCTAD   United Nations Conference on Trade and Development.

UNDP   United Nations Development Programme.

Index

Acknowledgments

I WOULD like to thank Kenneth Friedman, Robert Parra and Elizabeth Rabitsch for their insights and assistance in the preparation of this book. I would also like to thank my wife, Edna, for her invaluable editorial contributions. Finally, I would like to thank Margo Williams and Anne Young for their many hours of secretarial assistance in the preparation of the manuscript.

About the Author

IRVING S. FRIEDMAN has had over forty years of uniquely wide experience in international economics and finance. After receiving his doctorate from Columbia University, he served in senior positions in the U.S. Treasury, International Monetary Fund, World Bank, Citibank, First Boston Corporation, and more recently in senior advisory positions with the African, Asian, and Inter-American Development Banks and other public and commercial financial institutions.

In these positions he has originated policies and practices, advised and negotiated with countries throughout the world, and served as research director, senior advisor, and businessman. He has also been author, professor, lecturer, and leader in public affairs. His activities have involved extensive travels to countries throughout the world. His experience in international economics and finance has gained him a worldwide audience for his ideas and proposals, as well as numerous awards and honorary degrees.

Among his more recent books, published in numerous languages, are *Inflation: A World-Wide Disaster*, *The World Debt Dilemma*, and *The Emerging Role of Private Banks in the Developing World*.